JAPANESE 1
FROM ZERO!

Watch the JFZ! video series FREE!

LearnFZ.com/JFZvideo

George Trombley
Yukari Takenaka

W9-CLF-904

Japanese From Zero! Book 1
Proven Methods to Learn Japanese with integrated Workbook

DISTRIBUTION
Distributed in the UK & Europe by:
Bay Language Books Ltd.
Unit 4, Kingsmead, Park Farm,
Folkestone, Kent. CT19 5EU, Great Britain
sales@baylanguagebooks.co.uk

Distributed in the USA & Canada by:
From Zero LLC.
10624 S. Eastern Ave. #A769
Henderson, NV 89052, USA
sales@fromzero.com

PREFACE
Japanese From Zero! is a Japanese language book series built on Japanese grammar that makes sense! Each book is crafted page by page and lesson by lesson to have relevant (and sometimes fun) Japanese conversation and sentence structure patterns that enhance the Japanese learner's ability to speak Japanese faster and understand the small nuances of Hiragana and everyday Japanese speech.

DEDICATION
This book is dedicated and made for:

Japanese culture lovers, Japanese language learners, Japanese anime and drama watchers, Japanese beginners, JPOP music fans, people of Japanese heritage connecting to their history, and anyone planning travel to Japan!

I lived in Japan for 9 years and have been married to my Japanese wife, Yukari, for 20 years. When we began writing the Japanese From Zero series, it was out of frustration with current Japanese books on the market. I felt they were either too fast, too slow, or too complicated. Japanese has enriched my life so much and writing this series was a way to express my sincere appreciation to all that the country of Japan and the Japanese language can offer.

All of us on the Japanese From Zero! team wish you success on your road to Japanese fluency and hope this book is a solid first step!

Thanks for the nice comments! We love feedback!

These books and this website remain my nihongo bible!
Ray_San – YesJapan.com

The books are great! I like the way everything is explained, the examples, the lessons and reviews.
Eijioo – YesJapan.com

Japanese From Zero Book 1 and 2 are amazing books for beginners! Having tried other ways of learning Japanese from the beginning, I find that the Japanese from Zero series are incredibly user friendly.
Kurisuti.Chan – YesJapan.com

I love JFZ, because it's so so so easy to use compared to others I've tried! It's clear you put a lot of work into it and I'm very grateful. Even though I lead a busy life and can't find too much time to learn, JFZ makes it easy for me to pick up where I left off and revise what I might have forgotten. THANKS!! ☺
J. Brooks – Facebook

THANK-YOU JFZ!!!!!! I think Everything JFZ does is wonderful! It is the most helpful book I've come across!
Rukia Kuchiki – YesJapan.com

Thank you, I just finished the 2nd book and can't wait to start with the 3rd! Soon am getting my hands on the 4th!
religionflag – YesJapan.com

JFZ! is perfect. If you're a complete beginner, this book takes you through the bare basics and really helps you progress quickly. I highly recommend this.
F. Morgan – Good Reads review

The perfect Japanese textbook for young learners. One of the benefits of this book, which also slows it down, are the tangents it takes to explain the nuances of Japanese that a beginner might encounter.
Michael Richey – Tofugu.com

You really learn Japanese from zero – no prior knowledge at all required. The grammar is easy to understand.
Karl Andersson - karlandersson.se

As someone who owns the first three books, I can say the books are great.
Mastema – YesJapan.com

Email us here:
feedback@fromzero.com

Join our Discord
http://learnfz.com/JFZdiscord

Japanese From Zero! Book 1
– CONTENTS –

From Zero! LEARNING RESOURCES

❏ **100+ Japanese From Zero! Video Lessons on YouTube!**
There are over 100 videos for the Japanese From Zero! book series on our YouTube channel. Each grammar point is explained by one of the authors of the series.

Look for the "Japanese From Zero! Video Series" playlist.
▶ **http://youtube.com/yesjapan**

❏ **Online Courses**
All of the courses are available on our website. You can listen to the sound files, ask teachers questions, play games, and take lesson quizzes. Prices vary. Sign up today:
▶ **http://japanesefromzero.com**

❏ **Discord Server**
Talk to other students on our free Discord server. Join here:
▶ **http://learnfz.com/jfzdiscord**

❏ **Email etc.**
You can send book feedback here:
▶ **feedback@fromzero.com**

❏ **Wholesale Inquiries**
Inquiries about using our books / materials for your school or organization here:
▶ **sales@fromzero.com**

❏ **After Book 5**
Learn one of the most widely used Japanese dialects, *Kansai Dialect*, with our video-only course available at:
▶ **http://fromzero.com**

Lesson

0

Level ①

Welcome!

How this book works

---

0 | Introduction

❑ **Welcome to Lesson "Zero" of JAPANESE FROM ZERO!**

LEARNING JAPANESE can be intimidating at first, but don't worry! Our method is designed to lead you <u>step-by-step</u> through the basics of Japanese grammar.

Whether you're learning Japanese for business, travel, or to make new friends, we've created these lessons to make sure you feel confident in your ability to SPEAK, READ, and WRITE what you've learned.

❑ **Japanese characters**

WHAT ARE THESE STRANGE LETTERS? The Japanese language uses a set of symbols called *hiragana* (to spell Japanese words), *katakana* (to spell foreign words), and *kanji* (to represent entire words or names). Over the course of BOOK 1, we will teach you groups of hiragana piece-by-piece to gradually build up your understanding and familiarity.

Our lessons begin with *ro–maji* (Japanese words spelled with Roman letters), but as each lesson progresses, we will continually substitute the hiragana you've learned. By the end of this book, you'll not only be able to speak Japanese, but <u>read and write it too!</u>

❑ **Japanese punctuation facts**

HERE ARE SOME QUICK FACTS about Japanese writing to help you get started.

UPPERCASE/LOWERCASE
In English, we learn to write both *A* and *a*, but in Japanese, あ is always あ no matter where you find it in a sentence. There are no upper and lower cases in Japanese.

QUESTION MARKS
Written Japanese doesn't (normally) use the question mark punctuation (?). Instead the hiragana か (ka) is placed at the end of a sentence to indicate a question.

> **Example**
> Nan desu ka. = What is it?
> Both are questions, but in Japanese, using *ka* does the trick. (Details in Lesson 1.)

PERIODS (or "What's that funny-looking circle?")

> **Example**
> Kore wa hon desu. → converted to hiragana becomes → これは ほんです。

This punctuation mark 。 does exactly the same job as the period in English.

SPACES

Japanese normally doesn't contain spaces. We have added spaces to make sentences easier to read for you.

❑ About the pre-lessons

Before this book introduces grammar concepts in lesson 1, there will be 4 pre-lessons. The pre-lessons are designed to give you some of the tools needed to begin to interact with native Japanese speakers. You will learn pronunciation, basic counting, initial conversation phrases, and other basic concepts.

Once you complete the pre-lessons, you will learn many key Japanese grammar concepts and how to read and write hiragana.

❑ About the authors

For over 20 years I, George Trombley, worked as a simultaneous Japanese interpreter. I've interpreted for Japanese clients at corporations such as Microsoft, IBM, NTT DoCoMo, Lucent, and in countries throughout North America, Europe, Asia, and the Middle East.

In 1998, my wife, Yukari Takenaka, and I formed a Japanese Language School in Las Vegas, NV. Over the years the live classroom courses formed the basis for the *Japanese From Zero!* series and the courses on our website, YesJapan.com

❑ WRITE IN THIS BOOK!

This book is your tool to learning in a way that will stick! Learning Japanese is hard work so we want your knowledge to last forever. *Japanese From Zero!* is designed to be an interactive workbook where you can take personal notes, add new words or phrases of your own, and develop your writing skills from hopeless/crazy/illegible (we all start that way!) to expert-level.

Every time you write in this book, you're making your connection to Japanese a little bit stronger - we guarantee it!

Ganbatte kudasai!
George Trombley
Yukari Takenaka

Lesson **A** Level ①

Pronunciation Guide & The Basics

Understanding Japanese phonetics

A Why Learn Hiragana?

It's important to know how powerful your Japanese will be if you can read and write it. Learning to read and write Japanese gives your brain a turbo boost in comprehension. You will immediately see how knowing the hiragana benefits your Japanese pronunciation.

All of your life you have been reading the alphabet a certain way. You have learned that the letter combination "TO" sounds like the number 2. This instinct will be hard to overcome at first.
In Japanese, "TO" is read as "TOW". If you read this like you were taught in grade school your Japanese accent would be pretty bad! But don't worry - this book will teach you the correct way to read the Japanese hiragana writing system.

Before you can learn hiragana and katakana, you will need to know how Japanese is represented in the Roman alphabet. This lesson will teach you how Japanese is pronounced. Let's get started!

A The Japanese Writing Systems

There are three Japanese writing systems:
* hiragana (pronounced "hear-uh-gah-nah")
* katakana (pronounced "kah-tah-kah-nah")
* kanji (pronounced "kahn-jee")

Kanji are Chinese characters, and each one has a specific meaning. Many kanji have multiple meanings and can be read different ways. Hiragana and katakana are phonetic characters derived from the more complicated kanji. They each represent a sound and do not have meaning by themselves.

The three writing systems are used together to write Japanese. Hiragana and kanji are used together to form all Japanese words. Katakana is mostly used to represent words of foreign origin or any word that was not originally Japanese. In daily life the combination of these three systems, plus roman letters called "ro–maji", are used in all types of media.

A   Japanese Pronunciation

Anyone can sound great in Japanese. Although English is made up of over a thousand possible sounds, Japanese has many less. A little over a hundred sounds are all you need to speak Japanese.

For this reason, it is much easier for English-speaking people to learn natural Japanese pronunciation than it is for Japanese speakers to learn natural English pronunciation. With just a few exceptions, Japanese sounds are based on the following five vowel sounds:

❑ A-1. Normal vowels

These sounds are short and simple, with no glide or lengthening.

Roman Letter	Sounds Like	Example
a	**ah** as in f**a**ther	**a**ka (red)
i	**ee** as in s**ee**	**i**nochi (life)
u	**oo** as in z**oo**	**u**ma (horse)
e	**eh** as in m**e**n	**e**bi (shrimp)
o	**oh** as in b**oa**t	**o**toko (man)

Now let's look at some of the sounds that make up the Japanese language. Use the same pronunciation as above for the sound sets listed below.

ka, ki, ku, ke, ko	sa, shi, su, se, so	pa, pi, pu, pe, po
ga, gi, gu, ge, go	na, ni, nu, ne, no	ba, bi, bu, be, bo

The following phonetic sounds are based on the "normal vowel" sounds listed above. The only difference is how the sound starts.

Roman Letter	Sounds Like	Example
ka	kah	**ka** (mosquito)
shi	shee	**shi**ru (to know)
tsu	tsoo	**tsu**ru (crane bird)
ne	neh	**ne**ko (cat)
po	poh	tan**popo** (dandelion)

❏ A-2. Double vowels

In Japanese it's common that sounds are lengthened. For example, in some words you will see a sound such as KA followed by an A, or NE followed by E, etc., to lengthen the sound.

Some books will represent the lengthened sound with a straight line over the lengthened vowel. This method may help you verbally, but doesn't help you when learning how to read and write Japanese. In *Japanese from Zero!*, A, I, U, E, or O is added to the sound that is to be lengthened just as the actual hiragana symbols are added to the word when written in Japanese. Look at the possible long vowel sound combinations.

Roman Letters	Sound	Example
aa, a–	**ah** as in father	oka**a**san (mother)
ii, i–	**ee** as in see	oji**i**san (grandfather)
uu, u–	**oo** as in zoo	zu**tsuu** (headache)
ei, ee, e–	**eh** as in men	on**ee**san (older sister)
ou, oo, o–	**oh** as in boat	**mou**fu (blanket)

Words that are written in katakana use a "–" as the "lengthener" instead of a repeating vowel. You'll learn more about katakana in *Japanese From Zero!* book 2.

Example Words			
kyouts<u>uu</u>	common	ot<u>ou</u>san	father
sat<u>ou</u>	sugar	ob<u>aa</u>san	grandmother
h<u>ei</u>wa	peace	sens<u>ou</u>	war
yasash<u>ii</u>	kind	isogash<u>ii</u>	busy

❏ A-3. Long versus short sounds

The meaning of a Japanese word can be changed by lengthening just one syllable.

Examples		
	ie	house
	<u>ii</u>e	no
	obasan	aunt
	ob<u>aa</u>san	grandmother
	ojisan	uncle
	oj<u>ii</u>san	grandfather

❑ A-4. Double consonants

Some Japanese words use double consonant sounds. Double consonants such as 'kk', 'pp', 'tt', and 'cch' must be stressed more than a single consonant to show the correct meaning of a word.

Examples	
roku	number six
ro<u>kk</u>u	rock (music)
uta	a song
u<u>tt</u>a	sold (past tense verb)
mata	again
ma<u>tt</u>a	waited (past tense verb)

Lesson

B

Level ①

Basic Counting
0 to 9999

B   The Basic Numbers

❏ B-1. Single Numbers

Basic counting in Japanese is easy! All you have to do is remember the following list of numbers, a few rules, and you're on the way.

the single numbers – 0-10		
rei, maru, zero ☆	れい、まる、ゼロ	0
ichi	いち	1
ni	に	2
san	さん	3
shi, yon ☆	し、よん	4
go	ご	5
roku	ろく	6
shichi, nana ☆	しち、なな	7
hachi	はち	8
ku, kyuu ☆	く、きゅう	9
juu	じゅう	10

B   Culture Clip: Why Two Versions?

The numbers with a ☆ have more than one version. Sometimes one version must be used instead of the other, but many times the version used is a personal preference.

There are also some cultural reasons for the different versions. The number four in Japanese is *yon*, or *shi*. *Shi* also means death. The number nine in Japanese is *kyuu* or *ku*. *Ku* also means suffering.

For these reasons, four and nine are considered to be unlucky in Japan. Many apartment buildings in Japan do not have apartments numbered four or nine. The different versions are used extensively in Japanese, so make sure to remember them.

B   The Counting Units

❑ B-2. The teens

To form numbers from 11 to 19, start with juu (10) and place the additional number you need directly after it. It is much like counting with roman numerals.

the teens – 11-19		
juu ichi	じゅういち	11
juu ni	じゅうに	12
juu san	じゅうさん	13
juu yon, juu shi ☆	じゅうよん、じゅうし	14
juu go	じゅうご	15
juu roku	じゅうろく	16
juu nana, juu shichi ☆	じゅうなな、じゅうしち	17
juu hachi	じゅうはち	18
juu kyuu, juu ku ☆	じゅうきゅう、じゅうく	19

❑ B-3. The tens

The tens are formed by combining the single numbers with juu. For example, 20 is two tens (*ni juu*), and 50 is five tens (*go juu*). The concept is simple. Look at this chart:

the tens – 10-90			
juu		じゅう	10
ni juu		にじゅう	20
san juu		さんじゅう	30
yon juu	never "shi juu"	よんじゅう	40
go juu		ごじゅう	50
roku juu		ろくじゅう	60
nana juu	never "shichi juu"	ななじゅう	70
hachi juu		はちじゅう	80
kyuu juu	never "ku juu"	きゅうじゅう	90

❑ B-4. Combining tens and singles

To make a number like 31, just string the numbers 30 and 1 together.

Examples

31 is san *juu* (three tens)	+	ichi (one)	=	*san juu ichi*
52 is *go juu* (five tens)	+	*ni* (two)	=	*go juu ni*
87 is *hachi juu* (eight tens)	+	*nana* (seven)	=	*hachi juu nana*

the twenties – 21-29		
ni juu ichi	にじゅういち	21
ni juu ni	にじゅうに	22
ni juu san	にじゅうさん	23
ni juu yon / shi	にじゅうよん、にじゅうし	24
ni juu go	にじゅうご	25
ni juu roku	にじゅうろく	26
ni juu nana / shichi	にじゅうなな、にじゅうしち	27
ni juu hachi	にじゅうはち	28
ni juu ku / kyuu	にじゅうきゅう、にじゅうく	29

❏ **B-5. The hundreds and thousands**

With *hyaku* (hundreds) and *sen* (thousands), the pattern is basically the same, but there are some variations. The variations are marked with ☆.

the hundreds – 100-900				
hyaku			ひゃく	100
ni hyaku			にひゃく	200
san byaku ☆	never "san hyaku"		さんびゃく	300
yon hyaku	never "shi hyaku"		よんひゃく	400
go hyaku			ごひゃく	500
roppyaku ☆	never "roku hyaku"		ろっぴゃく	600
nana hyaku	never "shichi hyaku"		ななひゃく	700
happyaku ☆	never "hachi hyaku"		はっぴゃく	800
kyuu hyaku	never "ku hyaku"		きゅうひゃく	900

the thousands – 1000-9000				
sen, issen			せん、いっせん	1,000
ni sen			にせん	2,000
san zen ☆	never "san sen"		さんぜん	3,000
yon sen	never "shi sen"		よんせん	4,000
go sen			ごせん	5,000
roku sen			ろくせん	6,000
nana sen	never "shichi sen"		ななせん	7,000
hassen ☆	never "hachi sen"		はっせん	8,000
kyuu sen	never "ku sen"		きゅうせん	9,000

❏ B-6. Putting all the numbers together

Now that you know the hundreds and thousands, you can simply string the numbers together to say numbers up to 9,999. The first few examples below will use repeating numbers to help you get used to putting the numbers together.

Examples

1.	222	ni hyaku ni juu ni
2.	555	go hyaku go juu go
3.	888	happyaku hachi juu hachi
4.	4,444	yon sen yon hyaku yon juu yon
5.	7,777	nana sen nana hyaku nana juu nana

Now let's mix up the numbers. Make sure you understand the numbers with variations.

Examples

1.	639	roppyaku san juu kyuu
2.	360	sanbyaku roku juu
3.	2,512	ni sen go hyaku juu ni
4.	8,096	hassen kyuu juu roku
5.	9,853	kyuu sen happyaku go juu san

B   For practice れんしゅうのため

Practice saying your phone number, lock combinations, etc., in Japanese. Learn them forwards and backwards. Say private numbers in your head so some sneaky person doesn't learn your bank pin code!

When you are riding in your car, practice reading the numbers on other cars' license plates.

B | Lesson Activities

❑ 1. Number conversion
Write out the following numbers in Japanese.

1) 34 _____   2) 59 _____

3) 29 _____   4) 78 _____

5) 120 _____   6) 392 _____

7) 57 _____   8) 3,004 _____

9) 1,203 _____   10) 789 _____

11) 99 _____   12) 4,675 _____

13) 932 _____   14) 8,773 _____

❑ 2. Everyday Numbers
Follow the instructions for each task.

1. Write your home phone number in Japanese.

_____

2. Write your cellular number, or work phone number in Japanese.

_____

3. Write your license plate number in Japanese. (Write any letters in ro–maji)

_____

B Answer Key

❏ 1. Number conversion (answers)

1. san juu yon
2. go juu kyuu
3. ni juu kyuu
4. nana juu hachi
5. hyaku ni juu
6. san byaku kyuu juu ni
7. go juu nana
8. san zen yon
9. sen ni hyaku san
10. nana hyaku hachi juu kyuu
11. kyuu juu kyuu
12. yon sen roppyaku nana juu go
13. kyuu hyaku san juu ni
14. hassen nana hyaku nana juu san

❏ 2. Everyday numbers (answers)

1. (answer will vary)
2. (answer will vary)
3. (answer will vary)

First Meeting
Self introduction and basic greetings
Hajimemashite

About This Lesson このレッスンについて

If there is one thing you need to be good at, it is introducing yourself. You should practice this as often as you can. You only get one first impression.

The good news is that not being a Japanese speaker gives you an advantage. If you mess up your initial introduction, you will most likely be forgiven. You are not Japanese, and everyone will understand that you are still learning.

Culture clip: Bowing

In the next conversation you will be able to practice a first-meeting conversation, but what you cannot see in the text is the bow that each person does when they say, "*Hajimemashite.*" Bowing is as important to the Japanese as shaking hands is to others.

Many of us have always heard that the deeper you bow, the more respect you bestow upon the person to whom you are bowing. This is true, though the majority of students learning Japanese will not find themselves in a situation that warrants a deep bow. When first meeting someone, a 30-degree bow held for about two seconds is standard. But keep in mind that, as a foreigner to Japan, the Japanese do not expect you to know Japanese customs, and if you bow incorrectly, it will not be considered rude.

The most common everyday bow is an informal 15-degree bow held for one or two seconds. You will be bowed to no matter where you go. The next time you see a Japanese person talking on the phone, you might even see them bowing to the person on the other end of the conversation! It is not necessary to return bows to waiters or staff in department stores. A nod of the head will suffice.

Hands are normally kept near the body when bowing. Men tend to have their hands at their sides while, women will usually place them together on their thighs with the fingertips overlapping or touching.

C Conversation かいわ

❑ C-1. Meeting someone for the first time

Let's look at the phrases that will come up when you first meet someone.

1. **Hajimemashite**
   Nice to meet you. / How do you do?
   This phrase is only used when first meeting someone. When pronouncing "Hajimemashite" make sure that the "i" in "mashite" is silent to sound similar to "mashte".

2. ____**(name)**____ **to moushimasu.**
   I am ____(name)____.
   Although there are other ways to say your name, this is an excellent way to introduce yourself.
   It's very polite and humble at the same time. It is the equivalent to saying "I am called _____".

3. **Yoroshiku onegai shimasu.**
   Best regards.   / I look forward to working with you.
   It's amazing how many different meanings there are for this phrase. This phrase is multi-purpose and its meaning varies depending on the situation. When used as it is in Conversation 1, it means something to the effect of, "Let's be nice to each other."

Although this phrase is very common when speaking Japanese, there is not an English equivalent that properly sums up its many meanings. Now let's see the phrases we have learned in action.

Conversation 1: First meeting
This conversation is between people meeting for the first time. Mr. Smith (Sumisu) is American and Mr. Mori is Japanese.

Mr. Smith:	Hajimemashite. Sumisu to moushimasu.
Mr. Mori:	Hajimemashite. Mori to moushimasu. Yoroshiku onegai shimasu.
Mr. Smith:	Yoroshiku onegai shimasu.
Mr. Smith:	Nice to meet you. I am Smith (My name is Smith).
Mr. Mori:	Nice to meet you. I am Mori (My name is Mori). Best regards.
Mr. Smith:	Best regards.

❑ C-2. Asking someone their age

Early on in your quest to learn Japanese, your conversations will be limited to what you can reliably understand and say in Japanese. Although the topic of "age" is not normally discussed in first time situations (and might be especially awkward in a business meeting!), it isn't a strange topic to discuss when meeting new people outside of business.

1. **Nansai desu ka.**
   How old are you?

2. _____(years)_____ **sai desu.**
   I am   (years)   years old.
   If needed, please review the numbers you learned in the prior lesson. The word "*sai*" literally means, "years old." It must always come after the number representing your age.

Examples	3 years old	san sai
	15 years old	juu go sai

Conversation 2: How old are you?	
Mr. Smith:	Nansai desu ka.
Ms. Hayashi:	Ni juu go sai desu.
Mr. Smith:	How old are you?
Ms. Hayashi:	I am 25 years old.

❑ C-3. Learning to say your age

As previously stated, to say your age, just add *sai* after the number of years. Some ages are said differently than you might think. Use the chart below to learn the correct way.

years old - とし		
1-year-old	issai	never "ichi sai"
2 years old	ni sai	
3 years old	san sai	
4 years old	yon sai	never "shi sai"
5 years old	go sai	
6 years old	roku sai	
7 years old	nana sai	never "shichi sai"
8 years old	hassai	never "hachi sai"
9 years old	kyuu sai	never "kusai" (*kusai* means smelly!)
10 years old	jissai, jussai	never "juu sai"
11 years old	juu issai	never "juu ichi sai"
12 years old	juu ni sai	
13 years old	juu san sai	
14 years old	juu yon sai	never "juu shi sai"
15 years old	juu go sai	
16 years old	juu roku sai	
17 years old	juu nana sai	never "juu shichi sai"

18 years old	juu hassai	never "juu hachi sai"
19 years old	juu kyuu sai	
20 years old	hatachi	never "ni jussai" or "ni jissai"
21 years old	ni juu issai	never "ni juu ichi sai"
22 years old	ni juu ni sai	
23 years old	ni juu san sai	
24 years old	ni juu yon sai	never "ni juu shi sai"
25 years old	ni juu go sai	
26 years old	ni juu roku sai	
27 years old	ni juu nana sai	never "ni juu shichi sai"
28 years old	ni juu hassai	never "ni juu hachi sai"
29 years old	ni juu kyuu sai	never "ni juu ku sai"
30 years old	san jissai, san jussai	never "san juu sai"
40 years old	yon jissai, yon jussai	never "shi jissai" or "yon juu sai"
50 years old	go jissai; go jussai	never "go juu sai"
100 years old	hyaku sai	sometimes said as "hyakkusai"

Note: The first ten numbers set the pattern for all the numbers that follow.

❏ C-4. JU- vs JI- for "ten"

The ages, 10, 30, 40, 50 and so on all contain JISSAI, but you might commonly hear Japanese people pronounce it as JUSSAI. In some Japanese schools, JUSSAI would be marked wrong on a kanji test. This is because officially the kanji for "ten" in the case of JISSAI must be read as JI.

Some schools have recognized that since JUSSAI is commonly spoken and therefore shouldn't be marked wrong.

Later in the book, other counting examples will have the same issue to consider with how "ten" is read for kanji, vs how people actually say it.

❏ C-5. How old do I look?

In your beginning stages of learning Japanese, the following conversation will be a really fun way to break the ice with your new Japanese friends. It is especially fun since Westerners and Japanese have different perceptions about how old someone looks.

1. **Nansai ni miemasu ka.**   **How old do I look?**
   This is probably the most common response to "Nansai desu ka." Keep in mind that honesty can be brutal in any language, so be kind with your answer! This phrase is great because it gives you and your new friend an opportunity for fun.

2. ___(years)___ **sai ni miemasu.**
   You look ___(years)___ years old.

Conversation 3: How old do I look?	
Mr. Smith:	Nansai desu ka.
Ms. Hayashi:	Nansai ni miemasu ka.
Mr. Smith:	Hatachi ni miemasu.
Mr. Smith:	How old are you?
Ms. Hayashi:	How old do I look?
Mr. Smith:	You look 20 years old.

C   Speaking Naturally しぜんに はなすこと

As with any language, there is "grammatically correct" and "culturally correct". In this section you will learn how to sound more natural when speaking Japanese. In some cases you might even learn how to break a rule you just learned, and in some cases you might learn what is more commonly used.

❑ C-6. My name is...

Many new students of Japanese learn to say "Watashi no namae wa _____ desu", which means, "My name is _____." However, although grammatically correct, this way of introducing yourself is not common between Japanese people.

Conversation 4: My name is... (grammatically correct)	
Ms. Hayashi:	(O)namae wa nan desu ka.
Mr. Smith:	Watashi no namae wa Sumisu desu.
Ms. Hayashi:	What is your name?
Mr. Smith:	My name is Smith.

Conversation 5: My name is... (the natural way)	
Ms. Hayashi:	(O)namae wa nan desu ka.
Mr. Smith:	Sumisu to moushimasu.
Ms. Hayashi:	What is your name?
Mr. Smith:	I am Smith (My name is Smith).

C Lesson Activities

❑ 1. Japanese numbers

Translate the following Japanese into English.

1. nana juu go sai _____

2. yon juu hassai _____

3. hachi juu ni sai _____

4. hyaku nana sai _____

5. san juu yon sai _____

6. juu roku sai _____

7. go juu issai _____

8. hatachi _____

9. happyaku sai _____

10. issai _____

❑ 2. Question and answer 1

Answer the following question in Japanese.

1. Nansai desu ka.

_____

2. (O)namae wa nan desu ka.

_____

❑ **3. Question and answer 2**
For each of the pictures below answer the question:

Nansai ni miemasu ka.

1.

Answer: _____

2.

Answer: _____

3.

Answer: _____

4.

Answer: _____

5.

Answer: _____

6.

Answer: _____

C Answer Key

❑ 1. Japanese numbers (answers)

1. 75 years old
2. 48 years old
3. 82 years old
4. 107 years old
5. 34 years old

6. 16 years old
7. 51 years old
8. 20 years old
9. 800 years old
10. 1-year-old

❑ 2. Question and answer 1 (answers)

1. How old are you?
2. What is your name?

____sai desu.
____desu / ____to moushimasu.

❑ 3. Question and answer 2 (sample answers)

How old do I look?

go jissai/go jussai ni miemasu.

juu roku sai ni miemasu.

Lesson

D

Level ①

Coming and Going
Basic greetings and farewells

D About This Lesson このレッスンについて

In Japan, there are certain phrases used for coming and going that change depending on whether the location is your own home, someone else's home, or a place of business.

D New Phrases あたらしい ことば

❑ **D-1. Daily Greetings**

Try to use the new phrases below every day with your friends and family.

1. **Ohayou gozaimasu. / Ohayou.**
   Good morning.
   The short version of *ohayou gozaimasu* is *ohayou* and is normally only used with friends, family and people you have a casual relationship with.

2. **Konnichiwa.**
   Good afternoon.
   The sound of the double consonant 'nn' in *konnichiwa* is held longer than just one "n".

3. **Konbanwa.**
   Good evening.
   This is only used when you first meet with someone in the evening. It cannot be used at the end of an evening.

4. **Oyasuminasai. / Oyasumi.**
   Good night.
   The short version, *oyasumi*, should only be used with friends, family and people you have a casual relationship with.

5. **Arigatou gozaimasu. / Arigatou.**
   Thank you.
   Arigatou is very common as a short way to say "Thank you". In real life, you will rarely hear the often-taught version *Doumo arigatou gozaimasu*.

❑ D-2. Leaving and returning home

The following phrases are said everyday by millions of Japanese people as they leave and arrive home:

1. **itte kimasu.**
    I will go and come back. / I'll be back.
    This phrase is said when you leave your home. It can also be said when you are leaving any place to which you plan to return.

2. **itterasshai.**
    Have a good day. / Take care. / See you.
    This is the response to *itte kimasu*. This phrase is said to someone who is leaving and will be back. *itterasshai* is normally only used in situations when the person leaving will return in a relatively short time.

3. **Tadaima.**
    I'm home. / I'm back.
    This phrase is commonly used when arriving home. It can also be used when returning to a place you recently left.

4. **Okaerinasai.**
    Welcome back home.
    This is the response to *tadaima*. It can also be said to someone who has just returned to a place they have been before.

Conversation 1: Leaving home
The following conversation is between Jiro and his mother as Jiro leaves to go to school.

Jiro:	itte kimasu!
Jiro's mother:	itterasshai!

Conversation 2: Returning home
The following conversation is between Jiro and his mother as Jiro arrives back home from school.

Jiro:	Tadaima!
Jiro's mother:	Okaerinasai!

D   Speaking Naturally しぜんに はなすこと

❏ D-3. The silent "U" sound

Many phrases taught in this lesson end with "masu".

> **Examples**
> 1. Ohayou gozaimasu.
> 2. itte kimasu.
> 3. Arigatou gozaimasu.

In everyday spoken Japanese, the final "u" in words containing "masu" is silent and the word is pronounced as "mas". Practice your words and phrases with this pronunciation and you will sound more natural.

D   Lesson Activities

❏ 1. Japanese translation

Translate the following conversation into English.

1.	
Mari:	itte kimasu.
Mari's mother:	itterasshai.
Mari:	
Mari's mother:	

2.	
Kenji:	Tadaima.
Kenji's father:	Okaerinasai.
Kenji:	
Kenji's father:	

D Answer Key

☐ 1. Japanese translation (answers)

1. Mari: I will go and come back. / I'll be back.
    Mari's Mother: Have a good day. / Take care. / See you.

2. Kenji: I'm home. / I'm back.
    Kenji's Mother: Welcome back home.

Lesson E
Level ①

Typing Japanese
How to install and type Japanese

At the end of lesson 1, we start learning hiragana. You can **come back to this lesson later** to learn how to type Japanese on any of your devices. Or if you are super excited, read it now!

E   The Basics

❑ E-1. Adding a Japanese keyboard to ANY device

As of the printing of this book, almost any electronic device including PC, MAC, Linux, iOS, Android and probably any modern day operation system has the ability to add a Japanese keyboard.

STEP 1: Find Keyboard Settings

As long as you can find the keyboard settings, or input settings, or international settings or... whatever it's called on your device, you will be able to type in Japanese. A quick search on Google, or whatever searching tool you use yet to be invented, should come up with a way to get Japanese working on your device.

STEP 2: Choose Japanese

Most devices have all major and even minor languages available for installation. Depending on the device, there might be multiple options for keyboard type. For now choose Japanese since that is what we are learning in this book.

STEP 3: Choose Keyboard Type

If there are choices for keyboard types, I recommend that you install the "Romaji" or equivalent input. This will allow you to use the ABC alphabet to input Japanese. It will be easier than other keyboard types. After you know how to read all the hiragana, you can experiment with other keyboards.

STEP 1: Find Keyboard Settings

‹ Keyboards	**Keyboards**	Edit
English (US)		›
Emoji		
Add New Keyboard...		›

STEP 2: Choose Japanese

Cancel	**Add New Keyboard**	
Italian		
Japanese		
Kannada		
Kashmiri (Devanagari)		

STEP 3: Choose Keyboard Type

‹ Back	**Japanese**	Done
KEYBOARD		
Kana		
Romaji		✓

❑ E-2. Changing to Japanese keyboard

▶ iOS Devices
On iOS devices (as of this printing), there is a small world icon on the bottom left of the keyboard. Clicking that will open up a list of currently installed keyboards. You can then select Japanese and begin typing in Japanese.

▶ Windows
On Windows devices, there is a language icon on the bottom right of the screen near the clock. You can switch to Japanese here by clicking the icon.

NOTE: You won't be able to switch unless your cursor is in a box that you are able to type in.

Windows Keyboard Shortcuts
You can switch the language with the ALT + TAB shortcut. Once you are in Japanese mode, you can switch input modes from Japanese to English with ALT + ~ (top left key under esc key).

▶ Mac OS
Mac's language option is on the right side of the top bar. There are a variety of language related options here, including changing your input method to Japanese.

▶ Linux / Windows Alternative
If you search for "Google IME" you will find Google's version of a Japanese input system. This can be used instead of Windows IME. All Linux distributions should have Japanese input available during installation or as package update.

▶ Android
Android devices have a variety of keyboard selection methods. One of the most common methods is swiping the space key on the keyboard right or left.

iOS: Changing Keyboards

Windows: Changing Keyboards

MacOS: Changing Keyboards

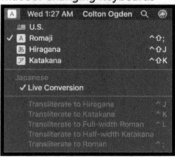

❑ E-3. Typing in Japanese using roma-ji

Roma-ji, as we will learn later, is just how Japanese looks when written using roman letters or as we call it "the English alphabet". If you can type in English, you can easily type in Japanese. Even the majority of Japanese people type using roman letters.

❑ E-4. Converting from roma-ji to hiragana and selecting kanji

Once you are in Japanese typing mode (see section E-2), you can just type the words and the keyboard will change the letters first into hiragana (taught at the end of lesson 1).

Typing Steps

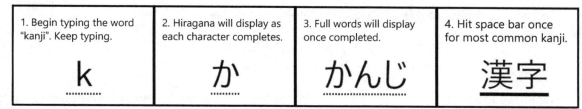

1. Begin typing the word "kanji". Keep typing.	2. Hiragana will display as each character completes.	3. Full words will display once completed.	4. Hit space bar once for most common kanji.
k	か	かんじ	漢字

If you want the "hiragana" only word, you can simply hit "enter" to accept at step 3. Or you can hit the space bar once to display the most common Kanji for the entered hiragana.

NOTE: If you select different kanji often, that kanji will become the first choice to appear.

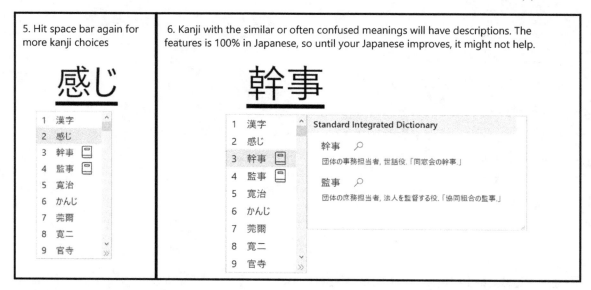

5. Hit space bar again for more kanji choices	6. Kanji with the similar or often confused meanings will have descriptions. The features is 100% in Japanese, so until your Japanese improves, it might not help.
感じ	幹事

1	漢字
2	感じ
3	幹事
4	監事
5	寛治
6	かんじ
7	莞爾
8	寛二
9	官寺

1	漢字
2	感じ
3	幹事
4	監事
5	寛治
6	かんじ
7	莞爾
8	寛二
9	官寺

Standard Integrated Dictionary

幹事 🔍
団体の事務担当者, 世話役。「同窓会の幹事。」

監事 🔍
団体の庶務担当者, 法人を監督する役。「協同組合の監事。」

Every time you hit the space bar, a different selection will display. Once you find the one you like, hit "enter".

NOTE: You can also type the number next to the selection to choose it.

❑ E-5. Typing full sentences in Japanese

You do not have to choose kanji word by word when typing Japanese. The auto-conversion is very smart when it comes to choosing the correct kanji for your sentence. Contrary to popular belief, almost all Japanese people use this method to type Japanese (on PCs).

For mobile phones, the hiragana keyboard is faily common as it's faster to type with than roma-ji for some people. Even though you might not understand what you are typing, let's type a full sentence. You can visit this lesson later after you know more Japanese!

On the keyboard, we will type the following sentence **without spaces**:
watashi no namae wa jo-ji desu. (My name is George.)

Something similar to this is what we will see on the screen.

わたしのなまえはじょーじです。

When we are at the end of the sentence, hit the space bar for the most common selections. You can keep hitting the space bar to cycle through each word in the sentence.

私の名前はジョージです。

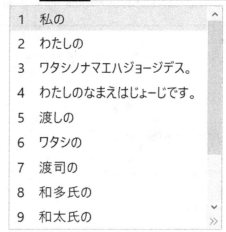

1	私の
2	わたしの
3	ワタシノナマエハジョージデス。
4	わたしのなまえはじょーじです。
5	渡しの
6	ワタシの
7	渡司の
8	和多氏の
9	和太氏の

❑ E-6. Japanese language bar shortcuts

A big pet peeve of mine is watching people change the language bar settings by manually clicking on them. It's time consuming if you are switching back and forth a lot.

You can easily switch language options and even input methods with these short cuts.

1. Change language on the fly.

ALT + SHIFT

NOTE: Japanese mode default setting is normally "half width alpha numeric". You can change this in the language bar properties. OR you can quickly switch to hiragana mode with the shortcut below.

2. Change input type (Hiragana, Alpha-numeric)

ALT + ~

NOTE: The '~' key is on the left side of the 1 key.
This is handy if you are already in Japanese input mode and want to switch back and forth between typing English and Japanese. It's quicker to use this shortcut when you have more than two languages installed.

3. Quick conversion

After typing a word, before you hit enter, you can force it into different versions using the function keys.

F7 - Full width katakana
F8 - Half width katakana
F9 - Full width alpha numeric
F10 - Half width alpha numeric (standard English text)

HAVE FUN TYPING JAPANESE!

Vocabulary Groups

During your studies you will soon realize that grammar points aren't so easily forgotten. But you need more than grammar to speak effectively – you need vocabulary too!

Throughout this book, we will introduce groups of words that are important to everyday Japanese speaking. You don't have to try to memorize them all at once. Just familiarize yourself with each group since they will be showing up in subsequent lessons.

❏ Explanation of Progressive, Kana and Kanji

When new words are introduced, multiple Japanese versions of each word will be introduced. This will make it easier to review once you know how to read more Japanese.

Progressive – As you learn hiragana throughout each lesson, the progressive version will slowly replace the English alphabet with hiragana that you have learned.

Kana – This version will be either hiragana or katakana characters depending on how the word is normally written in Japanese. Hiragana and katakana are collectively referred to as kana.

Kanji – When a word is normally written in kanji, it will be displayed here. If there is no kanji for that word, or if it's common to not use kanji, then the kana version will be repeated.

A the body

Progressive	Kana	Kanji	English
kuchi	くち	口	mouth
me	め	目	eye
mimi	みみ	耳	ear
hana	はな	鼻	nose
kao	かお	顔	face
te	て	手	hand
ashi	あし	足	foot; leg
yubi	ゆび	指	finger
atama	あたま	頭	head
ha	は	歯	tooth; teeth

B   bed and bath

Progressive	Kana	Kanji	English
makura	まくら	枕	pillow
beddo	ベッド	ベッド	bed
futon	ふとん	布団	futon
moufu	もうふ	毛布	blanket
taoru	タオル	タオル	towel
ofuro	おふろ	お風呂	bath
sekken	せっけん	石けん	soap
haburashi	ハブラシ	歯ブラシ	toothbrush
kagami	かがみ	鏡	mirror
mado	まど	窓	window

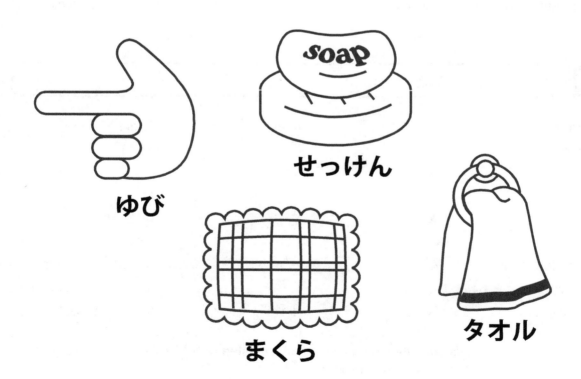

ゆび

せっけん

まくら

タオル

Lesson
1
Level ①

Creating Simple Sentences
What is it?

1   About This Lesson このレッスンについて

Before The Lesson

1. Review vocabulary groups A and B.
2. Make sure you understand the basics of Japanese pronunciation from Pre-Lesson A.

Lesson Goals

1. Learn how to ask and answer simple questions
2. Learn the question particle *ka*

From The Teachers

1. Remember the phrase *nan desu ka* (What is it?) and understand how *desu* is used.

1   New Words あたらしい ことば

Progressive	Kana	Kanji	English
nani	なに	何	What?
hai	はい	はい	yes
iie *	いいえ	いいえ	no
inu	いぬ	犬	dog
neko	ねこ	猫	cat
~san (after name)	さん	さん	Mr.; Ms.; Mrs.; Miss
Tanaka	たなか	田中	(a common last name)
Kobayashi	こばやし	小林	(a common last name)

* **NOTE:** In this book, *iie* and other Japanese words that start with "i" will be typed in lowercase to avoid confusion with lowercase "L".

1   New Phrases あたらしい かいわ

Each lesson will have several new phrases. At this point, don't worry about the grammar; simply memorizing the phrases will be more beneficial at this point.

1.	Do you understand?	Wakarimasu ka.
2.	Yes, I understand.	Hai, wakarimasu.
3.	No, I don't understand.	iie, wakarimasen.
4.	I don't understand. / I don't know. *	Wakarimasen.
5.	Please say it once again.	Mou ichido itte kudasai.
6.	Please speak more slowly.	Motto yukkuri itte kudasai.

* NOTE: Although *wakarimasen* means "I don't understand," it's frequently used to mean "I don't know."

1   Grammar ぶんぽう

❑ 1-1. Plurals

The Japanese language does not have plurals like English does. For example, *mimi* means "ear" or "ears," depending on the context of the sentence. Later you will learn that some words have plural forms, but for now remember that most words can be either plural or singular without any modification.

❑ 1-2. Using *desu* to make a simple statement

Desu (usually pronounced "des"), depending on the context, can mean: "it is," "this is," "they are," "these are," "I am," "you are," "he is," "she is" and "we are." It is always placed at the end of a sentence. Look at these examples to see how *desu* is used:

> **[word] + desu**

> **Example Sentences**
> 1. <u>It is</u> a pillow.   Makura <u>desu</u>.
> 2. <u>I am</u> Tanaka.   Tanaka <u>desu</u>.
> 3. <u>She is</u> Ms. Kobayashi.   Kobayashi san <u>desu</u>.
> 4. <u>It is</u> soap.   Sekken <u>desu</u>.

❑ 1-3. Making a question using *ka*

Ka is like the English question mark. To change a statement in Japanese to a question, you just add *ka* at the end.

> **[word] + desu ka**

Example Sentences

1. Is it a pillow?   Makura desu ka.
2. Are you Tanaka?   Tanaka san desu ka.
3. Is she Ms. Kobayashi?   Kobayashi san desu ka.
4. Is it soap?   Sekken desu ka.

❑ 1-4. The question word *nani*

The question word *nani* or *nan* means "what." The two versions are used differently. *Nani* can stand alone to simply mean "What?" *Nan* cannot be used alone. It is always used with other words such as *desu*, as in the sentence "Nan desu ka" ("What is it?").

Example Sentences

1. Nan desu ka.   What is it?
2. Nansai desu ka.   How old are you?
3. Nani iro desu ka. *   What color is it?
4. Nani ga suki desu ka. *   What do you like?

* NOTE: The grammar used in the example sentences 3 and 4 above using nani will be taught in later lessons. In the mean time, simply remember that you will see both NAN and NANI to mean "what".

1 Culture Clip: Using *san* for Mr., Mrs., etc.

It's a custom in Japan to add *san* to the end of someone's name. *San* means "Mr.," "Ms.," "Mrs.," and "Miss," and can be used on first or last names. It's considered rude not to use *san*, especially when talking to or about someone you are not close to, or to someone who is older or above you in status. You should <u>never</u> use *san* when referring to yourself or someone in your own family.

1   Q&A しつもんと こたえ

1. **What is it?**   Nan desu ka.
    It is a pillow.   Makura desu.
    It is soap.   Sekken desu.
    I don't know.   Wakarimasen.

2. **Is it (this) a mirror?**   Kagami desu ka.
    Yes, it is a mirror.   Hai, kagami desu.
    No, it is a window.   iie, mado desu.

3. **Is (this) a bed?**   Beddo desu ka.
    No, it is a futon.   iie, futon desu.
    Yes, it is a bed.   Hai, beddo desu.

4. **Is he Mr. Tanaka?**   Tanaka san desu ka.
    Yes, he is Mr. Tanaka.   Hai, Tanaka san desu.
    No, he is Mr. Kobayashi.   iie, Kobayashi san desu.

5. **Is it a head?**   Atama desu ka.
    No, it is a face.   iie, kao desu.
    Yes, it is a head.   Hai, atama desu.
    I don't know.   Wakarimasen.

6. **Do you understand?**   Wakarimasu ka.
    No, I don't understand.   iie, wakarimasen.
    Yes, I understand.   Hai, wakarimasu.
    No.   iie.

7. **What is it?**   Nan desu ka.
    It is a hand.   Te desu.
    It is a foot.   Ashi desu.
    It is a finger.   Yubi desu.
    It is a toothbrush.   Haburashi desu.

8. **Is she Ms. Kobayashi?**   Kobayashi san desu ka.
    I don't know.   Wakarimasen.
    No, she is Ms. Tanaka.   iie, Tanaka san desu.
    Yes, she is Ms. Kobayashi.   Hai, Kobayashi san desu.

Hiragana あいうえお

あ The goal ゴール

When you complete *Japanese From Zero!* you will be able to read and write all of the symbols below. This chart is read in traditional Japanese-style, from right-to-left and top-to-bottom.

Read right-to-left and top-to-bottom

⬅

わ wa	ら ra	や ya	ま ma	ぱ pa	ば ba	は ha	な na	だ da	た ta	ざ za	さ sa	が ga	か ka	あ a
	り ri		み mi	ぴ pi	び bi	ひ hi	に ni	ぢ ji	ち chi	じ ji	し shi	ぎ gi	き ki	い i
を wo	る ru	ゆ yu	む mu	ぷ pu	ぶ bu	ふ fu	ぬ nu	づ zu	つ tsu	ず zu	す su	ぐ gu	く ku	う u
	れ re		め me	ぺ pe	べ be	へ he	ね ne	で de	て te	ぜ ze	せ se	げ ge	け ke	え e
ん n	ろ ro	よ yo	も mo	ぽ po	ぼ bo	ほ ho	の no	ど do	と to	ぞ zo	そ so	ご go	こ ko	お o

あ How this book works

Japanese From Zero! uses our PROGRESSIVE SYSTEM when teaching hiragana. As you learn new hiragana, we will immediately replace the roman letters (ro–maji) with the hiragana you have just learned. For example, in this lesson we learn あいうえお, so any words containing those EXACT hiragana, will from that point forward use those hiragana.

English	Before this lesson	After this lesson	Complete hiragana
you	anata	あnata	あなた
dog	inu	いnu	いぬ
house	ie	いえ	いえ
mother	okaasan	おkaあsan	おかあさん

NOTE: This book will never partially display hiragana (no book ever would!). For example, the *ka* in "mother" will not be displayed as kあ since the full hiragana is か (taught in lesson).

あ   Some History れきし

Hiragana was created by a Buddhist monk over 1200 years ago (AD 774-835). At that time it was believed that women were not allowed to learn the very intricate kanji. After hiragana was introduced to women, they were able to express themselves in the written form. It is due to hiragana that women authored many of the first published works in Japan.

Hiragana character samples

あ か さ た な は ま や ら わ ん

Katakana was created by using portions of kanji, while the more rounded hiragana was created by simplifying kanji. Children in Japan learn hiragana first, then katakana, and finally kanji. Hiragana, with only 47 unique characters, can represent the entire Japanese language.

Katakana character samples

ア カ サ タ ナ ハ マ ヤ ラ ワ ン

Kanji, on the other hand, consists of over 10,000 characters. In 1981 the Japanese Ministry of Education announced 1,945 commonly used kanji called the *Joyou Kanji*. By the 6th grade, the average Japanese student knows half of the *Joyou Kanji*. Since this time more Kanji have been deemed necessary to learn and have been added to the *Joyou Kanji* list.

Kanji character samples

安 加 左 太 奈 波 末 也 良 和 毛

あ   **Writing Basics かくときの きほん**

❑ **1-5. What is a stroke?**

A stroke begins when the pen (or any other writing device) comes in contact with the paper. The stroke ends when the pen separates from the paper.

❑ **1-6. Why use brushes to write?**

Traditionally, Japanese was written with brushes. This book – and almost any book that teaches Japanese writing – uses the brush-written style for the Japanese characters. The brush-written style best represents how the characters should be written.

❑ **1-7. Different types of brush strokes**

There are three types of strokes. For ease of understanding we have named them *fade out*, *dead stop* and *bounce fade*. Whether writing with a brush, pen, or pencil, make sure that you pay attention to the stroke type. This will ensure that your writing is neat and proper.

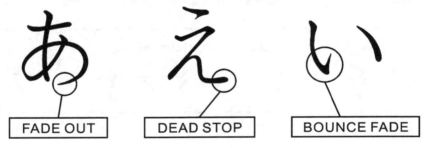

| FADE OUT | DEAD STOP | BOUNCE FADE |

あ   **New Hiragana あたらしい ひらがな**

The first five hiragana to learn are listed below. Notice the different stroke types. Make sure you learn the correct stroke order and stroke type.

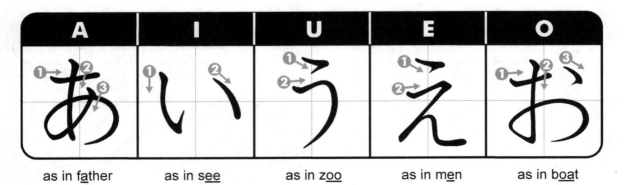

A	I	U	E	O
as in f<u>a</u>ther	as in s<u>ee</u>	as in z<u>oo</u>	as in m<u>e</u>n	as in b<u>oa</u>t

あ Various Styles スタイル

Look at the various possible styles for the hiragana in this lesson. Write each symbol as neatly as you can, then compare it to the different versions below.

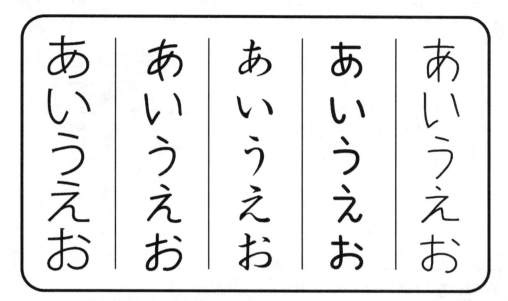

☐ 1-8. The importance of the various styles

It is important to always study the different styles of each character in the Various Styles section of the lessons to see what is allowed when writing. Remember that there are small differences between how the characters will look when writing with a brush and writing with a pen or pencil.

あ Writing Points かくポイント

☐ 1-9. The difference between あ (a) and お (o)

Be careful not to mix up あ and お. The second stroke of あ is curved while the second stroke for お is straight until the loop.

more curved
than お and
not connected
to the loop.

straighter
than あ and
connected to
the loop.

❏ **1-10. Writing left-to-right and top-to-bottom**

Before World War II, Japanese publications were written with each line going from top to bottom as shown in style 2 below. In modern Japan, both styles are common. Many times the style used is based solely on design choice, and in some cases (such as writing an e-mail) only style 1 is possible. Many Japanese writing books for children will use style 2. Even though *Japanese From Zero!* contains only style 1, both styles are acceptable.

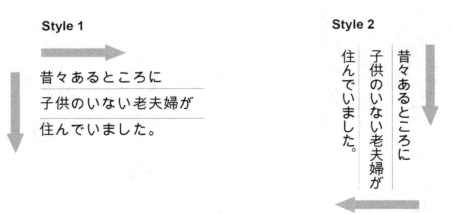

あ | **Writing Practice れんしゅう**

To practice correct stroke order, first trace the light gray characters, then write each character six times for practice.

a	あ	あ					
i	い	い					
u	う	う					
e	え	え					
o	お	お					

あ Word Practice ことばの れんしゅう

Fill in the appropriate hiragana in the blanks for each word.

1. __ka__san (mother)
   o   a

2. __ __ (house)
   i   e

3. __to__san (father)
   o   u

4. __ka __ (red)
   a   i

5. __mo__to (younger sister)
   i   u

6. ka__ (to buy)
   u

7. __sagi (rabbit)
   u

8. __npitsu (pencil)
   e

9. __ne__san (older sister)
   o   e

10. __moshiro__ (interesting)
    o   i

11. __su (chair)
    i

12. __kiru (to wake up)
    o

あ Words You Can Write かける ことば

Write the following words using the hiragana that you just learned. This is a great way to increase your Japanese vocabulary.

え
(a painting)

いい
(good)

おい
(nephew)

あい
(love)

えい
(a ray fish)

いいえ
(no)

おおい
(many)

あう
(to meet)

うえ
(up)

いう
(to say)

いえ
(house)

あお
(blue)

あ | **Everyday Hiragana Words にちじょうの ことば**

あkachan
baby

いnu
dog

うshi
cow

kaえru
frog

おkoru
to get mad

うchuう
space

あ Hiragana Matching ひらがな マッチング

Connect the dots between each hiragana and the correct ro–maji.

お・	・a
う・	・o
え・	・u
い・	・e
あ・	・i

1 Lesson Activities

❏ 1. Question and answer

Answer the following questions by looking at the pictures. You can check your answers in the answer key for this lesson.

1. **Nan desu ka?**

Answer: _____

2. **Taoru desu ka?**

Answer: _____

3. **Nan desu ka?**

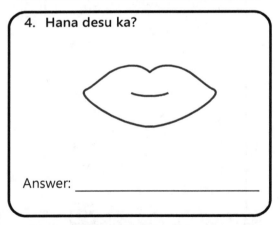

Answer: _____

4. **Hana desu ka?**

Answer: _____

5. **Tanaka san desu ka?**

Yamamoto san

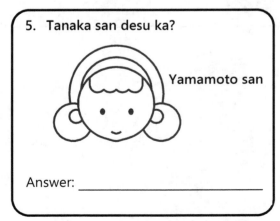

Answer: _____

6. **Nan desu ka?**

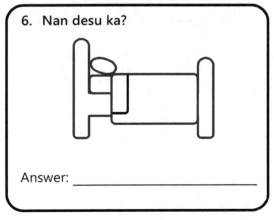

Answer: _____

❑ **2. Japanese translation**
Translate the following conversation into English.

1.	
Tanaka san:	Nan desu ka. Mo う fu desu ka.
Kobayashi san:	Moう いchido いtte kudasaい.
Tanaka san:	Moうfu desu ka.
Kobayashi san:	いいえ, taoru desu.
Tanaka san:	
Kobayashi san:	
Tanaka san:	
Kobayashi san:	

❑ **3. English translation**
Translate the following conversation into Japanese.

1.	
Kouichi:	Are you Masumi?
Yasuko:	No, I am Yasuko. Are you Yuusuke?
Kouichi:	No, I am Kouichi.
Kouichi:	
Yasuko:	
Kouichi:	

❑ **4. What would you say?**
What would you say in the following situations? Write the answer in Japanese.

1. When you want someone to repeat what they said:

_____

2. When you meet someone for the first time:

_____

3. When you want someone to guess your age:

_____

4. When you ask someone if he is Mr. Nakamura:

_____

5. When you ask someone to speak slower:

_____

1 Drill ドリル

If you know what these sentences mean, congratulations! You're already learning Japanese! If you don't know what they mean, we recommend that you review the lesson up to this point before continuing.

1. Nan desu ka.
2. Wakarimasu ka.
3. Haい, wakarimasu.
4. いnu desu ka.

5. Makura desu ka.
6. いいえ、neko desu.
7. Wakarimasen.
8. Hajimemashite.

1 Sentence Building ぶんのつくり

In each lesson, we will build on a previous sentence. Watch it grow and transform each time new concepts are introduced.

> Nan desu ka.
> What is it?

1 Answer Key

❑ Word practice (answers)

1. おkaあsan
2. いえ
3. おtoうsan
4. あkaい
5. いmoうto
6. kaう
7. うsagi
8. えnpitsu
9. おneえsan
10. おmoshiroい
11. いsu
12. おkiru

❑ Hiragana matching (answers)

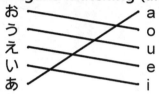

❑ 1. Question and answer (answers)

Question	Answer
1. What is it?	Haburashi desu.
2. Is it a towel?	いいえ、makura desu.
3. What is it?	いnu desu.
4. Is it a nose?	いいえ、kuchi desu.
5. Is she Ms. Tanaka?	いいえ、Yamamoto san desu.
6. What is it?	Beddo desu.

❑ 2. Japanese translation (answers)

1. Tanaka san: What is it? Is it a blanket?
   Kobayashi san: Please say it one more time.
   Tanaka san: Is it a blanket?
   Kobayashi san: No, it is a towel.

❑ 3. English translation (answers)

1. Kouichi: (あnata wa) Masumi san desu ka.
   Yasuko: いいえ、Yasuko desu. (あnata wa) Yuusuke san desu ka.
   Kouichi: いいえ、Kouichi desu.

❑ 4. What would you say? (sample answers)

1. Moう いchido いtte kudasaい.
2. Hajimemashite. _____to moushimasu. Yoroshiku おnegaい shimasu.
3. Nansaい ni miemasu ka.
4. Nakamura san desu ka.
5. Motto yukkuri いtte kudasai.

Lesson

2

Level ①

Working with a Topic

Which one?

---

2 | About This Lesson このレッスンについて

Before The Lesson

1. Be able to write and read あいうえお.
2. Understand how to use *desu* and the particle *ka*.

Lesson Goals

1. Learn how to work with a topic in simple sentences.
2. Learn how to use the topic marker *wa*.

From The Teachers

1. Remember the phrases "Dore desu ka" and "Docchi desu ka"
2. Memorize the *ko so a do* pattern. It'll come in handy later.

---

2 | New Words あたらしい ことば

Progressive	Kana	Kanji	English
dore	どれ	どれ	which one (three or more)
kore	これ	これ	this one
sore	それ	それ	that one
あre	あれ	あれ	that one over there
docchi	どっち	どっち	which one (two items)
kocchi	こっち	こっち	this one
socchi	そっち	そっち	that one
あcchi	あっち	あっち	that one over there
retasu	レタス	レタス	lettuce
banana	バナナ	バナナ	banana
yasaい	やさい	野菜	vegetable
furu–tsu	フルーツ	フルーツ	fruit *
kudamono	くだもの	果物	fruit *

sushi	すし	寿司	sushi
pen	ペン	ペン	pen
kuruma	くるま	車	car
konpyu–ta–	コンピューター	コンピューター	computer
hon	ほん	本	book
zasshi	ざっし	雑誌	magazine

* There are 2 ways to say "fruit" in Japanese. One came from English and one is native Japanese, but both are correct.

2 New Phrases あたらしい かいわ

At this point, don't worry about the grammar of the New Phrases; simply memorizing the phrases will be more beneficial at this point.

1. Can you speak Japanese?   Nihongo ga hanasemasu ka.
2. Can you speak English?   えいgo ga hanasemasu ka.
3. A little.   Sukoshi.
4. Not at all.   Zenzen.
5. I'm studying Japanese.   Nihongo o benkyou shiteいmasu.

2 Culture Clip: Sushi and Sashimi

Many foreigners to Japan don't know the difference between sushi and sashimi. Sushi is raw or cooked fish, eggs, or vegetables on rice. It is placed on top of a fist-full of rice, and normally between the fish and rice there is some *wasabi*. *Wasabi* is a Japanese horseradish. It is very pungent. Sashimi is just sliced raw fish. (Try it – you might like it!)

**Sushi is raw
fish on rice**

**Sashimi is sliced
raw fish**

2 | Cool Tools クール・ツール

In Japanese, there is a pattern of words that comes up many times. It is the *ko so a do* pattern. In this lesson there are two *ko so a do* patterns: <u>ko</u>re, <u>so</u>re, <u>a</u>re, <u>do</u>re, and <u>ko</u>cchi, <u>so</u>cchi, <u>a</u>cchi, <u>do</u>cchi. Notice that each word starts with *ko~*, *so~*, *a~* or *do~*. The following chart shows the distance relation of these words to the speaker.

Since the four words in a *ko-so-a-do* group are similar in sound, they are easy to mix up. The diagram on the right will help you remember the relation of each word in the group to the speaker. Remember this diagram, because there are more *ko-so-a-do* groups coming up.

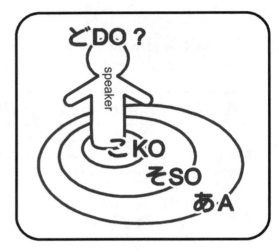

ko – Close enough to touch
so – Sort of close, but not enough to touch
a – In the distance. Definitely not close.
do – Question word.

2 | Grammar ぶんぽう

❑ **2-1. The topic marker *wa***

The particle *wa* is used to mark the topic of the sentence. It can be thought to mean, "Speaking of (the) ~," or "As for (the) ~," but it does not have any meaning in English. Generally, everything that comes before *wa* is the topic or part of the topic. Everything after the *wa* describes or asks a question about the topic.

> **[topic] + wa + [question or description]**

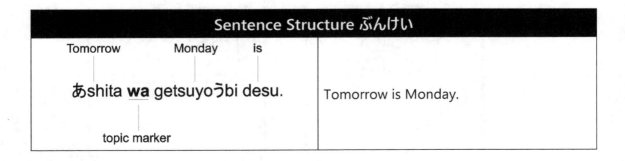

Sentence Structure ぶんけい	
Tomorrow Monday is **あshita wa getsuyoうbi desu.** topic marker	Tomorrow is Monday.

Yukari Japanese is **Yukari-san wa** nihonjin desu. topic marker	Yukari is Japanese.
Bananas yellow are **Banana wa** kiʼro desu. topic marker	Bananas are yellow.

❏ 2-2. Using *wa* in a variety of sentences

Remember that *wa* is used to mark the topic of a sentence. Read the examples to see how *wa* can be applied to the words that you already know. Don't forget that the word before the *wa* is the topic, and everything after *wa* is asking a question about or describing the topic.

Example Q&A

1. Kore <u>wa</u> nan desu ka.   What is this?
   Sore <u>wa</u> kagami desu.   That is a mirror.

2. Sore <u>wa</u> nan desu ka.   What is that?
   Sore <u>wa</u> pen desu.   That is a pen.
   あれ <u>wa</u> banana desu.   That over there is a banana.

3. Kore <u>wa</u> yasaい desu ka.   Is this a vegetable?
   いいえ、sore <u>wa</u> furu–tsu desu.   No, that is a fruit.

4. Banana <u>wa</u> nan desu ka.   What is a banana?
   Banana <u>wa</u> furu–tsu desu.   A banana is a fruit.

5. Retasu <u>wa</u> furu–tsu desu ka.   Is lettuce a fruit?
   いいえ、retasu <u>wa</u> yasaい desu.   No, lettuce is a vegetable.

❏ **2-3. The question words *dore* and *docchi***

Dore and *docchi* both mean "which one?" *Dore* is used with groups of three or more. If there are only two items, *docchi* is used.

> **[*topic*] + wa dore desu ka**
> **[*topic*] + wa docchi desu ka**
> **Which one is the/a [*topic*]?**

If there are three or more items, *dore* is used.

1. Kuruma wa dore desu ka. Which one is the car?
2. Furu–tsu wa dore desu ka. Which one is a fruit?
3. Yasaい wa dore desu ka. Which one is a vegetable?

If there are only two items, *docchi* is used.

1. Kuruma wa docchi desu ka. Which one is the car?
2. Furu–tsu wa docchi desu ka. Which one is a fruit?
3. Yasaい wa docchi desu ka. Which one is a vegetable?

❏ **2-4. Following the same pattern when answering**

Notice that the questions and answers in the Q&A below follow the same sentence pattern. When answering questions, remember that *90% of the answer is in the question.*

Also, when the question has *~cchi* in it, the answer should not change to *~re*. Try to keep response sentences in the same format as their question sentences.

Example Q&A

Question:	Kuruma	wa	dore	desu	ka.	Which one is a car?
Answer:	Kuruma	wa	kore	desu.		The car is this one.
Question:	Banana	wa	nan	desu	ka.	What is a banana?
Answer:	Banana	wa	furu–tsu	desu.		A banana is a fruit.
Question:	Kagami	wa	dore	desu	ka.	Which one is a mirror?
Answer:	Kagami	wa	sore	desu.		That one is a mirror.
Question:	Mado	wa	docchi	desu	ka.	Which one is a window?
Answer:	Mado	wa	あcchi	desu.		That one over there is a window.

❑ **2-5. Using what you know to learn more**

If you don't know a word, use the Japanese you know to ask someone what the word is. You can use the following sentence to ask what something is. For example, let's say that you don't know what えnpitsu means:

Examples

1. えnpitsu wa <u>nan</u> desu ka?
   What is "enpitsu"?

2. えnpitsu wa pencil desu.
   Enpitsu is a pencil.
---

2   Speaking Naturally しぜんに はなすこと

❑ **2-6. Dropping the topic of a sentence**

It's very common in Japanese to drop the topic of a conversation once it has been introduced. In English, we constantly restate the topic directly or use "he", "she", "they" as a substitute. Spoken Japanese is much more like a match of tennis.

In Japanese, a topic is served and then discussed back and forth. Normally a topic is not mentioned again until a new topic is served.

To illustrate this, look at the following statements about my friend Michiko:

---
1. My friend is Michiko.
2. She lives in Japan.
3. She is 18 years old.
4. She is a college student.

In English, the topic "My friend" is introduced in the first sentence. Then in each following sentence, "she" is used to continually restate the topic. In Japanese, it's more natural to not say "she" over and over again. Instead, what would be considered incomplete sentences in English are used. This makes for much more natural conversation.
The English equivalent if spoken in Japanese would look like this:

---
1. My friend is Michiko.	Watashi no tomodachi wa Michiko san desu.
2. Lives in Japan.	Nihon ni sundeいmasu.
3. Is 18 years old.	Juうhassaい desu.
4. Is a college student.	Daいgakuseい desu.

As you read the example Q&A in the next section, look for places where the topic is NOT repeated.

2   Q&A しつもんと こたえ English→Japanese

1. **Which one is it? (four items)**
   It is this one.
   It is that one.
   It is that one over there.

   Dore desu ka.
   Kore desu.
   Sore desu.
   あre desu.

2. **What is this?**
   This is a pillow.
   This is a computer.
   It's a blanket.

   Kore wa nan desu ka.
   Kore wa makura desu.
   Kore wa konpyu–ta– desu.
   Moうfu desu.

3. **Is this a vegetable?**
   Yes, it's a vegetable.
   No, it's a fruit.
   Yes, it's lettuce.

   Kore wa yasaい desu ka.
   Haい, yasaい desu.
   いいえ, furu–tsu desu.
   Haい, retasu desu.

4. **Which one is a vegetable? (two items)**
   This one is.
   That one is.
   I don't know.

   Yasaい wa docchi desu ka.
   Kocchi desu.
   Socchi desu.
   Wakarimasen.

5. **What is that?**
   That is soap.
   This is a towel.
   It's a futon.

   Sore wa nan desu ka.
   Sore wa sekken desu.
   Kore wa taoru desu.
   Futon desu.

か Hiragana かきくけこ

か New Hiragana あたらしい ひらがな

Make sure you learn the correct stroke order since correct stroke order will mean neater characters when writing quickly.

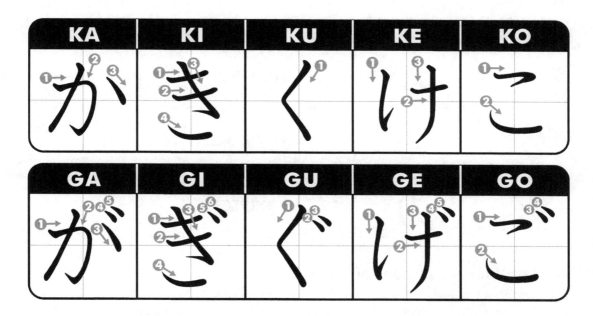

か Various Styles スタイル

Look at the various possible styles for the hiragana in this lesson. Write each symbol as neatly as you can, then compare it to the different versions below.

かきくけこ　かきくけこ　かきくけこ　かきくけこ　かきくけこ

がぎぐげご　がぎぐげご　がぎぐげご　がぎぐげご　がぎぐげご

か Writing Points かくポイント

❑ 2-7. The dakuten

The only difference between *ka ki ku ke ko* and *ga gi gu ge go* are the two small strokes in the right hand corner. Those strokes are called *dakuten*. You will see more in future lessons.

❑ 2-8. Writing が (ga) the correct way

When adding *dakuten* to か (ka) to make it が (ga), make sure that they are shorter than the third stroke. The third stroke of が should always be longer than the *dakuten*.

が	INCORRECT
が	INCORRECT
が	CORRECT

❑ 2-9. The different versions of き (ki)

You may have noticed in the *Various Styles* section of this lesson that there are two versions of *ki*. It is your choice which version you use. You will see both versions in Japan.

き	This version has four strokes and is very common when writing. Many Japanese people write using this version.
き	This version has combined the third and fourth strokes into one stroke. It is very common in printed text such as books and magazines.

❑ 2-10. Spaces in Japanese

Japanese does not normally use spaces. When sentences are written using all three writing systems, it's easy to see where words begin and end because of the kanji. However, since we are mixing roma-ji and hiragana, we will add spaces to make sentences easier to read. This book series will slowly remove spaces as you learn more.

か	Writing Practice れんしゅう

To practice correct stroke order, first trace the light gray characters, then write each character six times for practice.

ka	か	か						
ki	き	き						
ku	く	く						
ke	け	け						
ko	こ	こ						

ga	が	が						
gi	ぎ	ぎ						
gu	ぐ	ぐ						
ge	げ	げ						
go	ご	ご						

か   Word Practice ことばの れんしゅう

Fill in the appropriate hiragana in the blanks for each word.

1. __いro   (yellow)
   ki

2. __ __   (to listen)
   ki ku

3. __minari   (lightning)
   ka

4. __う__n   (air force)
   ku gu

5. __ __   (moss)
   ko ke

6. い__   (to go)
   ku

7. __mushi   (caterpillar)
   ke

8. __う__う   (airport)
   ku ko

9. __nいro   (silver color)
   gi

10. __n'ni__   (muscle)
    ki   ku

11. __ __   (afternoon)
    go go

12. __おri   (ice)
    ko

か   Words You Can Write かける ことば

Write the following words using the hiragana that you just learned. This is a great way to increase your Japanese vocabulary.

き
(tree)

か く
(to write)

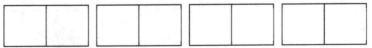

い か
(squid)

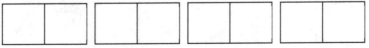

か ぎ
(key)

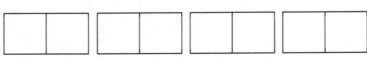

かお
(face)

かい
(shell)

あか
(red)

ごご
(afternoon)

がいこく
(foreign country)

おおきい
(big)

くうこう
(airport)

か **Everyday Hiragana Words にちじょうの ことば**

tsuき
the moon

けいtaいdenwa
cell phone

かぎ
key

cho**きん** ba**こ**
safe; piggy
bank

かく
to write

su**いか**
watermelon

| **か** | **Hiragana Matching ひらがな マッチング** |

Connect the dots between each hiragana and the correct ro–maji.

き ・　　　　　 ・ i

い ・　　　　　 ・ go

く ・　　　　　 ・ ka

か ・　　　　　 ・ ki

え ・　　　　　 ・ ku

ご ・　　　　　 ・ ke

け ・　　　　　 ・ e

2 Lesson Activities

❑ 1. Question and answer 1

Answer the following questions in Japanese by looking at the pictures.

1. これ wa nan desuか?

Answer: _____

2. これ wa nan desuか?

Answer: _____

3. これ wa かがmi desuか?

Answer: _____

4. これ wa yasaい desuか?

Answer: _____

☐ 2. Question and answer 2

Circle the correct item and answer with _これre desu_ or _こcchi desu_.

1. Hon wa dore desuか?

2. Yasaい wa dore desuか?

3. Furu–tsu wa docchi desuか?

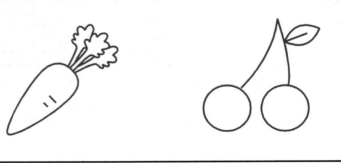

❏ 3. Question and answer 3

Fill in the question being asked by the girl (Q:) and the answer given by the woman (A:) in the following pictures. (Write your answers in Japanese)

1.

Q: _____

A: _____

2.

Q: _____

A: _____

3.

Q: _____

A: _____

4.

Q: _____

A: _____

❏ 4. Japanese translation
Translate the following conversation into English.

1.	
Sato こ san:	Sore wa hon desu か.
Sho う ta san:	いいえ, zasshi desu.
Sato こ san:	Mo う い chido い tte く dasa い. Nan desu か.
Sho う ta san:	こ re wa zasshi desu.
Satoこ san:	
Shoうta san:	
Satoこ san:	
Shoうta san:	

❏ 5. English translation
Translate the following conversation into Japanese.

1.	
Japanese:	Can you speak Japanese?
American:	A little.
Japanese:	What is that over there?
American:	That is a car.
Japanese:	Thank you.
Japanese:	
American:	
Japanese:	
American:	
Japanese:	

2 | Drill ドリル

If you're not sure what these sentences mean, we recommend that you review the lesson up to this point before continuing.

1. Retasu wa nan desuか。
2. Hon wa socchi desu.
3. Tadaいma.
4. Banana wa furu–tsu desu.
5. これ wa yasaい desuか。

6. Nihonご o benkyoう shiteいmasu.
7. あre wa かがmi desu.
8. くruma wa dore desuか。
9. Yasaい desu.
10. Nihonごが hanasemasuか。

2 | Sentence Building ぶんのつくり

In each lesson we build on a previous sentence. Watch it grow and transform each time new concepts are introduced.

The sentence from the previous lesson was: Nan desuか。 (What is it?). In this lesson we learned how to attach a topic to the question. Let's look at the new sentence:

> **これ wa nan desuか。**
> **What is this?**

Compare how the sentence has changed from the prior lessons:

Lesson 1:   Nan desuか。

          What is it?

2 | Answer Key

❑ Word Practice (answers)

1. きいro
2. きく
3. かminari
4. くうぐn
5. こけ
6. いく
7. けmushi
8. くうこう
9. ぎnいro
10. きn'niく
11. ごご
12. こおri

❑ Hiragana matching (answers)

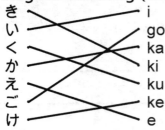

き   i
い   go
く   ka
か   ki
え   ku
ご   ke
け   e

❑ 1. Question and answer 1 (answers)

1. What is this?   (これ wa) くruma desu.
2. What is this?   (これ wa) konpyu–ta– desu.
3. Is this a mirror?   いいえ、(これ wa) mado desu.
4. Are these vegetables?   いいえ、(これ wa) furu–tsu desu.

❑ 2. Question and answer 2 (answers)

1. Which is a book?   (1st picture) これ desu.
2. Which is a vegetable?   (middle picture: onion) これ desu.
3. Which is a fruit?   (2nd picture: cherries) こcchi desu.

❑ 3. Question and answer 3 (answers)

1. Q: What is that over there?   A: That's a dog.
   (あれ wa) nan desuか。   あれ wa いnu desu.

2. Q: Is this a toothbrush?   A: Yes, that's a toothbrush
   これ wa haburashi desuか。   Haい、sore wa haburashi desu.

3. Q: What is that?   A: This is a towel.
   Sore wa nan desuか。   (これ wa) taoru desu.

4. Q: What is that?   A: This is a book.
   Sore wa nan desuか。   (これ wa) hon desu.

❑ 4. Japanese translation (answers)

1. Satoko san: Is that a book?
   Shouta san: No, it is a magazine.
   Satoko san: Please say it one more time. What is it?
   Shouta san: This is a magazine.

❑ 5. English translation (answers)

1. Japanese person: (あnata wa) nihonご が hanasemasuか。
   American person: Suこshi.
   Japanese person: あre wa nan desuか。
   American person: あre wa くruma desu.
   Japanese person: あriが toう。

Vocabulary Groups

C   family

Progressive	Kana	Kanji	English
おかあsan	おかあさん	お母さん	mother
おtoうsan	おとうさん	お父さん	father
おjiいsan	おじいさん	おじいさん	grandfather
おbaあsan	おばあさん	おばあさん	grandmother
あかchan	あかちゃん	赤ちゃん	baby

D   greetings and farewells

Progressive	Kana	Kanji	English
あриがtoう	ありがとう	ありがとう	thank you; thanks
おhayoうごzaいmasu	おはよう ございます	おはよう ございます	good morning
おyasuminasaい	おやすみなさい	お休みなさい	good night
こnnichiwa	こんにちは	今日は	good afternoon
sayoうnara	さようなら	さようなら	good bye; farewell

おとうさん

おはよう ございます

おかあさん

Lesson 3 Level ①

Possession
Whose is this?

---

3 About This Lesson このレッスンについて

Before The Lesson

1. Be able to write and read かきくけこ, がぎぐげご
2. Understand how to use the question words *dore* and *docchi* and the topic marker *wa*
3. Review vocabulary groups C and D.

Lesson Goals

1. Learn to show possession using the particle *no*
2. Learn how to use the subject marker が

From The Teachers

1. It's common to mix up *dare* (who) and *dore* (which one). It's also common to mix up *watashi* (me) and あ*nata* (you). Try to avoid these mistakes.

---

3 New Words あたらしい ことば

Progressive	Hiragana	Kanji	English
dare	だれ	誰	who?
watashi	わたし	私	I; me (male or female)
boく	ぼく	僕	I; me (males only)
あnata	あなた	貴方	you
かnojo	かのじょ	彼女	her; she; girlfriend
かre	かれ	彼	him; he; boyfriend
namaえ	なまえ	名前	name
tomodachi	ともだち	友達	friend
tabun	たぶん	多分	maybe
がkkoう	がっこう	学校	school

tori	とり	鳥	bird
senseい	せんせい	先生	teacher
nihonご no senseい	にほんごの せんせい	日本語の先生	Japanese teacher

3 New Phrases あたらしい かいわ

1. **Soうdesu.**
   That's right.
   This phrase is used to affirm that something said is true or correct. It doesn't need to always be translated as "That's right." It can be translated into a variety of similar phrases such as: "You are right," "It is," or even just simply "Yes."

2. **Chiがいmasu.**
   That's wrong.
   This phrase is used when something is false or incorrect. It doesn't always have to be translated as "That's wrong." It can mean a variety of similar phrases such as: "It's different," "It isn't," and "No."

3 Culture Clip: Interesting information about boく

boく

The word *boく* means "me" or "I," and normally only males use it. It can be masculine or cute depending on the usage. It should only be used in casual conversation.

Also, when talking to little boys, it is very common to call them *boく* when their name is not known. For example, if someone is talking to a little boy and you hear them say, "Boく wa nansaい desuか," it means "How old are you?" and not "How old am I?"

Can girls use *boく*?
Even though *boく* is normally a male word, you might hear it in songs sung by female singers. This sometimes done when the girl is singing from a male perspective or when the girl is trying to sound boyish. Despite this, you might never hear a girl use *boく* in conversation. However, you will often hear young girls say *あtashi* as an informal and cute way of saying *watashi*.

3 Grammar ぶんぽう

❑ 3-1. The question word *dare*

You can use the question word *dare* just as *nan*, *dore* and *docchi* are used.

Example Q&A

1. <u>Nan</u> desuか。   <u>What</u> is it?
   くruma desu.   It is a car.

2. <u>Dore</u> desuか。   <u>Which one</u> is it?
   Sore desu.   It is that one.

3. <u>Dare</u> desuか。   <u>Who</u> is it?
   Tanaかsan desu.   It is Mr. Tanaka.

❑ 3-2. Using *wa* with *dare*

As we learned in lesson 2, you can specify a topic using the topic marker *wa*. Look at how the new question word *dare* (who) is used.

Example Q&A

1. あnata wa <u>dare</u> desuか。   <u>Who</u> are you?
   Watashi wa こbayashi desu.   I am Kobayashi.

2. かre wa <u>dare</u> desuか。   <u>Who</u> is he?
   かre wa tomodachi desu.   He is a friend.

3. Senseい wa <u>dare</u> desuか。   <u>Who</u> is the teacher?
   Yamada san desu.   It's Yamada san.

4. Tanaかsan wa <u>dare</u> desuか。   <u>Who</u> is Tanaka san?
   Nihonご no senseい desu.   (She's / He's) a Japanese teacher.

❑ 3-3. Assuming the topic based on context

Japanese conversation relies heavily on the context or "circumstances" of the conversation. Let's look at the sentence **Dare desuか** which in the prior example was translated as "Who is it?". You might have noticed that there isn't any specific topic in this sentence.

It's not uncommon for sentences to lack a topic in Japanese. And as stated in the prior lesson, it isn't natural to continually say, "he, she, you, I" in Japanese as we do in English.

Look at how the translation of *Dare desuか* changes depending on the context.

Example Conversations

1. **Context:** Looking at an unknown person in a photograph.
    A: Dare desuか。   Who is this person?
    B: Tanaかsan desu.   It is Mr. Tanaka.

    The topic "this person" is assumed and doesn't need to be said.

2. **Context:** Someone you don't know calls you on the phone.
    A: Dare desuか。   Who are you?
    B: Tanaか desu.   It's Tanaka.

    You could have added **あnata wa** in front of the question, but the person knows you're speaking directly to him, so the topic can be dropped.

3. **Context:** Looking at a girl in the hallway.
    A: Dare desuか。   Who is she?
    B: Mayumi desu.   She is Mayumi.

    You could have added **かnojo wa** in front of both of these sentences, but the conversation would not sound natural. The "she" part of the conversation does not need to be stated since the topic is obvious.

❑ 3-4. Starting sentences with or without question words

In English it's common to start sentences with a question word. Look at the following English sentences that start with question words:

Example Sentences

1. <u>What</u> is this?
2. <u>Which one</u> is your car?
3. <u>Who</u> are you?

Since it's so common to start sentences in English with a question word, many students of Japanese mistakenly believe you can always do the same thing in Japanese, but this is not the case.

In the following examples you will notice that the Japanese sentences DO NOT start with a question word even though the English sentences do. The question words have been underlined in both sentences.

Example Sentences

1. Kore wa <u>nan</u> desuか。
   <u>What</u> is this?

2. Kuruma wa <u>dore</u> desuか。
   <u>Which one</u> is a car?

3. Tanakaさん wa <u>dare</u> desuか。
   <u>Who</u> is Tanaka?

❑ 3-5. How to start a sentence with a question word using が

Even though you don't generally start a Japanese sentence with a question word, there are times when this is acceptable or necessary.

When a question word is the topic of the sentence, or when a question word is the FIRST word in a sentence, the topic/subject marker が instead of *wa* <u>must</u> be used.

However, if the items you are talking about have already been introduced or are in front of you, you can start a sentence with a question word as the topic.

In the following examples, the question words have been underlined in both sentences.

Example Sentences

1. <u>Dore</u>が Kuruma desuか。
   <u>Which one</u> is a car?

2. <u>Dare</u>が Tanakaさん desuか。
   <u>Who</u> is Tanaka?

Remember that the answer must follow the same pattern as the question, and therefore the answer must also use が as the topic/subject marker.

> **Example Conversations**
>
> 1. A: <u>Dore</u>が くruma desuか。   <u>Which one</u> is a car?
>   B: Soreが くruma desu.   That's a car.
>
> 2. A: <u>Dare</u>が Tanaかsan desuか。   <u>Who/which</u> is Tanaka?
>   B: Tanaかsanが tomodachi desu.   Tanaka is a friend.

❑ 3-6. Making words possessive with the particle *no*

It is easy to convert words into their possessive form by adding *no* after them.

> **Examples**
>
> | | |
> |---|---|
> | mine | watashi <u>no</u> |
> | mine | boく <u>no</u> |
> | yours | あnata <u>no</u> |
> | hers | かnojo <u>no</u> |
> | his | かre <u>no</u> |
> | whose | dare <u>no</u> |

No also acts like the possessive *'s* in English when it follows a person's name and other words.

> Examples
>
> | | |
> |---|---|
> | Akiko<u>'s</u> | あきこ <u>no</u> |
> | Jeff<u>'s</u> | Jefu <u>no</u> |
> | Mr. Tanaka<u>'s</u> | Tanaかsan <u>no</u> |
> | Father<u>'s</u> | おとうsan <u>no</u> |
> | Mother<u>'s</u> | おかあsan <u>no</u> |
> | Grandfather<u>'s</u> | おjiいsan <u>no</u> |
> | Grandmother<u>'s</u> | おbaあsan <u>no</u> |

Using this concept in conversation is easy. If someone asks, **これ wa dare no desu か** (Whose is this?) as they hold an object in their hand, you can use any of the following answers:

Example Answers

1. Watashi no desu.   It's mine.
2. あnata no desu.   It's yours.
3. Tanaか san no desu.   It's Mr. Tanaka's.
4. かnojo no desu.   It's hers.
5. おba あsan no desu.   It's grandmother's.
6. かre no desu.   It's his.
7. おか あsan no desu.   It's mother's.

❏ 3-7. Showing possession of objects using *no*

In the prior grammar section, you learned that the particle ***no*** is used to change words into their possessive form. The possessive form can be used by itself or followed by another word to show ownership. Try thinking of ***no*** as the glue that holds nouns together. You add objects after the possessive form as follows:

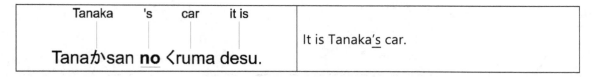

Tanaka	's	car	it is	
Tana か san **no** くruma desu.				It is Tanaka's car.

Examples

my dog	watashi <u>no</u> いnu
your mother	あnata <u>no</u> おか あsan
her cat	かnojo <u>no</u> neこ
his dog	かre <u>no</u> いnu
father's pen	おto うsan <u>no</u> pen

The particle ***no*** is not limited to linking only two items. It can be used to further clarify the object or item being discussed.

Examples

あnata no かnojo no nama え	your girlfriend's name
おか あsan <u>no</u> neこ <u>no</u> nama え	mother's cat's name

Now let's put your new knowledge of *no* into practice. These sentences may appear long at first, but they're using the simple grammar you've learned already.

Example Sentences

1. あnata <u>no</u> かnojo <u>no</u> namaえ wa nan desuか。
    What is your girlfriend's name?

2. Tanaかsan no おかあsan wa nansai desuか。
    How old is Tanaka san's mother?

3. こbayashi san no おtoうsan wa dare desuか。
    Who is Kobayashi san's father?

---

3   Q&A しつもんと こたえ English→Japanese

1. **Who is it?**   **Dare desuか。**
    It's me.   Watashi desu.
    It's Hideko.   Hideこ desu.
    It's Mom.   おかあsan desu.

2. **Whose car is it?**   **Dare no くruma desuか。**
    It's my car.   Watashi no くruma desu.
    It's mine.   Watashi no desu.
    It's Mr. Takada's car.   Taかda san no くruma desu.
    I don't know.   Waかrimasen.

3. **Which one is your rabbit?**   **Docchiが あnata no うsaぎ desuか。**
    That one over there is my rabbit.   あcchiが watashi no うsaぎ desu.
    It's that one.   Socchi desu.

4. **Is this your car?**   **こre wa あnata no くruma desuか。**
    Yes, it is.   Haい, soう desu.
    No, it's my friend's car.   いいえ、tomodachi no くruma desu.
    No, it's her car.   いいえ、かnojo no くruma desu.
    No, it's hers.   いいえ、かnojo no desu.

5. **Which one is your bird?**   **あnata no tori wa dore desuか。**
    My bird is that one.   Boく no tori wa sore desu.

3 | Q&A しつもんと こたえ Japanese→English

1. **あnata no neこ wa dore desuか。**
   Watashi no neこ wa sore desu.
   Watashi no neこ wa あre desu.

   Which one is your cat?
   My cat is that one.
   My cat is that one over there.

2. **おかあsan no namaえ wa nan desuか。**
   Maria desu.
   Yoshiこ desu.

   What is (your) mother's name?
   It's Maria.
   It's Yoshiko.

3. **Sore wa かnojo no taoru desuか。**
   いいえ、かre no taoru desu.
   いいえ、Mamiこsan no taoru desu.

   Is that her towel?
   No, it's his towel.
   No, it's Mamiko's towel.

4. **あnata no tomodachi no いnu no namaえ wa nan desuか。**
   いnu no namaえ wa Pochi desu.
   Waかrimasen.

   What is your friend's dog's name?

   The dog's name is Pochi.
   I don't know.

3 | Reading Comprehension どっかい

Read the sentences below. Use the information to answer the reading comprehension questions later in this lesson.

① Watashi no namaえ wa Honda desu.

② Sanjuうごsaい desu.

③ Watashi no かnojo no namaえ wa Terada desu.

④ かnojo wa nijuうkyuうsaい desu.

Hiragana さしすせそ

さ New Hiragana あたらしい ひらがな

Make sure you learn the correct stroke order since correct stroke order will mean neater characters when writing quickly.

さ Various Styles スタイル

Look at the various possible styles for the hiragana in this lesson. Write each symbol as neatly as you can, then compare it to the different versions below.

さしすせそ さしすせそ さしすせそ さしすせそ さしすせそ

ざじずぜぞ ざじずぜぞ ざじずぜぞ ざじずぜぞ ざじずぜぞ

さ Writing Points かくポイント

❏ 3-8. The different versions of さ (sa) and そ (so)

You may have noticed in the *Various Styles* section of this lesson that there are two versions of *sa* and *so*. You can write whichever version you choose, so long as it is legible.

Different versions of さ (sa)	
さ	This version has three strokes and is very common when writing. Most Japanese people use this version when writing.
さ	This version has combined the second and third strokes into one stroke. It is very common in printed text.

Different versions of そ (so)	
そ	This version has two strokes and is common when writing. Many Japanese people write using this version.
そ	This version similar to version above except that the first and second stroke are touching.
そ	This version has only one stroke and is very common in printed text. It is also acceptable for writing.

さ Writing Practice れんしゅう

To practice correct stroke order, first trace the light gray characters, then write each character six times for practice.

sa	さ	さ					
shi	し	し					
su	す	す					
se	せ	せ					
so	そ	そ					

za	ざ	ざ					
ji	じ	じ					
zu	ず	ず					
ze	ぜ	ぜ					
zo	ぞ	ぞ					

さ   Word Practice ことばの れんしゅう

Fill in the appropriate hiragana in the blanks for each word.

1. mura___き   (purple)
         sa

2. ___ ___   (to point)
    sa su

3. ___ro   (white)
    shi

4. ___tsugyoう   (graduation)
    so

5. ___ ___   (sushi)
    su shi

6. ___かn   (time)
    ji

7. ___ ru   (monkey)
    sa

8. お___い___n   (grandfather)
        ji   sa

9. あ___   (sweat)
        se

10. あn___n   (safety)
         ze

11. ___う   (elephant)
     zo

12. げn___い   (currently; at present)
         za

さ   Words You Can Write かける ことば

Write the following words using the hiragana that you have just learned. This is a great way to increase your Japanese vocabulary.

しか
(deer)

すし
(sushi)

すずしい
(cool)

おそい
(slow/late)

あし
(legs/feet)

いす
(chair)

すき
(like)

すうじ
(number)

すいか
(watermelon)

せかい
(world)

かず
(numbers)

うし
(cow)

さ Everyday Hiragana Words にちじょうの ことば

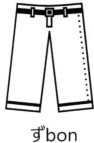

ずbon
pants

しnbun
newspaper

tsuくえ
desk

さmuい
cold

waくせい
planet

すし
sushi

さ   **Hiragana Matching ひらがな マッチング**

Connect the dots between each hiragana and the correct ro–maji.

す・	・za
し・	・su
え・	・ku
こ・	・shi
ざ・	・i
あ・	・e
く・	・ko
い・	・a

3 Lesson Activities

❏ 1. Question and answer 1
Answer the following questions in Japanese by looking at the pictures.

1. Dare deすか。

Yoshida

Answer: _____

2. Jenny さん deすか。

Monica

Answer: _____

3. Dare no tori deすか。

Takako

Answer: _____

4. Dare no おかあさn deすか。

Makoto

Answer: _____

❏ 2. Question and answer 2
Answer the following questions in Japanese as if they were being asked to you directly. Use the hiragana that you have learned when writing your answers.

1.   あnata no namaえ wa nan deすか。

_____

2. おbaあさn no namaえ wa nan deすか。

_____

3. おかあさn no くruma wa nan deすか。

_____

4. おじいさn wa nanさい deすか。

_____

5. おtoうさn wa nanさい deすか。

_____

❑ 3. Japanese translation
Translate the following conversation into English.

1.	
こ baya し さ n:	これ wa dare no hon de すか。
Na か ya さ n:	Wa か rima せ n, tabun Tana かさ n no hon de す。
こbayaし さn:	
Naかʸya さn:	

❑ 4. English translation
Translate the following conversation into Japanese.

1.	
Terada san:	Are you Mr. Tanaka?
Yamada san:	No, I am Yamada. Who is Mr. Tanaka?
Terada san:	Mr. Tanaka is Ms. Kobayashi's friend.
Terada san:	
Yamada san:	
Terada san:	

❑ 5. Reading comprehension questions

Answer the following questions about the reading comprehension in this lesson.

1. Hondaさん no かnojo no namaえ wa Tanaかさん deすか。

_____

2. Teradaさん wa dare deすか。

_____

3. Teradaさん wa Yamadaさん no かnojo deすか。

_____

4. Teradaさん wa nanさい deすか。

_____

_____

❑ 6. What would you say?

What would you say in the following situations?

1. when you are saying good bye

_____

2. when you greet someone in the morning

_____

3. when you don't know the answer to a question

_____

4. when you want to show your thanks to someone

_____

_____

❑ 7. Short dialogue

Mr. Yoshida saw Ms. Ueki on the street and they started a conversation.

Yoしdaさn:	うえきさn、こnnichiwa.
うえきさn:	こnnichiwa、Yoしdaさn.
	おhiさしburi deす。
	おtoうさn wa げnき deすか。
Yoしdaさn:	Haい、げnき deす。
	(looking at the big bag Ueki-san is holding)
	そre wa nan deすか。
うえきさn:	こre wa kamera deす。
	Wataし no shumi deす。
Yoしdaさn:	すごい deす ne。
うえきさn:	Yoしdaさn no shumi wa nan deすか。
Yoしdaさn:	Wataし no shumi wa gorufu deす。

New words and expressions in the dialogue

Progressive	English
おhiさしburi deす。	It's been a long time. / Long time no see.
_____wa げnき deすか。	Is _____ healthy / doing fine? (Are you fine?)
げnき deす。	They're fine. / I'm fine.
kamera	camera
shumi	hobby
すごい deす ne。	That's great. / That's awesome.
gorufu	golf

❑ 8. Short dialogue activities

Practice reading the dialogue in pairs.
Change the dialogue to add your own hobbies (*shumi*) .

3   Drill ドリル

If you're not sure what these sentences mean, we recommend that you review the lesson up to this point before continuing.

1. これ wa あnata no neこ deすか。
2. あnata no tomodachi no namaえ wa nan deすか。
3. いいえ、chiがいmaす。
4. それ wa dare no くruma deすか。
5. Tanaかさn wa wataし no tomodachi deす。

3   Sentence Building ぶんのつくり

In each lesson we build on a previous sentence. Watch it grow and transform each time new concepts are introduced. In this lesson we learned possession concepts. Let's look at the new sentence:

> **これ wa あnata no おかあさn no くruma deすか。**
> **Is this your mother's car?**

Compare how the sentence has changed from the prior lessons:

Lesson 1:   Nan deすか。

              What is it?

Lesson 2:   これ wa nan deすか。

              What is this?

3 Answer Key

❑ Reading comprehension (translation)
① My name is Honda.
② I am 35 years old.
③ My girlfriend's name is Terada.
④ She is 29 years old.

❑ Word practice (answers)
1. muraさき
2. さす
3. しro
4. そtsugyoう
5. すし
6. じかn
7. さru
8. おじいさn
9. あせ
10. あnぜn
11. ぞう
12. げnざい

❑ Hiragana matching (answers)

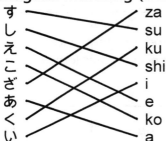

す ——— za
し ——— su
え ——— ku
こ ——— shi
ざ ——— i
あ ——— e
く ——— ko
い ——— a

❑ 1. Question and answer 1 (answers)

Question
1. Who is this?
2. Is this Jenny?
3. Whose bird is this?
4. Whose mother is this?

Answer
Yoしda さん deす。
いいえ、Monika さん deす。
Taかこ さん no tori deす。
Maこto (くn) no おかあさn deす。

❑ 2. Question and answer 2 (sample answers)

Question
1. What's your name?
2. What's your grandmother's name?
3. What's your mother's car?
4. How old is your grandpa?
5. How old is your dad?

Answer
Yamada Yoしこ deす。
Yamada Maさmi deす。
Toyota deす。
Nanajuう ごさい deす。
ごjuう niさい deす 。

❑ 3. Japanese translation (answers)
1. Kobayashi san: Whose book is this?
   Nakaya san: I don't know, maybe it is Mr. Tanaka's book.

❑ 4. English translation (answers)
1. Terada san: Tanaか さん deすか。
   Yamada san: いいえ、Yamada deす. Tanaか さん wa dare deすか。
   Terada san: (Tanaか さん wa) こbayaし さん no tomodachi deす。

❑ **5. Reading comprehension questions (answers)**

Question	Answer
1. Is Honda's girlfriend's name Tanaka?	いいえ、Terada deす。*
2. Who is Terada?	Honda さん no かnojo deす。
3 Is Terada Yamada's girlfriend?	いいえ、Honda さん no かnojo deす。 **OR** いいえ、chiがいmaす。
4. How old is Ms. Terada?	Nijuう kyuう さい deす。

* (Note: **いいえ、Honda san no かnojo no nameえ wa** in front of the answer above would be unnaturally long. Try to keep the answers simple.)

❑ **6. What would you say? (sample answers)**
1. さyoうnara. (later you will learn いtte きmaす)
2. おhayoう ございmaす.
3. Waかrimaせn.
4. あriがtoう ございmaす.

❑ **7. Short dialogue (translation)**

Yoshida san:	Good afternoon, Ms. Ueki.
Ueki san:	Good afternoon, Mr. Yoshida. It's been a long time. Is your father doing well?
Yoshida san:	Yes he is fine. What is that?
Ueki san:	This is a camera. It's my hobby.
Yoshida san:	That's great!
Ueki san:	What is your (Yoshida san's) hobby?
Yoshida san:	My hobby is golf.

Vocabulary Groups

E animals

Progressive	Kana	Kanji	English
いnu	いぬ	犬	dog
neこ	ねこ	猫	cat
ぞう	ぞう	象	elephant
うma	うま	馬	horse
うさぎ	うさぎ	兎	rabbit
panda	パンダ	パンダ	panda
neずmi	ねずみ	鼠	mouse
raion	ライオン	ライオン	lion
きrin	きりん	麒麟	giraffe
うし	うし	牛	cow
さru	さる	猿	monkey
hitsuじ	ひつじ	羊	sheep
きtsune	きつね	狐	fox
くma	くま	熊	bear

パンダ

うし

うさぎ

Lesson 4 Level ①

Colors and Adjectives
Making lists

4 About This Lesson こののレッスンについて

Before The Lesson

1. Be able to write and read さしすせそ, ざじずぜぞ .
2. Understand how to use the question word *dare* and the particles *no* and が .
3. Review vocabulary group E.

Lesson Goals

1. Learn how to use the noun and adjective forms of colors.
2. Learn how to use the Japanese version of "and".

From The Teachers

1. Memorize the colors.
2. Make sure that you understand the different types of adjectives introduced in this lesson.

4 New Words あたらしい ことば

Progressive	Kana	Kanji	English
naniいro	なにいろ	何色	what color?
いro	いろ	色	color
あか	あか	赤	red
あお	あお	青	blue
くro	くろ	黒	black
しro	しろ	白	white
chaいro	ちゃいろ	茶色	brown
きいro	きいろ	黄色	yellow
orenji	オレンジ	オレンジ	orange

muraさき	むらさき	紫	purple
pinku	ピンク	ピンク	pink
guree	グレー	グレー	gray
haいいro	はいいろ	灰色	gray
miずいro	みずいろ	水色	light blue
midori	みどり	緑	green
きnいro	きんいろ	金色	gold
ぎnいro	ぎんいろ	銀色	silver
toうmeい	とうめい	透明	clear

4 New Phrases あたらしい かいわ

1. Excuse me. / I'm sorry.   すみmaせn。
2. I am sorry. / Please forgive me.   ごmen naさい。

3. What is it in Japanese?   Nihonごde nan deすか。
4. What is it in English?   えいごde nan deすか。

5. It's _____ in English.   えいごde _____deす。
6. It's _____ in Japanese.   Nihonごde _____deす。

4 Culture Clip: Green is Blue?

Blue apples?

Japanese people sometimes refer to what we call "green" as "blue." For example, in Japan, when vegetables are not ripe they are referred to as blue, not green. A green apple isn't green – it's blue. Green traffic lights are called "blue" even though the colors used for traffic lights in Japan are exactly the same as in America. So keep this in mind when someone yells to you, "Hey, let's go! The light is *blue*!"

There is a prefecture in the northern part of Japan's main island Honshuu called Aomori, which literally means "blue forest." Well then, what color is the sky in Japan, you ask? Blue, of course!

4 Grammar ぶんぽう

❑ 4-1. The particle *to*

To is the equivalent of English "and." It must come between every word in a list. *To* cannot be used to link sentences together.

Examples

1. あお <u>to</u> muraさき <u>to</u> pinku   blue, purple, and pink
2. wataし <u>to</u> あnata <u>to</u> tanaかさん   me, you, and Tanaka san
3. いnu <u>to</u> neこ <u>to</u> うma <u>to</u> buta   a dog, a cat, a horse, and a pig

Example Sentences

1. Wataし no くruma wa くro to ぎnいro deす。
   My car is black and silver.

2. Tomodachi no neこ wa chaいro to しro deす。
   My friend's cat is brown and white.

rinご **to** すいか **to** banana   いnu **to** neこ **to** うさぎ

❑ 4-2. Making nouns into adjectives using no

Up until now, *no* has been used to mark possession. *No* is also used to create a "noun adjective" or what we call a "*no* adjective". When *no* is added after a noun, that noun becomes an adjective. The noun before the *no* modifies or "describes" the following noun.

> [noun 1] + no + [noun 2]

Examples

1. Japanese food
   nihon (Japan) + tabemono (food) = nihon <u>no</u> tabemono

2. American cars
   Amerika (America) + くruma = Amerika no くruma

3. Japanese book
   nihonご (Japanese language) + hon (book) = nihonご <u>no</u> hon

❏ 4-3. Using colors to describe

In this lesson, the colors are introduced in their noun form. To make a color an adjective you must link the words with *no*. To say "green car" in Japanese, you would say: **midori no ˂ruma.** This type of adjective is called a *no* adjective. With the noun forms of colors you CANNOT say, for example, **midori ˂ruma** to mean "green car."

English	incorrect	correct
what color car?	naniいro ˂ruma	naniいro <u>no</u> ˂ruma
a white towel	しro taoru	しro <u>no</u> taoru
a brown monkey	chaいro さru	chaいro <u>no</u> さru
a black dog	˂ro いnu	˂ro <u>no</u> いnu
a green pillow	midori ma˂ra	midori <u>no</u> ma˂ra

Example Sentences

1. あか no ˂ruma wa あnata no deすか。   Is the red car yours?
2. Dare no pinku no いえ deすか。   Whose pink house is that?
3. Pinku no ma˂ra wa bo˂no deす。   The pink pillow is mine.

❏ 4-4. Colors with い adjective forms

Six of the Japanese colors also have an い adjective form.

Japanese Colors with い adjective Forms			
Progressive	Kana	Kanji	English
しroい	しろい	白い	white
˂roい	くろい	黒い	black
chaいroい	ちゃいろい	茶色い	brown
あかい	あかい	赤い	red
あおい	あおい	青い	blue
きいroい	きいろい	黄色い	yellow

い adjectives always end with い and never require *no* to modify other words – they are simply put in front of the word being modified.

Examples

1. <u>あかい</u> ˂ruma   a <u>red</u> car
2. <u>あおい</u> pen   a <u>blue</u> pen
3. <u>chaいroい</u> neこ   a <u>brown</u> cat
4. <u>しroい</u> いnu   a <u>white</u> dog

When directly modifying, using い adjective or *no* adjective version of a color is your choice. Just remember that only the six colors mentioned above have い adjective versions.

English	い adjective	NO adjective
a yellow giraffe	きいろい きrin	きいろ no きrin
a blue car	あおい くruma	あお no くruma
a brown horse	chaいろい うma	chaいろ no うma
a red fruit	あかい furu-tsu	あか no furu-tsu

❑ 4-5. When to use adjective and noun versions of the colors

The six colors, white, black, brown, red, blue, and yellow are unique because they have adjective and noun versions. It can create confusion as to which version should be used. Here are some basic rules to help avoid confusion:

1. When you are directly modifying a noun you can use EITHER version. **あか no くruma** AND **あかい くruma** are BOTH correct.

2. When answering a direct question about color, such as **Naniいro deすか** (What color is it?), it's better to answer with the NOUN version.

Example Q&A

The noun version sounds better here because we are directly asking about color.

1. あnata no くruma wa naniいro deすか。 　　What color is your car?
   きいro deす。 　　　　　　　　　　　　　It's yellow.
   しro deす。 　　　　　　　　　　　　　　It's white.

Noun and いadjective version work here because we are directly modifying.

2. あre wa nan deすか。 　　　　　　　　　What is that over there?
   しroい maくra deす。 　　　　　　　　　It's a white pillow.
   しro no maくra deす。 　　　　　　　　　It's a white pillow.

いadjective form can be used since we aren't asking directly about color.

3. これ wa あnata no neこ deすか。 　　　　Is this your cat?
   いいえ、wataし no neこ wa chaいろい deす。 　No, my cat is brown.

NOTE: Don't worry too much about which version you use, since Japanese people themselves wouldn't be able to explain the differences unless they really thought about it.

4   Q&A しつもんと こたえ English→Japanese

1. **What color is it?**
    It's black.
    It's pink.
    It's purple and orange.

    Naniいro deすか。
    くro deす。
    Pinku deす。
    Muraさきto orenji deす。

2. **What color car is it?**
    It's a green car.
    It's a red and blue car.
    It's a yellow car.

    Naniいro no くruma deすか。
    Midori no くruma deす。
    あか to あお no くruma deす。
    きいro no くruma deす。

3. **Is your toothbrush blue?**
    No, mine is white.
    No, mine is yellow.

    あnata no haburashi wa あお deすか。
    いいえ、waたし no wa しro deす。
    いいえ、waたし no wa きいro deす。

4. **What color is this?**
    This is blue.
    It's purple.

    これ wa naniいro deすか。
    これ wa あお deす。
    Muraさき deす。

5. **Is your cat black and white?**
    No, it is brown and grey.

    あnata no neこ wa くro to しro deすか。
    いいえ、chaいro to guree deす。

6. **Whose car is the silver car?**
    Maybe it is Yoshida san's.

    ぎnいro no くruma wa dare no deすか。
    Tabun Yoしdaさん no deす。

4   Q&A しつもんと こたえ Japanese→English

1. **あか deすか。**
    Haい、そうdeす。
    いいえ、chiがいmaす。

    Is it red?
    Yes, it is.
    No, it's not.

2. **Moうfu wa naniいro deすか。**
    しro deす。
    あか deす。
    あお to midori deす。

    What color is the blanket?
    It's white.
    It's red.
    It's blue and green.

3. **Koppu wa chaいro deすか。**
    Haい、そう deす。
    いいえ、chiがいmaす。

    Is the cup brown?
    Yes, it is.
    No, it isn't.

4. **Maくra wa naniいro deすか。**
    Maくra wa midori deす。
    Muraさき deす。
    くro deす。
    Waかrimaせん.

    What color is the pillow?
    The pillow is green.
    It's purple.
    It's black.
    I don't know.

5. **Chaいro no うma wa あnata no deすか。**
    いいえ、しro no うma deす。

    Is the brown horse yours?
    No, it's the white horse.

6. **あnata no おかあさん no うさぎ wa naniいro deすか。**
    Waかrimaせん.
    しro to chaいro deす。

    What color is your mother's rabbit?
    I don't know.
    It's white and brown.

4 **Reading Comprehension どっかい**

Read the sentences below. Use the information to answer the reading comprehension questions later in this lesson.

① Junこさん wa nijuうごさい deす。

② かnojo no おtoうさん wa ごjuうniさい deす。

③ おtoうさん no namaえ wa Yoしhiro deす。

④ Junこさん to Junこさん no おtoうさん no くruma wa Honda deす。

⑤ おtoうさん no くruma wa muraさき deす。

⑥ Junこさん no くruma wa pinku to あお deす。

Hiragana たちつてと

た New Hiragana あたらしい ひらがな

Make sure you learn the correct stroke order since correct stroke order will mean neater characters when writing quickly.

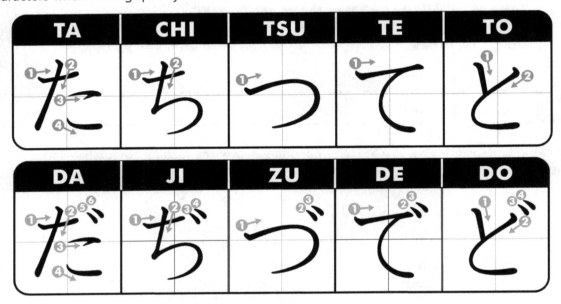

TA	CHI	TSU	TE	TO
た	ち	つ	て	と

DA	JI	ZU	DE	DO
だ	ぢ	づ	で	ど

た Various Styles スタイル

Look at the various possible styles for the hiragana in this lesson. Write each symbol as neatly as you can, then compare it to the different versions below.

た	た	た	た	た
ち	ち	ち	ち	ち
つ	つ	つ	つ	つ
て	て	て	て	て
と	と	と	と	と

だ	だ	だ	だ	だ
ぢ	ぢ	ぢ	ぢ	ぢ
づ	づ	づ	づ	づ
で	で	で	で	で
ど	ど	ど	ど	ど

た Writing Points かくポイント

❑ 4-5. The double consonants

The double consonants (*kk, pp, tt, cch*) are stressed with a slight pause before the consonant. To represent them in hiragana, a small つ is used.* The small つ is always placed in front of the hiragana that needs to be doubled.

> **Examples**
>
> | | | |
> |---|---|---|
> | school | ga<u>kk</u>ou | が_っこう |
> | magazine | za<u>ss</u>hi | ざ_っし |
> | postage stamp | ki<u>tt</u>e | き_って |

* Make sure to write the つ smaller than normal to avoid confusion with a normal つ.

❑ 4-6. The double consonant sound analysis

If you look at the sound wave for a word that has a double consonant, you will see a pause or visible space before the consonant. Look at the two samples below:

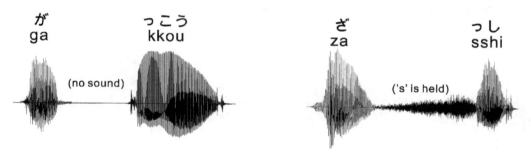

❑ 4-7. Which version of *zu* and *ji* should be used?

There are two versions of *zu* and *ji*. The first set was in Lesson 3 and the second set is taught in this lesson. ず and じ from Lesson 3 are the most commonly used versions. づ and ぢ are used in only a few words, such as **はna ぢ** (nosebleed), **ちぢmu** (to shrink), and **つづく** (to continue).

As you learn more vocabulary, pay attention to the hiragana that's used when you see these sounds. If you're not sure about what version to use, try ず and じ and 90% of the time you will be correct.

た Writing Practice れんしゅう

To practice correct stroke order, first trace the light gray characters, then write each character six times for practice.

ta	た	た					
chi	ち	ち					
tsu	つ	つ					
te	て	て					
to	と	と					

da	だ	だ					
ji	ぢ	ぢ					
zu	づ	づ					
de	で	で					
do	ど	ど					

た Word Practice ことばの れんしゅう

Fill in the appropriate hiragana in the blanks for each word.

1. wa___し (me; I)
      ta

2. ___ ___ (free; no charge)
   ta da

3. ___ ___ (to stand)
   ta tsu

4. ___ ___ぜn (all of a sudden)
   to tsu

5. ___ ___mu (to shrink)
   chi ji

6. ___ ___ ___う (to help)
   te tsu da

7. い___い (it hurts; ouch)
      ta

8. お ___うさn (father)
        to

9. hana___ (nose bleed)
         ji

10. いき___mari (dead end)
           do

11. ___nwa (telephone)
    de

12. ___ ___く (to reach; arrive)
    to do

た Words You Can Write かける ことば

Write the following words using the hiragana that you just learned.

た だ
(free)

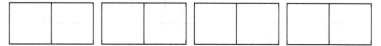

つ ぎ
(next)

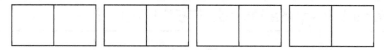

ち ず
(map)

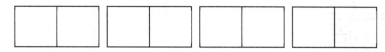

か ど
(corner)

ち ち
(my father)

た つ
(to stand)

ざ っ し
(magazine)

き っ て
(postage stamp)

あ つ い
(hot)

た い い く
(phys. ed.)

つ づ き
(continuation)

と お い
(far)

た | Everyday Hiragana Words にちじょう の ことば

でんしrenji
microwave oven

honだna
bookshelf

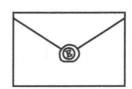

fuうとう
envelope

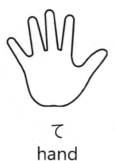

て
hand

たmaご
eggs

くつした
socks

た　Hiragana Matching ひらがな マッチング

Connect the dots between each hiragana and the correct ro–maji.

て・	・tsu
つ・	・da
さ・	・chi
ち・	・te
す・	・u
ぢ・	・ji
う・	・sa
だ・	・su

4 | **Lesson Activities**

❑ 1. Question and answer 1
Answer the following questions by looking at the pictures.

1. これ wa nihonごで nanですか。

Answer: _____

2. これ wa nihonごで nanですか。

Answer: _____

3. これ wa えいごで nanですか。

Answer: _____

4. これ wa えいごで nanですか。

Answer: _____

❑ 2. Question and answer 2
Answer the following questions as if they were being asked to you directly. Use the hiragana that you know.

1. あなた no くruma wa naniいro ですか。

_____

2. あなた no haburashi wa naniいro ですか。

_____

3. Panda wa naniいro ですか。

_____

4. Banana wa naniいro ですか。

_____

5. ぞう wa gure– ですか。

_____

❑ **3. What would you say?**
What would you say in the following situations?

1. after you stepped on someone's foot by mistake

_____

2. when you want to know what color someone's dog is

_____

3. when someone asks you if you are Mr. Tanaka

_____

4. when you want to know how to say something in Japanese

_____

❑ 4. Japanese translation

Translate the following conversations into English. Then, in the space after the number write where you think the conversation is taking place and if it is polite, informal or mixed.

1.
たかださn:　くruma wa naniいro ですか。
かどたさn:　Waたし no くruma ですか。
たかださn:　Haい。
かどたさn:　Muraさきです。あnaた no くruma wa...？
たかださn:　Waたし no くruma wa ぎnいro と きnいro です。
たかださn:
かどたさn:
たかださn:
かどたさn:
たかださn:

❑ 5. Reading comprehension questions

Answer the following questions about the reading comprehension in this lesson.

1.　Junこさn no くruma wa naniいro ですか。

_____

2.　だre no くrumaが Honda ですか。

_____

3.　だre no くrumaが muraさき ですか。

_____

4.　Junこさn wa nanさい ですか。

_____

5.　だreが ごjuうniさい ですか。

_____

❑ 6. Short dialogue

Mr. Tanaka and Mr. Kobayashi are talking about their cars.

> こbayaしさn: たnaかさn の くruma wa nan ですか。
>
> たnaかさn: Waたしの ①<u>くruma</u> wa ②<u>Nissan</u> です。
> あnaたno wa?
>
> こbayaしさn: Waたしの ①<u>くruma</u> wa ③<u>Mitsubishi</u> です。
> いro wa ④<u>あか</u>です。
>
> たnaかさn: そうですか。
> Waたしの ①<u>くruma</u> wa ⑤<u>しro</u> です。

❑ 7. Short dialogue activity

Practice reading the above dialogue in pairs OR by yourself with a funny voice :-)
Substitute ①~⑤ using the words below and try the conversation again.

1. ① Dog
   ② (your choice)
   ③ (your choice)
   ④ Brown
   ⑤ Black and white

2. ① Cat
   ② (your choice)
   ③ (your choice)
   ④ Gray
   ⑤ Brown and white

3. ① Cell Phone (けいたいでnwa)
   ② (your choice)
   ③ (your choice)
   ④ Red
   ⑤ Blue

❑ **8. More words you can write**

You should practice writing these words a minimum of five times each. Not only will you be practicing the new hiragana, but you will also learn new words.

えきたい	liquid; fluid	ちえ	wisdom
ちいき	region	ていあつ	low pressure
こうあつ	high pressure	げっこう	moonlight

4 Drill ドリル

If you're not sure what these sentences mean, we recommend that you review the lesson up to this point before continuing.

1. すみまaせn。
2. Nihonごで nan ですか。
3. Naniいro ですか。
4. Waたし no くruma wa あかと くro です。
5. たnaかさn no くruma wa あおい Toyota です。

4 Sentence Building ぶんのつくり

In each lesson we will build on a previous sentence. Watch it grow and transform each time new concepts are introduced.

> あnaた no おかあさn no くruma wa しro ですか。
> **Is your mother's car white?**

Compare how the sentence has changed from the prior lessons:

Lesson 1: Nan ですか。

What is it?

Lesson 2: これ wa nan ですか。

What is this?

Lesson 3: これ wa あnaた no おかあさn no くruma ですか。

Is this your mother's car?

4 Answer Key

❏ Word practice (answers)

1. waたし
2. ただ
3. たつ
4. とつぜn
5. ちぢmu
6. てつだう
7. いたい
8. おとうさn
9. hanaぢ
10. いきどmari
11. でnwa
12. とどく

❏ Hiragana matching (answers)

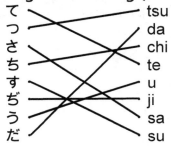

て — tsu
つ — da
さ — chi
ち — te
す — u
ぢ — ji
う — sa
だ — su

❏ Reading comprehension (translation)

① Junko is 25 years old.
② Her dad is 52 years old.
③ Her dad's name is Yoshihiro.
④ Junko's car and her dad's car are Hondas.
⑤ Dad's car is purple.
⑥ Junko's car is pink and blue.

❏ 1. Question and answer 1 (answers)

Questions

1. What is this in Japanese?
2. What is this in Japanese?
3. What is this in English?
4. What is this in English?

Answers

うさぎです。
うしです。
「Panda」です。
「Lion」です。

❏ 2. Question and answer 2 (sample answers)

1. What color is your car?　　　　　＿＿＿です。
2. What color is your toothbrush?　[any color] です。
3. What color are pandas?　　　　しro と くro です。
4. What color are bananas?　　　　きいro です。
5. Are elephants grey?　　　　　Haい、そうです。/ Haい、gure– です。

❏ 3. What would you say? (sample answers)

1. ごmennaさい。/ すmimaせn。
2. ＿＿＿さn no いnu wa naniいro ですか。
3. いいえ、ちがいmaす。(Haい、そうです. if you ARE Tanaka san)
4. ＿＿＿wa、nihonご で nan ですか。

❏ 4. Japanese translation (answers)

1. Takada san:　　　　　What color is (your) car?
   Kadota san:　　　　　My car?

Takada san:	Yes.
Kadota san:	It's purple. How about your car?
Takada san:	My car is silver and gold.

❑ 5. Reading comprehension questions (answers)

Question	Answer
1. What color is Junko's car?	Pinku と あお です。
2. Whose car is the Honda?	Junこ さん と Junこ さん no おとうさん no くruma です。
4. Whose car is purple?	おとう さん no くruma です。
5. How old is Junko?	Ni juうごさい です。
6. Who is 52 years old?	Junこ さん no おとうさん です。

❑ 6. Short dialogue (translation)

Mr. Kobayashi:	What (kind of) car is your car, Mr. Tanaka?
Mr. Tanaka:	My car is a Nissan.
	What about yours?
Mr. Kobayashi:	My car is a Mitsubishi. Its color is red.
Mr. Tanaka:	I see. My car is white.

Vocabulary Groups

F things around the house

Progressive	Kana	Kanji	English
koppu	コップ	コップ	cup; glass
supu–n	スプーン	スプーン	spoon
fo–ku	フォーク	フォーク	fork
(お)さra	(お)さら	(お)皿	plate
(お)chawan	(お)ちゃわん	(お)茶わん	bowl
(お)haし	(お)はし	(お)箸	chopsticks
reいぞうこ	れいぞうこ	冷蔵庫	refrigerator
とけい	とけい	時計	clock
terebi	テレビ	テレビ	television
zubon	ズボン	ズボン	pants
くつ	くつ	靴	shoe(s)
しnbun	しんぶん	新聞	newspaper

コップ

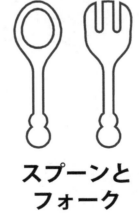

**スプーンと
フォーク**

ズボン

Lesson

5

Level ①

Likes and Dislikes

Making nouns negative

5 About This Lesson このレッスンについて

Before The Lesson

1. Be able to write and read たちつてと, だぢづでど.
2. Understand how to use the question word naniいro and the particle と.
3. Review vocabulary group F.

Lesson Goals

1. Learn how to say you like or dislike something.
2. Learn how to use janaい.

From The Teachers

1. Know すき, きraい and janaい like the back of your hand since they are used so much in daily conversation.

5 New Words あたらしい ことば

Progressive	Kana	Kanji	English
すき	すき	好き	like
きraい	きらい	嫌い	dislike; hate
だいすき	だいすき	大好き	really like; like a lot
だいきraい	だいきらい	大嫌い	really dislike; really hate
さとこ	さとこ	聡子	a girl's first name
Yoしお	よしお	良夫	a boy's first name
かいmono	かいもの	買い物	shopping
かnこう	かんこう	観光	sightseeing
ryoこう	りょこう	旅行	travel
shuくだい	しゅくだい	宿題	homework

しごと	しごと	仕事	work
さかna	さかな	魚	fish
chikin	チキン	チキン	chicken
nihonご	にほんご	日本語	Japanese language
jaあ	じゃあ	じゃあ	well then...

5 New Adjectives あたらしい けいようし

Progressive	Kana	Kanji	English
おいしい	おいしい	美味しい	tastes good; delicious
おいしくnaい	おいしくない	美味しくない	doesn't taste good

5 Grammar ぶんぽう

❑ 5-1. The particle が with すき and きraい

To say you like or dislike something with すき (like) and きraい (dislike), the subject particle が is used after the thing that is liked or disliked.

> **[noun] が すき／きraいです。**
> **like / dislike a [noun]**

Examples

1. Waたし wa いちごが すきです。   I like strawberries.
2. Waたし wa うさぎが すきです。   I like rabbits.

3. Waたし wa すいかが きraいです。   I dislike watermelons.
4. Waたし wa いnuが きraいです。   I dislike dogs.

5. Waたし wa chikinが だいすきです。   I really like chicken.
6. Waたし wa さかnaが だいすきです。   I really like fish.

7. Waたし wa retasuが だいきraいです。   I hate lettuce.
8. Waたし wa かいmonoが だいきraいです。   I hate shopping.

❑ 5-2. Using janaい to make things negative

Janaい means "not" or "don't" depending on the context of the sentence. **Janaい** is the informal version of **ja あrimaせn, でwa あrimaせn,** or **でwa naい**; however, the informal version is most commonly used in everyday conversation. **Janaい** on its own is informal, but can be made polite by adding です. It must always follow the word it is modifying.

> **[word] janaいです。**
> **It's not a [word].**

Examples
1. あか <u>janaい</u> です。   It's <u>not</u> red.
2. Waたし <u>janaい</u> です。   It's <u>not</u> me.
3. たnaかさn <u>janaい</u> です。   It is <u>not</u> Mr. Tanaka.
4. そre <u>janaい</u> です。   It's <u>not</u> that one.
5. すき <u>janaい</u> です。   I <u>don't</u> like it.
6. きraい <u>janaい</u> です。   I <u>don't</u> dislike it.

❑ 5-3. The "one" pronoun

When the particle **no** comes after the noun version of a color or after an adjective, it transforms the word into what is called the "one" pronoun.

Examples
1. あか no   (a / the) red one
2. chaいro no   (a / the) brown one
3. おいしい no   (a / the) good tasting one
4. nihon no   (a / the) Japanese one
5. muraさきと きいro no   (a / the) purple and yellow one

Example Q&A
1. どre が すきですか。   **Which one do you like?**
   あか <u>no</u> が すきです。   I like the red <u>one</u>.
   おいしい <u>no</u> が すきです。 I like the delicious <u>one</u>.

2. あnaた no neこ wa どreですか。 **Which one is your cat?**
   Chaいro <u>no</u> です。   It's the brown <u>one</u>.
   くro と orenji <u>no</u> です。   It's the black and orange <u>one</u>.

❑ 5-4. Using *ja*あ to say "Well then..."

Jaあ is a very well used word in Japanese. It's said at the beginning of a sentence, normally when asking a follow-up question.

Example Conversations

1. A: Neこが すきですか。   Do you like cats?
   B: いいえ、だいきraい です。   No, I hate them!
   A: Jaあ、いnuが すき ですか。   Well then, do you like dogs?
   B: Haい、だいすき です。   Yes, I love (like a lot) them!

2. A: あreが あnaた no くruma ですか。   Is that your car?
   B: いいえ、ちがいmaす。   No, it's not.
   A: Jaあ、どre ですか。   Well then, which one is it?
   B: あre です。   It's that one over there.

3. A: あかが すきですか。   Do you like red?
   B: いいえ、あかが きraいです。   No, I dislike red.
   A: Jaあ、naniいroが すきですか。   Well then, what color do you like?
   B: Miどriと muraさきが すきです。   I like green and purple.

5 Speaking Naturally しぜんに はなすこと

❑ 5-5. Using きraい versus すきjanaい

When speaking in Japanese, you should be careful when using **きraい** and **だいきraい**. In Japanese culture, these words sound a bit harsh. If you don't like something, then you should use **すきjanaい** instead of **きraい** in everyday conversations.

5 Q&A しつもんと こたえ English→Japanese

1. **Do you like it?**   すきですか。
   Yes, I like it.   Haい、すきです。
   No, I don't like it.   いいえ、すきjanaいです。
   Yes, I really like it.   Haい、だいすきです。

2. **Do you dislike it?**   きraい ですか。
    Yes, I dislike it.   Haい、きraいです。
    No, I don't dislike it.   いいえ、きraいjanaい です。
    No, I like it.   いいえ、すきです。

3. **What do you like?**   Naniが すき ですか。
    I like shopping.   かいmonoが すきです。
    I like travel.   Ryoこうが すきです。
    I like Japanese (language).   Nihonごが すきです。

4. **What do you dislike?**   Naniが きraいですか。
    I dislike homework.   Shuくだいが きraいです。
    I dislike work.   しごとが きraいです。
    I dislike fish.   さかnaが きraいです。

5. **Which one do you like? (two items)**   どっちが すきですか。
    I like the red one.   あかnoが すきです。
    I like the green one.   Miどri noが すきです。
    I like this one.   こっちが すきです。

5   Q&A しつもんと こたえ Japanese→English

1. **さかnaが すき ですか。**   Do you like fish?
    Haい、さかnaが すきです。   Yes, I like fish.
    いいえ、さかnaが きraいです。   No, I dislike fish.
    Haい、さかnaが だいすきです。   Yes, I really like fish.
    いいえ、すきjanaい です。   No, I don't like it.
    いいえ、おいしくnaい です。   No, it doesn't taste good.

2. **Waたし no くrumaが すきですか。**   Do you like my car?
    Haい、だいすき です。   Yes, I like it a lot.
    いいえ、だいきraい です。   No, I hate it.

3. **Bananaが きraい ですか。**   Do you dislike bananas?
    Haい、きraい です。   Yes, I dislike them.
    いいえ、bananaが すきです。   No, I like bananas.
    Bananaが きraいjanaい です。   I don't dislike bananas.

4. **Ryoこう が すきですか。**
   Haい、すきです。
   いいえ、すきjanaいです。

   Do you like (to) travel?
   Yes, I do.
   No, I don't like it.

5. **Naniが きraいですか。**
   Chaいroい bananaが だいきraいです。
   かいmono が きraいです。

   What do you dislike?
   I really hate brown bananas.
   I hate shopping.

5 Reading Comprehension どっかい

Read the sentences below. Use the information to answer the reading comprehension questions later in this lesson.

① さとこさn no かre no namaえ wa たnaか yoしお です。

② さとこさn wa 25さい です。

③ Yoしおさn wa 27さい です。

④ さとこさn wa かいmonoが だいすきです。

⑤ Yoしおさn wa かいmonoが すきjanaい です。

⑥ Yoしおさn wa しごとが すきです。

⑦ さとこさn wa しごとが きraいです。

⑧ さとこさnと yoしおさn wa ryoこうが だいすきです。

Hiragana なにぬねの

な New Hiragana あたらしい ひらがな

Make sure you learn the correct stroke order since correct stroke order will mean neater characters when writing fast.

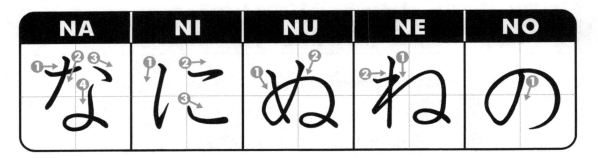

NA	NI	NU	NE	NO
な	に	ぬ	ね	の

な Various Styles スタイル

Look at the various possible styles for the hiragana in this lesson. Write each symbol as neatly as you can, then compare it to the different versions below.

なにぬねの	なにぬねの	なにぬねの	なにぬねの	なにぬねの

な Writing Practice れんしゅう

To practice correct stroke order, first trace the light gray characters, then write each character six times for practice.

na	な	な						
ni	に	に						
nu	ぬ	ぬ						
ne	ね	ね						
no	の	の						

な Word Practice ことばの れんしゅう

Fill in the appropriate hiragana in the blanks for each word.

1. ___つ (summer)
   na

2. ___hon (Japan)
   ni

3. ___こ (cat)
   ne

4. yo___か (middle of the night)
   na

5. ___mu (to drink)
   no

6. ___ru (to sleep; to go to bed)
   ne

7. ___ ___ (what?)
   na ni

8. ___いぐrumi (stuffed animal)
   nu

9. __がい (bitter tasting)
ni

10. お__えさn (older sister)
ne

11. __ぐ (to take off clothes)
nu

12. __ru (to ride)
no

な Everyday Hiragana Words にちじょうの ことば

いぬ
dog

ながい
long

にwaとri
chicken

のru
to ride

ぬru
to paint

ねこ
cat

な Words You Can Write かける ことば

Write the following words using the hiragana that you just learned. This is a great way to increase your Japanese vocabulary.

なに
(what)

ねこ
(cat)

なな
(seven)

にし
(west)

なつ
(summer)

あなた
(you)

ねつ
(fever)

いぬ
(dog)

のど
(throat)

かに
(crab)

にっき
(diary)

にく
(meat)

にじ
(rainbow)

な Hiragana Matching ひらがな マッチング

Connect the dots between each hiragana and the correct ro–maji.

な ・	・ no
の ・	・ ni
か ・	・ ta
す ・	・ na
ぬ ・	・ ka
ね ・	・ nu
に ・	・ ne
た ・	・ su

5 Lesson Activities

❏ **1. Question and answer 1**
Answer the following questions by looking at the pictures. Use ~jaない です when answering the following questions:

1a. これ wa さかな ですか。

_____

1b. Jaあ ("Well then")、なn ですか。

_____

2a. これ wa hon ですか。

_____

2b. Jaあ、なn ですか。

_____

3a. これ wa (お)chawanと
supu–n ですか。

_____

3b. Jaあ、なn ですか。

_____

4a. これ wa くつ ですか。

_____

4b. Jaあ、なn ですか。

_____

❑ **2. Question and answer 2**

Pick one of the pictures and say, [item] が すきです or [item] が きraいです.

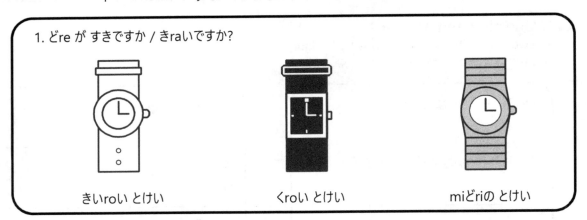

1. どre が すきですか / きraいですか?

きいroい とけい　　　くroい とけい　　　miどriの とけい

2. どre が すきですか / きraいですか?

しごと　　　shuくだい　　　かいmoの

❑ **3. Question and answer 3**

Answer the following questions as though they were being asked to you directly. Use the hiragana that you know when writing your answer.

1.　Ryoこう が すきですか。

_____

2.　ねこが きraいですか。

_____

3. Yaさいが すきですか。

_____

4. にhonごが すきですか。

_____

5. (お)すし wa おいしいですか。

_____

❑ 4. Japanese translation
Translate the following example into English.

1. Yoしおさn wa くrumaが だいすきです。 2. Yoしおさnの くruma wa あかと しroです。 3. かreの しroい くruma wa honだ です。 4. あかの wa Toyotaです。 5. Yoしおさnの おとうさn wa くrumaが だいすきです。 6. おとうさnの くruma wa きnいroの くrumaと きいroい くruma です。 7. おかあさn wa きいroい くrumaが すきjaないです。
1.
2.
3.
4.
5.
6.
7.

❑ **5. Reading comprehension questions**
Answer the following questions about the reading comprehension in this lesson.

1. さとこさんの かre wa、だreですか。

_____

2. Yoしおさん wa しごとが きraいですか。

_____

3. さとこさん wa なnさいですか。

_____

4. だreが かいmoの が すきですか。

_____

5. だreが ryoこうが すきですか。

_____

❑ **6. Short dialogue**

Ms. Mori and Ms. Nishida are talking about movies.

Mori さn:	にしださn wa えいがが すきですか。
にしだ さn:	Haい、だいすきです。
Mori さn:	Waたしmoです。 Haいyuう wa だreが すきですか。
にしだ さn:	Harison Fo–do が すきです。
Mori さn:	そうですか。 Waたしwa Buraddo Pittoが すきです。
にしだ さn:	Waたしmo Buraddo Pittoが すきです。

New words and expressions in the dialogue

Progressive	Kana	Kanji	English
えいが	えいが	映画	movie
haいyuう	はいゆう	俳優	actor
Harison Fo–do	ハリソン・フォード	ハリソン・フォード	Harrison Ford (actor)
Buraddo Pitto	ブラッド・ピット	ブラッド・ピット	Brad Pitt (actor)
mo	も	も	also; too (particle)

❑ **7. Short dialogue activities**

1. Practice reading the dialogue in pairs.
   (I really hope you have a friend or this will be awkward!)
2. Talk about your most/least favorite movie(s).
3. Talk about your most/least favorite actor(s).

❏ **8. More words you can write**
You should practice writing these words a minimum of five times each. Not only will you be practicing the new hiragana, but you will also learn new words.

ぬぐ	to undress	かね	bell; chime
にっき	diary	にく	meat
ねじ	a screw	ねぎ	green onion
ねあげ	a rise in price	なつかしい	dear; longed for

5 Drill ドリル

If you're not sure what these sentences mean, we recommend that you review the lesson up to this point before continuing.

1. なにが すきですか。
2. しごとが だいすきです。
3. さかな to yaさいが すきjaない です。
4. Waたしの くruma wa muraさきjaない です。
5. あなたの とmoだちの くruma wa あおjaない ですか。

5 Sentence Building ぶんのつくり

In each lesson, we will build on a previous sentence. Watch it grow and transform each time new concepts are introduced.

> あなたの おかあさn wa なにいroの くrumaが すきですか。
> **What color car does your mother like?**

あか   しro

Compare how the sentence has changed from the prior lessons:

Lesson 2:   こre wa なn ですか。

　　　　　　What is this?

Lesson 3:   こre wa あなたの おかあさnの くruma ですか。

　　　　　　Is this your mother's car?

Lesson 4:   あなたの おかあさnの くruma wa しro ですか。

　　　　　　Is your mother's car white?

5 Answer Key

❑ Word practice (answers)

1. なつ
2. にhon
3. ねこ
4. yoなか
5. のmu
6. ねru
7. なに
8. ぬいぐrumi
9. にがい
10. おねえさn
11. ぬぐ
12. のru

❑ Hiragana matching (answers)

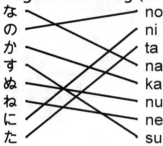

な — no
の — ni
か — ta
す — na
ぬ — ka
ね — nu
に — ne
た — su

❑ Reading comprehension (translation)

① Satoko's boyfriend's name is Yoshio Tanaka.
② Satoko is 25 years old.
③ Yoshio is 27 years old.
④ Satoko likes shopping a lot.
⑤ Yoshio doesn't like shopping.
⑥ Yoshio likes work.
⑦ Satoko dislikes work.
⑧ Satoko and Yoshio like (to) travel a lot.

❑ 1. Question and answer 1 (answers)

Question	Answer
1a. Is this fish?	いいえ、さかな jaないです。
1b. Well then, what is it?	Chikin です。
2a. Is this a book?	いいえ、hon jaないです。
2b. Well then, what is it?	しnbun です。
3a. Is this a bowl and a spoon?	いいえ、(お)chawanと supu–n jaないです。
3b. Well then, what are they?	(お)chawanと (お)haしです。
4a. Are these shoes?	いいえ、くつjaないです。
4b. Well then, what are they?	ずbonです。

❑ 2. Question and answer 2 (sample answers)

1. Which one do you like/dislike?   これがすき／きraいです。／くroいのが すきです。
2. Which one do you like/dislike?   これがすき／きraいです。／かいmoのが すきです。

❑ 3. Question and answer 3 (sample answers)

Question	Answer
1. Do you like traveling?	Haい、すきです / いいえ、きraいです。
2. Do you dislike cats?	Haい、きraいです / いいえ、すきです。
3. Do you like vegetables?	Haい、すきです / いいえ、すきjaないです。
4. Do you like Japanese?	Haい、だいすきです / いいえ、だいきraいです。
5. Does sushi taste good?	Haい、おいしいです / いいえ、おいしくないです。

❑ 4. Japanese translation (answers)

1. Yoshio san likes cars a lot.
2. Yoshio san's cars are red and white.
   (this sentence could mean, "Yoshio's car is red and white," but from the context of the other sentences we see that he has two cars.)
3. His white car is a Honda.
4. The red one is a Toyota.
5. Yoshio's father likes cars a lot.
   (This would be better as "Yoshio's father <u>also</u> likes cars a lot," but we haven't learned the "also" particle.)
6. His father's cars are a gold car and a yellow car.
7. His mother does not like the yellow car.

❑ 5. Reading comprehension questions (answers)

Question	Answer
1. Who is Satoko's boyfriend?	たなか yoしおさんです。
2. Does Yoshio dislike his work?	いいえ、しごとが すきです。
3. How old is Satoko?	にjuう ごさいです。
4. Who likes shopping?	さとこさんが （かいmoのが） すきです。
5. Who likes traveling?	さとこさんと yoしおさんが （ryoこうが） すきです。

❑ 6. Short dialogue (translation)

Ms. Mori:	Do you like movies, Ms. Nishida?
Ms. Nishida:	Yes, I like them a lot.
Ms. Mori:	Me, too. As for actors, who do you like?
Ms. Nishida:	I like Harrison Ford.
Ms. Mori:	Is that so? I like Brad Pitt.
Ms. Nishida:	I like Brad Pitt, too.

Vocabulary Groups

G   sports and entertainment

Progressive	Kana	Kanji	English
basuketto booru	バスケットボール	バスケットボール	basketball
gyanburu	ギャンブル	ギャンブル	gambling
sakka–	サッカー	サッカー	soccer

H   fruit

Progressive	Kana	Kanji	English
いちご	いちご	苺	strawberry
miかn / orenji	みかん / オレンジ	みかん / オレンジ	orange
rinご	りんご	りんご	apple
banana	バナナ	バナナ	banana
すいか	すいか	西瓜	watermelon
remon	レモン	レモン	lemon
momo	もも	桃	peach
buどう	ぶどう	ぶどう	grapes

Lesson

6

Level ①

Wanting and Not Wanting

Conjugating adjectives

6 | About This Lesson このレッスンについて

Before The Lesson

1. Be able to write and read なにぬねの.
2. Understand how to use すき, きらい and jaない.
3. Review vocabulary group G and H.

Lesson Goals

1. Learn how to say you want or don't want something.
2. Learn how to conjugate adjectives into the negative form.

From The Teachers

1. Don't confuse the usage of jaない, and くない. Remember that jaない is used with nouns and くない is used with いadjectives.

6 | New Words あたらしい ことば

Progressive	Kana	Kanji	English
hoしい	ほしい	欲しい	want
doru	ドル	ドル	dollars
えn	えん	円	yen
inta–netto	インターネット	インターネット	internet
おかね	おかね	お金	money
moちron	もちろん	もちろん	of course
ko–ra	コーラ	コーラ	cola
miず	みず	水	water
のmimoの	のみもの	飲み物	a drink; drinks

6 | Culture Clip カルチャー クリップ

You might see くん or *chan* added to the end of last or first names. They are both used to show affection, but are not limited to just that. *Chan* is mostly used after girls' names and くん after boys' names. *Chan* is used quite often after children's names, regardless of the sex of the child. It is also not unusual for a higher-up in a company to refer to the female staff members with a くん following their names.

When NOT to use
Chan and くん should *never* be used when addressing people above you in social status. If you ever hear someone addressing another person with くん or *chan*, you can assume that the speaker is equal or higher in status.

 kun

 chan

6 | New Phrases あたらしい かいわ

1. けっこうです。   I'm fine. (No thanks)

6 | New Adjectives あたらしい けいようし

The following are all いadjectives and always end in い. の is not needed to make them into adjectives. They are simply be placed in front of a word to modify it. They can be considered *true adjectives* because they stand alone as adjectives without any help.

Progressive	Kana	Kanji	English
あたraしい	あたらしい	新しい	new
furuい	ふるい	古い	old
あつい	あつい	暑い	hot
さmuい	さむい	寒い	cold
つmeたい	つめたい	冷たい	cold to the touch
ぬruい	ぬるい	温い	warm; lukewarm

6 Grammar ぶんぽう

❑ 6-1. Making adjectives negative

In the prior lesson, you learned how to make nouns negative with jaない. For example, いぬ jaないです, means "it's not a dog." ~jaない can NOT be used to make い adjectives negative.

Remember that all "true" adjectives (い adjectives) end with an い. To make them negative, drop the last い then add くない.

> **(い adjective) minus い, add くない**
> **It's not (adjective).**

Examples

1. あたらしい = new
    あたらし<u>くない</u> = <u>not</u> new

2. おいしい = delicious
    おいし<u>くない</u> = <u>not</u> delicious

3. さむい = cold
    さむ<u>くない</u> = <u>not</u> cold

4. あつい = hot
    あつ<u>くない</u> = <u>not</u> hot

5. つめたい = cold to the touch
    つめた<u>くない</u> = <u>not</u> cold to the touch

6. furuい = old
    furu<u>くない</u> = <u>not</u> old

❑ 6-2. The colors as negative adjectives

The same thing can be done with the adjective forms of colors.

Examples

1. あかい = red
    あか<u>くない</u> = <u>not</u> red

2. あおい = blue
    あお<u>くない</u> = <u>not</u> blue

3. chaいroい = brown
    chaいro<u>くない</u> = <u>not</u> brown

4. きいroい = yellow
    きいro<u>くない</u> = <u>not</u> yellow

❑ 6-3. Wanting and not wanting

The particle が is used with ほしい (want) in the same way it is used with すき and きらい. が is used to mark the thing that you want or don't want.

[*thing*] が ほしい です。
I want [*thing*]

To change "want" into "don't want," drop the い then add くない.

[*thing*] が ほし<u>くない</u> です。
I don't want [*thing*]

Example Sentences

1. あたらしい terebi<u>が</u> ほしい です。
   I want a new television.

2. つめたい のmimoのが ほしい です。
   I want a cold drink.

3. Furuい くrumaが ほしくない です。
   I don't want an old car.

❑ 6-4. Tricky uses of the particle の

The particle の that we learned in other lessons is used to show possession (as in the sentence **わたしの くruma です** – "it's my car"). More importantly, we learned that の can be used to make any noun into an adjective just by coming after the noun, as in **にhonごの hon** (a Japanese language book).

The usage described above is simple, but sometimes when you have a string of words separated by の it can be tricky. Look at the following sentence:

1. <u>Waたしの とmoだちの あきこさn</u> wa にjuうごさい です。
   <u>My friend Akiko</u> is 25 years old.

This sentence may look confusing, but remember that the key function of の is to make the noun or word it comes after into a modifier (no-adjective). Waたしの とmoだちの あきこさn simply means, "my friend Akiko." Waたしの とmoだちの is just modifying あきこさn.

❑ 6-5. Numbers and money

If you want to say 100 dollars or 100 yen, you just add *doru* or えn after the number. The particle の is not required.

> **Examples**
> 1. 100 yen.
>   Hyaくえn.
>
> 2. 1000 dollars.
>   せn doru.

❑ 6-6. Counting above 10,000 (Numbers Part II)

The 1,000 unit in Japanese ends at 9,000. In other words, you can NEVER say JUU SEN to mean 10,000. After 9,000, Japanese begins counting in units of 10,000. Each unit of 10,000 is called MAN. So, 20,000 is にman because it is 2 (に) units of 10,000 (man). And 50,000 is ごman because it is 5 (ご) units of 10,000 (man).

the ten thousands (10,000-90,000)			
Number	Progressive	Hiragana	Never
10,000	いちman	いちまん	
20,000	にman	にまん	
30,000	さん man	さんまん	
40,000	yon man	よんまん	✘ しman
50,000	ごman	ごまん	
60,000	roくman	ろくまん	
70,000	ななman	ななまん	✘ しちman
80,000	haちman	はちまん	
90,000	kyuうman	きゅうまん	✘ くman

In English, we can have up to 999 units of 1000. This is why we can say 999,000. But as mentioned above, Japanese can NEVER have more than 9 units of 1000. It can have up to 9999 units of MAN (10,000). For English speakers the MAN unit is a new concept. This is hard to get used to at first, but imagine how Japanese feel about LOSING a counter and using 1000 in English ☺.

You can have up to 9999 units of 10,000 which is 99,990,000. Knowing this, and with practice you can now count up just under 100 million.

Examples

1. juう man (10 man)   100,000 (100 thousand)
2. ごjuう man (50 man)   500,000 (500 thousand)
3. hyaく man (100 man)   1,000,000 (1 million)
4. ななhyaく man (700 man)   7,000,000 (7 million)
5. にせn man (2000 man)   20,000,000 (20 million)
6. ごせn man (5000 man)   50,000,000 (50 million)
7. kyuうせn kyuう hyaく kyuう juうkyuう man   99,990,000
    (9999 man)   (99 million 990 thousand)

6   Q&A しつもんと こたえ Japanese→English

1. **なにが hoしい ですか。**   **What do you want?**
    あたraしい くrumaが hoしい です。   I want a new car.
    いちman doruが hoしい です。   I want 10,000 dollars.
    かのjoが hoしい です。   I want a girlfriend.
    つmeたい ko–raが hoしい です。   I want a cold cola.

2. **どreが hoしい ですか。**   **Which one do you want?**
    これ と これが hoしい です。   I want this one and this one.
    あかのが hoしい です。   I want the red one.
    Miどriと あおのが hoしい です。   I want the green and blue one.

3. **あなたのくruma wa あたraしい ですか。**   **Is your car new?**
    いいえ、furuい です。   No, it's old.
    いいえ、あたraしくない です。   No, it's not new.

4. **Konpyu–ta–が hoしい ですか。**   **Do you want a computer?**
    いいえ、hoしくない です。   No, I don't want one.
    Haい、hoしい です。   Yes, I want one.

6   Q&A しつもんと こたえ English→Japanese

1. **What color car do you want?**   **なにいroの くrumaが hoしい ですか。**
    I want a silver car.   ぎnいroの くrumaが hoしい です。
    I don't want a car.   くrumaが hoしくない です。

2. **Don't you want a new refrigerator?**　　あたraしい reいぞうこが hoしくない ですか。
   Of course, I want one.　　　　　　　Moちron、hoしい です。

3. **Is your drink cold?**　　　　　　あなたの のmimoの wa つmeたい ですか。
   No, it's not cold.　　　　　　　　いいえ、つmeたくない です。
   No, it's warm.　　　　　　　　　　いいえ、ぬruい です。

4. **Do you want a newspaper?**　　　しnbunが hoしい ですか。
   Yes, I want the Yomiuri Newspaper.　　Haい、Yomiうri しnbunが hoしい です。

   NOTE: Yomiuri is a popular newspaper in Japan.

6　Reading Comprehension どっかい

Read the sentences below. Use the information to answer the reading comprehension questions later in this lesson.

① Boくの なmaえ wa maつmoと です。

② Inta–nettoが すきです。

③ Konpyu–ta–が hoしい です。

④ Boくの とmoだちの たしroくn wa konpyu–ta–が hoしくないです。

⑤ たしroくn wa あかい くrumaが hoしい です。

⑥ Boく wa あかい くrumaが すきjaないです。

⑦ しroい くrumaが すきです。

Hiragana はひふへほ

は   New Hiragana あたらしい ひらがな

Make sure you learn the correct stroke order since correct stroke order will mean neater characters when writing quickly.

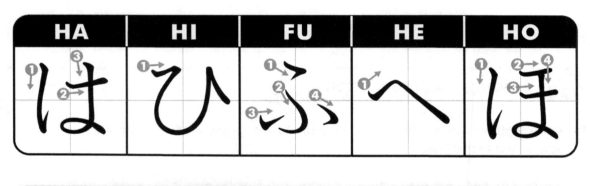

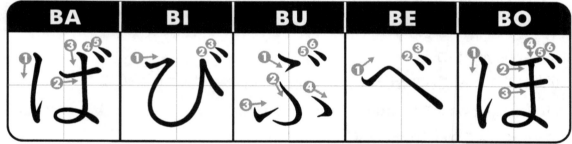

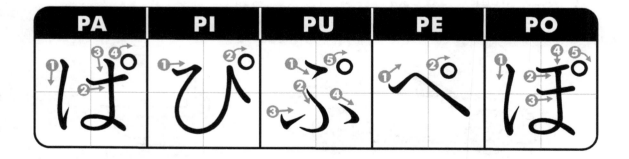

は Various Styles スタイル

Look at the various possible styles for the hiragana in this lesson. Write each symbol as neatly as you can, then compare it to the different versions below.

は	は	は	は	は
ひ	ひ	ひ	ひ	ひ
ふ	ふ	ふ	ふ	ふ
へ	へ	へ	へ	へ
ほ	ほ	ほ	ほ	ほ

ば	ば	ば	ば	ば
び	び	び	び	び
ぶ	ぶ	ぶ	ぶ	ぶ
べ	べ	べ	べ	べ
ぼ	ぼ	ぼ	ぼ	ぼ

ぱ	ぱ	ぱ	ぱ	ぱ
ぴ	ぴ	ぴ	ぴ	ぴ
ぷ	ぷ	ぷ	ぷ	ぷ
ぺ	ぺ	ぺ	ぺ	ぺ
ぽ	ぽ	ぽ	ぽ	ぽ

は **Writing Points かくポイント**

❏ **6-7. What is that circle?**

The *pa pi pu pe po* hiragana are made by adding a circle in the area where *dakuten* normally would go. The circle should be written clockwise and is always the last stroke. Most Japanese people refer to this as simply *maru*, which means "circle." The official name for it is *handakuten*.

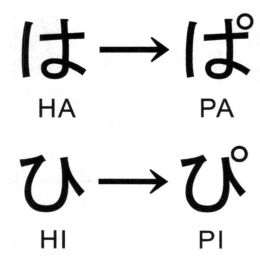

HA   PA

HI   PI

❏ **6-8. Why isn't ふ written as *HU*?**

Japanese From Zero! represents ふ as *FU* instead of *HU* in ro–maji. Japanese people will sometimes represent ふ as *HU* in ro–maji, however, the pronunciation of ふ is closer to *FU*. The F sound in ふ should be voiced softer than the F sound in an English word.

❏ **6-9. The easy way to write ふ (fu)**

ふ tends to be difficult to write, but there is an easy way: connect the first and second stroke into what looks like a number "3."

The 3 Version   Actual Font Versions

は Writing Practice れんしゅう

To practice correct stroke order, first trace the light gray characters, then write each character six times for practice.

ha	は	は					
hi	ひ	ひ					
fu	ふ	ふ					
he	へ	へ					
ho	ほ	ほ					

ba	ば	ば					
bi	び	び					
bu	ぶ	ぶ					
be	べ	べ					
bo	ぼ	ぼ					

pa	ぱ	ぱ						
pi	ぴ	ぴ						
pu	ぷ	ぷ						
pe	ぺ	ぺ						
po	ぽ	ぽ						

は Special Usage とくべつな つかいかた

❑ **6-10. The topic marker は (wa)**

A topic marker in Japanese identifies the subject of a sentence. The topic marker "wa" is written using the は (ha) character and can never be written using the わ (wa) character. In all other situations, は (ha) is always read as "ha."

> **Example Sentences**
> 1. あなたは (wa) だれ ですか。   Who are you?
> 2. Bananaは (wa) きいろ です。   Bananas are yellow.

❑ **6-11. The direction marker へ (e)**

The direction marker "e" is written using the へ (he) character and can never be written using the え (e) character. In all other situations, へ (he) is always read as "he."

NOTE: This grammar point is covered in Lesson 12.

> **Example Sentences**
> 1. がっこうへ (e) いきます。   I am going towards (to) school.
> 2. とうkyoうへ (e) いきます。   I am going towards (to) Tokyo.

は Word Practice ことばの れんしゅう

Fill in the appropriate hiragana in the blanks for each word.

1. __ru   (spring)
   ha

2. __ruご__n   (lunch)
   hi   ha

3. __yu   (winter)
   fu

4. __いwa   (peace)
   he

5. え__n   (picture book)
   ho

6. がn__ru   (to do your best)
   ba

7. __な__   (fireworks)
   ha bi

8. かmi__くro   (paper bag)
   bu

9. __とme__re   (love at first sight)
   hi   bo

10. くra__ru   (to compare)
    be

11. __ __な   (electric spark)
    hi ba

12. えn__つ   (pencil)
    pi

は Words You Can Write かける ことば

Write the following words using the hiragana that you just learned. This is a great way to increase your Japanese vocabulary.

は し
(chopsticks)

へ そ
(belly button)

は と
(pigeon; dove)

ぶた
(pig)

ひ と
(people)

しっぽ
(tail)

とうふ
(tofu)

はっぱ
(leaf)

ほっぺ
(cheeks)

ぼうし
(hat)

きっぷ
(ticket)

は な び
(fireworks)

は Everyday Hiragana Words にちじょうの ことば

ひしょ
secretary

ふくろう
owl

おばけ
monster

ほうたい
bandage

はしru
to run

てっぽう
pistol; gun

は | **Hiragana Matching ひらがな マッチング**

Connect the dots between each hiragana and the correct ro–maji.

ふ ·	· pi
ペ ·	· pe
ぜ ·	· bo
ぼ ·	· gi
は ·	· fu
た ·	· ze
ぴ ·	· ta
ぎ ·	· ha

6 Lesson Activities

❑ 1. Question and answer 1

Pick one of the pictures and say 〜が ほしいです / ほしくないです.

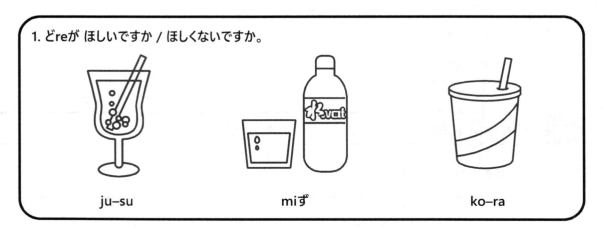

1. どれが ほしいですか / ほしくないですか。

ju–su   miず   ko–ra

2. どれ が ほしいですか / ほしくないですか。

うma   ねこ   いぬ

❑ 2. Question and answer 2

Answer the following questions as if they were being asked to you directly. Use the hiragana that you have learned when writing your answers.

1. なにいroの くrumaが すきですか。

_____

2. にほnの ざっしが ほしいですか。

_____

3. つmeたい ko-raが ほしいですか。

_____

4. あなたの terebiは あたraしいですか。

_____

_____

❑ 3. Question and answer 3

Using _____が ほしいです, make a conversation for the following pictures:

1. What are Ichiro and Yumiko saying in this picture?

Ichiro:_____

Yumiko: _____

2. What are the nurse and the patient saying
 in this picture?

Nurse: _____

Patient: _____

❏ 4. English translation

Translate the following conversation into Japanese.

1.
George さn: What is your name?   **Yuかri さn:**   It is Yukari. What is yours?   **George さn:** My name is George. I am 34 years old. How old are you?   **Yuかri さn:**   I am 26 years old.
George さn:
Yuかri さn:
George さn:
Yuかri さn:

❏ 5. Reading comprehension questions

Answer the following questions about the reading comprehension in this lesson.

1. Maつmoとくn は、なにが すきですか。

    _____

2. Maつmoとくnの とmoだちの なmaえは、なnですか。

    _____

3. たしro くnは、なにが ほしいですか。

    _____

4. Maつmoとくnは、あかい くrumaが すきですか。

    _____

5. Maつmoとくnは、なにいroの くrumaが すきですか。

    _____

❑ 6. Short dialogue
Mr. Yoshida is welcoming Karen to his house.

Yoしだ さn:	Karen さn、どうぞ。
Karen:	はい、おjamaしmaす。
Yoしだ さn:	のmimoのは なにが ほしいですか。
Karen:	そうですね...。Ko–raが ほしいです。
Yoしだ さn:	Choっと maってください。
	はい、どうぞ。 (serving a bottle of cola)
Karen:	あriがとうございmaす。

New words and expressions in the dialogue

Progressive	Kanji	English
どうぞ。	どうぞ。	Please come in.
おjamaしmaす。	お邪魔します。	I will come in.

(literally, "I will bother you," when entering someone's house)

そうですね...	そうですね...	Let's see...
Choっと maってください。	ちょっと待って下さい。	Please wait a moment.
(はい) どうぞ。	(はい) どうぞ。	Here you are.

(when serving/giving something to someone)

❑ 7. Short dialogue activities
Practice reading the dialogue in pairs. Certainly you have a friend by now! No... dang.
Suppose someone is visiting your house. Ask him/her what he/she wants for a drink.

orenji ju–su?

miず?

rinご ju–su?

❑ **8. More words you can write**

You should practice writing these words a minimum of five times each. Not only will you be practicing the new hiragana, but you will also learn new words.

しばふ	grass	ふうふ	married couple
はこぶ	to move an item	へいたい	soldier
すなば	sand box	こうべ	Kobe (city)
ばくはつ	explosion	ぴかぴか	shiny
てっぽう	gun		

6   Drill ドリル

If you're not sure what these sentences mean, we recommend that you review the lesson up to this point before continuing.

1. なにが ほしい ですか。
2. つめたい miずが ほしい です。
3. あかくない rinごが すきjaない です。

6   Sentence Building ぶんのつくり

In each lesson we will build on a previous sentence. Watch it grow and transform each time new concepts are introduced.

> **あなたの おかあさnは なにいroの くrumaが ほしいですか。**
> **What color car does your mother want?**

Compare how the sentence has changed from the prior lessons:

Lesson 3:   こreは あなたの おかあさn の くruma ですか。
Is this your mother's car?

Lesson 4:   あなたの おかあさnの くrumaは しro ですか。
Is your mother's car white?

Lesson 5:   あなたの おかあさnは なにいroの くrumaが すき ですか。
What color car does your mother like?

6 Answer Key

❑ Word Practice (answers)

1. はru
2. ひruごはn
3. ふyu
4. へいwa
5. えほn
6. がnばru
7. はなび
8. かmiぶくro
9. ひとmeぼre
10. くraべru
11. ひばな
12. えnぴつ

❑ Hiragana matching (answers)

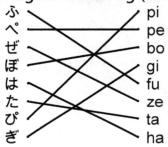

ふ — fu
ぺ — pe
ぜ — bo
ぼ — ze
は — ha
た — ta
ぴ — pi
ぎ — gi

❑ Reading comprehension (translation)

① My name is Matsumoto.
② I like the internet.
③ I want a computer.
④ My friend Tashiro doesn't want a computer.
⑤ Tashiro wants a red car.
⑥ I don't like red cars.
⑦ I like white cars.

❑ 1. Question and answer 1 (sample answers)

1. Which one do/don't you want?   Ju–su が ほしいです／みずが ほしくないです。
2. Which one do/don't you want?   うmaが ほしいです／いぬが ほしくないです。

❑ 2. Question and answer 2 (sample answers)

1. What color car do you like?
   しroい くrumaが すきです。

2. Do you want a Japanese magazine?
   はい、ほしいです／いいえ、ほしくないです。

3. Do you want a cold cola?
   はい、つmeたい ko–raが ほしいです。
   いいえ、ko–raが きraいです。

4. Is your TV new?
   はい、あたraしいです。／いいえ、あたraしくないです。

❑ 3. Question and answer 3 (answers may vary)

1. Ichiro: なにが ほしいですか。
   Yumiko: Konpyu–ta–が ほしいです。

2. Nurse: Maくraが ほしいですか。
   Patient: いいえ、ほしくないです。

❑ 4. English translation (answers)

George: なまえは なnですか。
Yuかri: Yuかriです。あなたの なまえは なnですか。
George: Jo–jiです。さnjuう yonさいです。なnさいですか。
Yuかri: にjuう roくさいです。

❑ 5. Reading comprehension questions (answers)

1. What does Matsumoto like? Inta–nettoが すきです。
2. What is Matsumoto's friend's name? たしro（くn）です。
3. What does Tashiro want? あかい くrumaが ほしいです。
4. Does Matsumoto like red cars? いいえ、すきjaないです。
5. What color car does Matsumoto like? しroい くrumaが すきです。

❑ 6. Short dialogue (translation)

Mr. Yoshida: Please come in, Karen.
Karen: Thank you (I will come in) .
Mr. Yoshida: What drink would you like?
Karen: Let's see... I want cola.
Mr. Yoshida: Wait a minute. Here you are.
Karen: Thank you.

Vocabulary Groups

I transportation

Progressive	Kana	Kanji	English
くruma	くるま	車	car
ひこうき	ひこうき	飛行機	airplane
でnsha	でんしゃ	電車	train
basu	バス	バス	bus
ふね	ふね	船	ship; boat
さnrinsha	さんりんしゃ	三輪車	tricycle
shoうぼうsha	しょうぼうしゃ	消防車	fire truck
じてnsha	じてんしゃ	自転車	bicycle
しnかnせn	しんかんせん	新幹線	bullet train
patoka–	パトカー	パトカー	patrol car

バス

じてんしゃ

ひこうき

Lesson 7 Level ①

Locations
Where is it?

7 | About This Lesson このレッスンについて

Before The Lesson

1. Be able to write and read はひふへほ, ばびぶべぼ, ぱぴぷぺぽ.
2. Understand how make a noun into a modifying word using the particle の.
3. Review vocabulary group I.

Lesson Goals

1. Learn how to say where an item is.
2. Learn when to use は (wa) or が.

From The Teachers

1. The こそあど diagram in Lesson 2 for will be helpful in understanding the distance relationships for ここ, そこ, and あそこ words in the どこ word group in this lesson.

7 | New Words あたらしい ことば

Progressive	Kana	Kanji	English
どこ	どこ	どこ	where? what place?
ここ	ここ	ここ	here; this place
そこ	そこ	そこ	there; that place
あそこ	あそこ	あそこ	over there; that place over there
そと	そと	外	outside
なか	なか	中	inside
resutoran	レストラン	レストラン	restaurant
にほn	にほん	日本	Japan
amerika	アメリカ	アメリカ	America
でmo	でも	でも	but
おcha	おちゃ	お茶	tea

7 | New Adjectives あたらしい けいようし

Progressive	Kana	Kanji	English
いい、yoい	いい 、よい	いい、良い	nice; good
おおきい	おおきい	大きい	big
ちいさい	ちいさい	小さい	small

7 | Culture Clip: Japanese Tea

Japanese people love tea. When you visit a Japanese home, you will often be offered tea and a snack. The snack is often a variety of rice cracker called, せnべい. Any one of the following teas might be offered:

ryoくcha	りょくちゃ	緑茶	green tea (leaves)
まccha	まっちゃ	抹茶	green tea (powdered)
ほうじcha	ほうじちゃ	ほうじ茶	green tea (roasted)
こうcha	こうちゃ	紅茶	black tea
u-ron cha	ウーロンちゃ	ウーロン茶	oolong tea
むぎcha	むぎちゃ	麦茶	wheat tea

Green tea is popular having a variety of types. These teas might be simply referred to as, おcha, despite the variety.

7 | New Phrases あたらしい かいわ

1. おなかが すいていmaす。   I'm hungry.
   This literally means, "My stomach is empty."

2. おなかが いっぱい です。   I'm full.
   This literally means, "My stomach is full."

3. のどが かwaいていmaす。   I'm thirsty.
   This literally means, "My throat is dry."

7   Word Usage ことばの つかいかた

❑ 7-1. Yoくない vs いくない

In Lesson 6 you learned how to make any adjective negative by dropping the い and adding くない.

> **Examples**
> 1. おおきい = big
>   おおき<u>くない</u> = <u>not</u> big
>
> 2. ちいさい = small
>   ちいさ<u>くない</u> = <u>not</u> small

いい is an exception to the normal pattern. Both いい and yoい mean "nice; good". And even though you will sometimes hear people say いくない to mean "not good" in a casual conversation, it's not commonly used and generally not considered standard Japanese. Instead, yoくない should be used to say "not good".

7   Grammar ぶんぽう

❑ 7-2. Using でmo

でmo is used to connect two complete sentences together. The second sentence begins with でmo.

> (Sentence 1). でmo, (Sentence 2).
> (Sentence 1). But (Sentence 2).

> **Example sentences**
> 1. Furu–tsuは おいしいです。<u>でmo</u>、おなかが いっぱいです。
>   Fruits are delicious. <u>But</u> I am full.
>
> 2. のどが かwaいています。<u>でmo</u>、ko–raは つめたくない です。
>   I'm thirsty. <u>But</u> the cola isn't cold.
>
> 3. Waたしの konpyu–ta–は ふるいです。<u>でmo</u>、あたraしいのは ほしくない です。
>   My computer is old. <u>But</u> I don't want a new one.

❑ 7-3. The rules for using は (wa) and が (ga)

In this lesson, we will discuss some differences between は (wa) and が. This topic tends to stress out new students of Japanese, but there is nothing to worry about if you learn these simple rules!

#1. You can NEVER use は (wa) immediately after a question word.

This is a simple rule with no exceptions.

INCORRECT
1. なには すきですか。
2. どれ は いぬですか。
3. なにいro は すき ですか。

CORRECT
なにが すきですか。
どれ が いぬですか。
なにいro が すき ですか。

#2. は (wa) is used for comparison and emphasis.

Generally speaking, adjectives such as ほしい, すき, and きら い use が to mark the item being discussed. However, when comparing items or emphasizing, は is used instead of が.

Examples (emphasis)

1. すいかは おいしいです。

   Watermelons are delicious. (You are emphasizing how tasty watermelons are.)

2. Totoro (anime character)は おおきいです！

   Totoro is big!

Examples (comparison)

1. Moうふが ほしい です。でmo、maくra は ほしくない です。

   I want a blanket. But I don't want a pillow.

2. Rinごが すきです。でmo、banana は きraい です。

   I like apples. But I dislike bananas.

3. ねこが ほしくない です。でmo、いぬは ほしい です。

   I don't want a cat. But I want a dog.

#3. は (wa) and が can both be in the same sentence.

When は (wa) and が are in the same sentence, は marks the topic and が marks the object.

Examples

1. Waたしは ねこが すきです。
   I like cats.

2. Yoしおさん は banana が ほしい です。
   Yoshio wants a banana.

#4. は (wa) should be used with new topics and conversations.

Even though your sentence will still be understood if you mix up は (wa) and が, you should always use は when introducing new topics of discussion.

As discussed in Lesson 2, after the topic is introduced, it can be dropped from the rest of the conversation. But if the topic needs to be restated OR you change topics, don't forget that は (wa) should be used.

#5. は (wa) and が are often dropped in casual conversations.

Until your Japanese is really good, we don't recommend that you drop any particles, but from time to time, you will hear casual Japanese conversations where は (wa) or が have been dropped.

WITH THE PARTICLE

1. ねこが すきです。
   I like cats.

2. おかあさんは なnさい ですか。
   How old is your mother?

WITHOUT THE PARTICLE

ねこ すきです。
I like cats.

おかあさん なnさい ですか。
How old is your mother?

7 Q&A しつもんと こたえ English→Japanese

1. **Where is it?** どこ ですか。
It's here. ここ です。
It's there. そこ です。
It's outside. そと です。
It's inside. なか です。

2. **Is it here?** ここ ですか。
Yes, it's here. はい、ここです。
No, it's not here. いいえ、ここjaない です。
No, it's over there. いいえ、あそこです。

3. **Is it over there?** あそこ ですか。
Yes, it's over there. はい、あそこです。
No, it's there. いいえ、そこです。
No, it's not over there. いいえ、あそこjaない です。

4. **Where is the dog?** いぬは どこですか。
The dog is over there. いぬは あそこです。
The dog is outside. いぬは そとです。
The dog isn't inside. いぬは なかjaない です。

7 Q&A しつもんと こたえ Japanese→English

1. **いいですか** **Is it good?**
はい, いいです。 Yes, it's good.
いいえ、yoくないです。 No, it's not good.

2. **どこが いいですか。** **What place is good?**
ここが いいです。 This place is good.
そこが いいです。 That place is good.

3. **おいしい resutoranは どこですか。** **Where is a good (-tasting) restaurant?**
ごめんなさい、わかrimaせn. I'm sorry, I don't know.
おいしい resutoranは あそこです。 A good restaurant is over there.
あそこが いいです。 That place over there is good.

4. **にほnの くrumaが ほしい ですか。** **Do you want a Japanese car?**
はい、にほnの くrumaが だいすき です。 Yes, I really like Japanese cars.
いいえ、ほしくない です。 No, I don't want one.

7　Mini Conversation ミニかいわ Japanese→English

1. **Conversation between friends**
   A:　おなかが すいていmaす。
   B:　Pizaが ほしい ですか。
   A:　いいえ、すしが ほしい です。

   A:　I'm hungry!
   B:　Do you want pizza?
   A:　No, I want sushi.

2. **Conversation at school between friends**
   A:　たなか せnせいが すき ですか。
   B:　だいすきです。あなたは？
   A:　すきjaない です。
   B:　Jaあ、だreが すき ですか。
   A:　こばyaし せnせいが すき です。

   A:　Do you like Mrs. Tanaka?
   B:　I love her! What about you?
   A:　I don't like (her).
   B:　Well then, who do you like?
   A:　I like Mr. Kobayashi.

   NOTE: When addressing a teacher, you just add せnせい after their family name. In English we translate せnせい to "Mr.", "Mrs." etc. instead of just "teacher" in this case.

3. **Conversation between friends.**
   A:　あなたの くrumaは おおきいですか。
   B:　いいえ、ちいさいです。でmo、おとうさnの くrumaは おおきい です。
   A:　なにいro ですか。
   B:　しro です。

   A:　Is your car big?
   B:　No, it's small. But my father's car is big.
   A:　What color is it?
   B:　It's white.

Hiragana まみむめも

ま New Hiragana あたらしい ひらがな

Make sure you learn the correct stroke order since correct stroke order will mean neater characters when writing quickly.

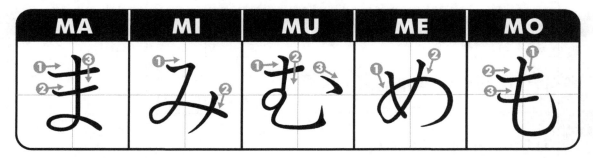

ま Various Styles スタイル

Look at the various possible styles for the hiragana in this lesson. Write each symbol as neatly as you can, then compare it to the different versions below.

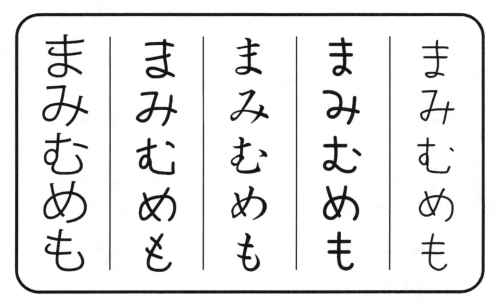

ま Writing Practice れんしゅう

To practice correct stroke order, first trace the light gray characters, then write each character six times for practice.

ma	ま	ま						
mi	み	み						
mu	む	む						
me	め	め						
mo	も	も						

ま Word Practice ことばの れんしゅう

Fill in the appropriate hiragana in the blanks for each word.

1. ___ri (forest)
   mo

2. ___ ___じ (maple leaf)
   mo mi

3. ___ri (impossible)
   mu

4. ___だつ (to stand out)
   me

5. ___ru (to see; to watch)
   mi

6. ___がね (eye glasses)
   me

7. たべ___の (food)
   mo

8. ___ ___ru (to protect)
   ma mo

9. の__ __の　(a drink)
　　　mi mo

10. __しあつい　(humid)
　　　mu

11. __ほう　(magic)
　　　ma

12. __ __ず　(earthworm)
　　　mi mi

ま　Everyday Hiragana Words にちじょうの ことば

yoむ
to read

のみもの
a drink

しつもん
question

なみだ
tears

うま
horse

あめ
candy

ま　Words You Can Write かける ことば

Write the following words using the hiragana that you just learned. This is a great way to increase your Japanese vocabulary.

ま ど
(window)

も も
(peach)

むし
(insect)

かみ
(paper; hair)

だめ
(no good)

みせ
(store)

あたま
(head)

まじめ
(serious)

さしみ
(sashimi)

むすこ
(son)

むすめ
(daughter)

ものさし
(ruler)

みじかい
(short)

ま | Hiragana Matching ひらがな マッチング

Connect the dots between each hiragana and the correct ro–maji.

に ·   · mu

む ·   · mi

も ·   · nu

ぬ ·   · ni

み ·   · o

ま ·   · mo

お ·   · me

め ·   · ma

7 Lesson Activities

❑ 1. Sentence creation
Create a sentence about the pictures using でも. Pay attention は and が particle usage.

Example

like→   BUT   dislike→

ex. <u>Chikin</u>が すきです。でも、さかなは きraいです。

like→   BUT   don't like→

1. _____

want→   BUT   don't want→

2. _____

←are delicious **BUT**   ←are not

3. _____

❏ 2. What would you say?
Use the hiragana to answer these questions as if they were directly asked to you.

1. おいしい resutoranは どこですか。

   _____

2. あなたの いえは、どこですか。

   _____

3. にほnの くruまが ほしいですか。

   _____

4. みどriの rinごが すきですか。

   _____

5. あなたの terebiは あたraしいですか。

   _____

6. あなたの じてnshaは、なにいroですか。

   _____

7. つめたいみずが ほしいですか。

   _____

❏ 3. Short dialogue 1
Mr. Tanaka is driving Mike (Maiku) home and asking which house is Mike's house.

たなかさn:	Maikuさnのうちは ①<u>あそこ</u>ですか。
Maiku:	いいえ、ちがいます。②<u>そこ</u>です。
たなかさn:	えっ、どこですか。Waかriません。 ③<u>みどri</u>の うちですか。
Maiku:	いいえ、③<u>みどriの</u> うちは、ともだちの うちです。 ④<u>きいroい</u> うちが waたしのです。
たなかさn:	ああ、waかriました。

New words and expressions in the dialogue

Progressive	Kana	Kanji	English
うち	うち	家	house
えっ	えっ	えっ	Eh?
ああ、waかriました。	ああ、わかりました。	ああ、分かりました。	Oh, I see. / I got it.

❑ 4. Short dialogue 1 activities

1. Practice reading the dialogue in pairs.
2. Substitute the words numbered ①~④ using the words below and try the conversation again.

A) ① There   B) ① There
    ② Here   ② Over there
    ③ Brown   ③ White
    ④ Blue   ④ Gray

❑ 5. Short dialogue 2

Mr. Tanaka is taking Mike to a sushi bar.

たなか さn:	Maikuさnは (お)すしが すきですか。
Maiku:	はい、だいすきです。
たなか さn:	なにが すきですか。
Maiku:	まぐroと えびが すきです。
たなか さn:	そうですか。Waたしは、ひraめと いかが すきです。にほnの おchaが、すきですか。
Maiku:	いいえ。にほnの おchaが すき jaないです。でも、ko–raは すきです。

New words and expressions in the dialogue

Progressive	Kana	Kanji	English
まぐro	まぐろ	鮪	tuna
えび	えび	海老	shrimp
ひraめ	ひらめ	平目	halibut
いか	いか	イカ	squid

❑ 6. Short dialogue 2 activities
1. Practice reading the dialogue in pairs.
2. Talk about your most/least favorite sushi.
3. Talk about your most/least favorite beverage.

❑ 7. More words you can write
You should practice writing these words a minimum of five times each. Not only will you be practicing the new characters, but you will also learn new words.

もしもし	hello (on the phone)	しも	frost
みみ	ear	め	eye
めだつ	to stand out	むね	chest
ひま	free time	むずかしい	difficult
もくじ	contents	ななめ	diagonal
まね	imitation		

7 Drill ドリル

If you're not sure what these sentences mean, we recommend that you review the lesson up to this point before continuing.

1. あなたの いえは どこですか。
2. Waたしは でnshaが すきです。でも, ひこうきは だいきraいです。

7 | Sentence Building ぶんのつくり

In each lesson we build on a previous sentence. Watch it grow and transform each time new concepts are introduced.

> ### あなたの おかあさnの くruまは どこですか。
> ### Where is your mother's car?

Compare how the sentence has changed from the prior lessons:

Lesson 4:   あなたの おかあさnの くruまは しro ですか。
             Is your mother's car white?

Lesson 5:   あなたの おかあさnは なにいroの くruまが すきですか。
             What color car does your mother like?

Lesson 6:   あなたの おかあさnは なにいroの くruまが ほしいですか。
             What color car does your mother want?

7 Answer Key

❏ **Word practice (answers)**

1. もri
2. もみじ
3. むri
4. めだつ
5. みru
6. めがね
7. たべもの
8. まもru
9. のみもの
10. むしあつい
11. まほう
12. みみず

❏ **Hiragana matching (answers)**

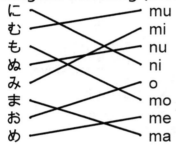

に — mu
む — mi
も — nu
ぬ — ni
み — o
ま — mo
お — me
め — ma

❏ **1. Sentence creation (answers)**

1. みかnが すきです。でも、rinごは すきjaないです。
2. いぬが ほしいです。でも、ねこは ほしくないです。
3. いちごが おいしいです。でも、remonは おいしくないです。

❏ **2. What would you say? (sample answers)**

1. Where is a good (delicious) restaurant?   _____ です。
2. Where is your house?   とうkyoう です。
3. Do you want a Japanese car?   はい、ほしいです。/ いいえ、ほしくないです。
4. Do you like green apples?   はい、すきです。/ いいえ、すきjaないです。
5. Is your TV new?   はい、あたraしいです。/ いいえ、ふruいです。
6. What color is your bicycle?   あか(い) です。
7. Do you want cold water?   はい、ほしいです。
   いいえ、ju–suが ほしいです。

❏ **3. Short dialogue 1 (translation)**

Mr. Tanaka:	Is your house over there, Mike?
Mike:	No, it's there.
Mr. Tanaka:	Huh? Where is it? I don't know (which one?) Is it the green house?
Mike:	No, the green house is my friend's house. The yellow house is mine.
Mr. Tanaka:	Oh, I see.

❏ **5. Short dialogue 2 (translation)**

Mr. Tanaka:	Do you like sushi, Mike?
Mike:	Yes, I love it.
Mr. Tanaka:	What do you like?
Mike:	I like tuna and shrimp.
Mr. Tanaka:	I see. I like halibut and squid. Do you like Japanese tea?
Mike:	No. I don't like Japanese tea. But I like cola.

Vocabulary Groups

J more animals

Progressive	Kana	Kanji	English
きngyo	きんぎょ	金魚	goldfish
かめ	かめ	亀	tortoise; turtle
かえru	かえる	蛙	frog
ぶた	ぶた	豚	pig
はと	はと	鳩	pigeon; dove
あひru	あひる	あひる	duck
かに	かに	蟹	crab
へび	へび	蛇	snake
とri	とり	鳥	bird
robusuta–	ロブスター	ロブスター	lobster
とかげ	とかげ	とかげ	lizard
さかな	さかな	魚	fish
kyoうryuう	きょうりゅう	恐竜	dinosaur

さかな

かえる

とり

Lesson 8
Level ①

Dates and Past Tense
The calendar

8 About This Lesson このレッスンについて

Before The Lesson

1. Be able to write and read まみむめも
2. Understand how to use the question word どこ and how the particle は is used for emphasis.
3. Review vocabulary group J.

Lesson Goals

1. Learn the months, days of the month, and how to use でした.

From The Teachers

1. There are three new question words in this lesson. Many people get them mixed up. Concentrate on learning them.

2. The first ten days of the month might be somewhat difficult to remember. There is no internal pattern to them, so just memorize them. They are important because they set the pattern for other areas of counting.

8 New Phrases あたらしい かいわ

1. たんjoうび おめでとう。   Happy Birthday.

2. あけまして おめでとう。   Happy New Year.

3. おめでとう。   Congratulations.

Note: You can also add ございます after おめでとう to sound more polite, but with friends and family it isn't required.

8   New Words あたらしい ことば

Progressive	Kana	Kanji	English
いつ	いつ	いつ	when?
なnにち	なんにち	何日	what day of the month?
なnがつ	なんがつ	何月	what month?
kyoう	きょう	今日	today
あした	あした	明日	tomorrow
きのう	きのう	昨日	yesterday
たnjoうび	たんじょうび	誕生日	birthday
kurisumasu	クリスマス	クリスマス	Christmas
どくriつ きねnび	どくりつきねんび	独立記念日	Independence Day
purezento	プレゼント	プレゼント	present; gift
go–ruden wi–ku	ゴールデンウィーク	ゴールデンウィーク	Golden Week
けnぽうきねnび	けんぽうきねんび	憲法記念日	Constitution Day
こどものひ	こどものひ	子供の日	Children's Day
ぶnかのひ	ぶんかのひ	文化の日	Culture Day
たいいくのひ	たいいくのひ	体育の日	Sports Day

8   Culture Clip: Christmas and other holidays in Japan

❏ 8-1. Christmas and other holidays in Japan

Japan celebrates Christmas every year, just as many westerners do. In Japan, though, it is a custom to eat a "Christmas cake" on Christmas Eve with the entire family, and on Christmas day they eat chicken. Let's look at some other Japanese holidays:

Constitution Day (May 3)   Children's Day (May 5)
Culture Day (November 3)   Sports Day (2nd Monday in October)

Golden Week, a period of consecutive holidays, happens in the first week of May. During this week, many people return to their home towns to celebrate with family.

Days of the Month にち

1st	ついたち	ついたち	一日
2nd	ふつか	ふつか	二日
3rd	みっか	みっか	三日
4th	yoっか	よっか	四日
5th	いつか	いつか	五日
6th	むいか	むいか	六日
7th	なのか	なのか	七日
8th	yoうか	ようか	八日
9th	ここのか	ここのか	九日
10th	とおか	とおか	十日
11th	juういちにち	じゅういちにち	十一日
12th	juうににち	じゅうににち	十二日
13th	juうさnにち	じゅうさんにち	十三日
14th	juうyoっか	じゅうよっか	十四日
15th	juうごにち	じゅうごにち	十五日
16th	juうroくにち	じゅうろくにち	十六日
17th	juう(しち/なな)にち	じゅう(しち/なな)にち	十七日
18th	juうはちにち	じゅうはちにち	十八日
19th	juうくにち	じゅうくにち	十九日
20th	はつか	はつか	二十日
21st	にjuういちにち	にじゅういちにち	二十一日
22nd	にjuうににち	にじゅうににち	二十二日
23rd	にjuうさnにち	にじゅうさんにち	二十三日
24th	にjuうyoっか	にじゅうよっか	二十四日
25th	にjuうごにち	にじゅうごにち	二十五日
26th	にjuうroくにち	にじゅうろくにち	二十六日
27th	にjuうしちにち	にじゅうしちにち	二十七日
28th	にjuうはちにち	にじゅうはちにち	二十八日
29th	にjuうくにち	にじゅうくにち	二十九日
30th	さnjuうにち	さんじゅうにち	三十日
31st	さnjuういちにち	さんじゅういちにち	三十一日

8 | Cool Tools クール・ツール

❏ 8-2. Memorizing the 4th and the 8th

The fourth day (yoっか) and the eighth day of the month (yoうか) are often confused because they sound alike.

This hint might help: the "yo" in yoっか is short, while the "yo" in yoうか has an う after it which makes it double in length. Understanding this, remember that 8 is double 4 in order to remember that the eighth day of the month has the longer sound.

On the previous page, the 14th, 20th and 24th have been highlighted. Pay attention to those three numbers, as they do not follow the pattern you might expect.

8 | Grammar ぶんぽう

❏ 8-3. The months

The Japanese months are created with numbers and the Japanese kanji symbol for the moon, 月. The days of the month taught on the previous page are created with numbers and the Japanese kanji symbol for the sun, 日.

Months つき		
January	いちがつ	いちがつ	一月
February	にがつ	にがつ	二月
March	さnがつ	さんがつ	三月
April	しがつ	しがつ	四月
May	ごがつ	ごがつ	五月
June	roくがつ	ろくがつ	六月
July	しちがつ	しちがつ	七月
August	はちがつ	はちがつ	八月
September	くがつ	くがつ	九月
October	juうがつ	じゅうがつ	十月
November	juういちがつ	じゅういちがつ	十一月
December	juうにがつ	じゅうにがつ	十二月

❑ 8-4. Making sentences in the past tense

でした is the past tense of です. It's used exactly like です except that it makes the sentence past tense. です means, "is, am, are," etc., and でした means "was, were," etc.

> [sentence] でした。
> It was [sentence]

> [sentence] でしたか。
> Was it [sentence]?

Examples Q&A

1. くruまは あか でしたか。   Was the car red?
   あかの くruま でした。   It was a red car.

2. Waたし でしたか。   Was it me?
   あなた でした。   It was you.

3. きのうは ついたち でしたか。   Was yesterday the 1st?
   ふつか でした。   It was the 2nd.

❑ 8-5. Saying dates with month and day of the month

When saying full dates – for example, "December 10th," or "the 20th of January" – you must always say the month first and then the day of the month.

> MONTH + DAY OF MONTH

Examples

1. January 5th   いちがつ いつか
2. May 9th   ごがつ ここのか
3. the 22nd of December   Juうにがつ にjuうににち

8 Q&A しつもんと こたえ Japanese→English

1. いつですか   **When is it?**
   あした です。   It's tomorrow.
   Kyoう です。   It's today.
   きのう でした。   It was yesterday.

2. なnにち ですか。
   Yoっか です。
   にjuうくにち です。
   ついたち です。

   What day of the month is it?
   It's the 4th.
   It's the 29th.
   It's the 1st.

3. なnがつ ですか。
   しちがつ です。
   Juうにがつ です。
   しがつ です。

   What month is it?
   It's July.
   It's December.
   It's April.

4. あしたは なnにちですか。
   あしたは juうににち です。
   あしたは さnjuうにち です。
   たぶn、なのか です。

   What day of the month is tomorrow?
   Tomorrow is the 12th.
   Tomorrow is the 30th.
   Maybe, it is the 7th.

5. たnjoうびは なnがつ ですか。
   くがつ です。
   きのう でした。
   あした です。

   What month is (your) birthday?
   It's September.
   It was yesterday.
   It's tomorrow.

6. たなかさnの たnjoうびは いつですか。
   Juうがつ にjuうroくにち です。
   はちがつ ふつか です。
   ごがつ juうyoっか です。

   When is Tanaka's birthday?
   It's October 26th.
   It's August 2nd.
   It's May 14th.

8   Q&A しつもんと こたえ English→Japanese

1. **What month and day is Children's Day?**
   Children's Day is May 5th.

   こどものひは なnがつ なnにち ですか。
   こどものひは ごがつ いつか です。

2. **When is Culture Day?**
   It's November 3rd.
   I don't know. But my birthday
   is September 5th.

   ぶnかのひ は いつ ですか。
   Juういちがつ みっか です。
   Waかriません。 でも、waたしの たnjoうびは
   くがつ いつか です。

3. **Is father's birthday on May 10th?**
   Yes, it is.
   No, it isn't.
   No, it is on the 11th of March.

   おとうさnの たnjoうびは ごがつ とおかですか。
   はい、そうです。
   いいえ、ちがいます。
   いいえ、さnがつ juういちにちです。

4. **When is (your) birthday?**   たnjoうびは いつ ですか。
    It's October 1st.   Juうがつ ついたち です。
    It's February 7th.   にがつ なのか です。

5. **What was the date yesterday?**   きのうは なnにち でしたか。
    Yesterday was the 14th.   きのうは juうyoっか でした。
    I don't know.   Waかりませn。

6. **Is Golden Week in July?**   Goruden wi–kuは しちがつ ですか。
    No, it's in May.   いいえ、ごがつ です。
    No, it's not in July.   いいえ、しちがつ jaない です。

7. **Was yesterday the 5th?**   きのうは いつか でしたか。
    No, it was the 9th.   いいえ、ここのか でした。

---

8   Reading Comprehension どっかい

Read the sentences below. Use the information to answer the reading comprehension
questions later in this lesson.

①   Waたしの なまえは kimuです。

②   きのうは waたしの たnjoうび でした。

③   にjuうななさいです。

④   Waたしの たnjoうびは kurisumasu です。

⑤   ともだちの purezentoは あかい おはし でした。

⑥   おとうさnの purezentoは にほnごの ほん でした。

⑦   Waたしは にほnが だいすきです。

Hiragana やゆよわをん

や New Hiragana あたらしい ひらがな

Make sure you learn the correct stroke order.

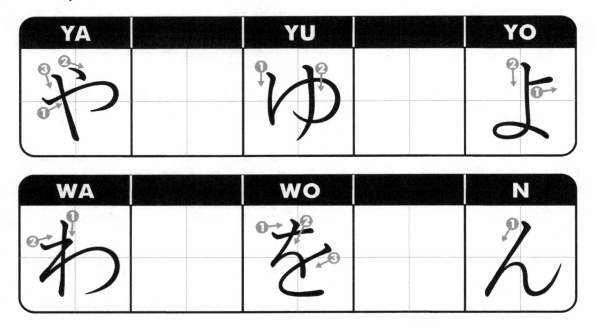

や Various Styles スタイル

Look at the various possible styles for the hiragana in this lesson. Write each symbol as neatly as you can, then compare it to the different versions below.

や	や	や	や	や
ゆ	ゆ	ゆ	ゆ	ゆ
よ	よ	よ	よ	よ

わ	わ	わ	わ	わ
を	を	を	を	を
ん	ん	ん	ん	ん

や Writing Practice れんしゅう

To practice correct stroke order, first trace the light gray characters, then write each character six times for practice.

ya	や	や					
yu	ゆ	ゆ					
yo	よ	よ					
wa	わ	わ					
wo	を	を					
n	ん	ん					

や Word Practice ことばの れんしゅう

Fill in the appropriate hiragana in the blanks for each word.

1. ___raう (to laugh)
   wa

2. だいこ___ (radish)
   n

3. みず___のむ (to drink water)
   wo

4. ___ruい (bad)
   wa

5. ___たし (me; I)
   wa

6. ほ___ ___かう (to buy a book)
   n wo

7. こ___ ___ (tonight; this evening)
      n   ya

8. ___す reru (to forget)
    wa

9. えいが ___み ru (to watch a movie)
       wo

10. き___ぞく (metal)
    n

11. か___た___ (easy)
    n   n

12. すし___たべ ru (to eat sushi)
     wo

や Special Usage とくべつな つかいかた

❏ 8-6. The particle を (wo)

The hiragana を is only used as a particle (object marker). It is never used for any other purpose. Even though "wo" is normally pronounced "o", お can never replace を as a particle.

Example Sentences
1. てがみを (wo) かきます。   I will write a letter.
2. えんぴつを (wo) ください。   Give me a pencil, please.

や Words You Can Write かける ことば

Write the following words using the hiragana that you just learned. This is a great way to increase your Japanese vocabulary.

わに
(alligator)

やね
(roof)

ゆび
(finger)

ゆうべ
(last night)

わかめ
(seaweed)

こんや
(tonight)

かんたん
(easy)

うわさ
(rumor)

ゆびわ
(ring)

や **Everyday Hiragana Words にちじょうの ことば**

たいよう
the sun

うわぎ
jacket

ゆかた
light kimono

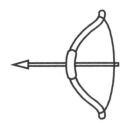

ゆみや
bow and arrow

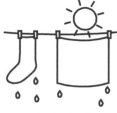

かわかす
to dry

じてんsha
bicycle

や | Hiragana Matching ひらがな マッチング

Connect the dots between each hiragana and the correct ro–maji.

は ·	· yu
よ ·	· to
ゆ ·	· n
わ ·	· wo (o)
と ·	· ha
や ·	· wa
を ·	· yo
ん ·	· ya

8 Lesson Activities

❑ 1. Questions
Answer the following questions as if they were being asked to you directly. Use the hiragana that you have learned when writing your answers.

1. おとうさんの たんjoうびは いつ ですか。

_____

2. Kurisumasuは、なんがつ なんにち ですか。

_____

3. なんがつが すき ですか。

_____

4. Kyoうは、なんがつ なんにち ですか。

_____

5. きのうは、なんがつ なんにち でしたか。

_____

6. こどものひは しちがつよっか ですか。

_____

❑ 2. Dates
Write the following dates in Japanese.

1. あなたの おかあさんの たんjoうび

_____

2. けんぽう きねんび

_____

3. March 15

    _____

4. ぶんかのひ

    _____

5. こどものひ

    _____

6. April 20

    _____

❑ **3. Japanese translation**

Translate the following conversations into English. Then, in the space after the number write where you think the conversation is taking place and if it is polite, informal or mixed.

1.
いまいさん:　たん jo うびは いつ ですか。 やまださん:　さんがつ に ju うさんにち です。あなたのは？ いまいさん:　わたしの たん jo うびは あしたです。 やまださん:　おめでとう！ なんさい ですか。 いまいさん:　さん ju う はっさい です。
いまいさん:
やまださん:
いまいさん:
やまださん:
いまいさん:

❏ **4. Reading comprehension questions**
Answer the following questions about the reading comprehension in this lesson.

1. Kimuさんの たんjoうびは いつ でしたか。

   _____

2. Kimuさんは なんさい ですか。

   _____

3. ともだちの purezentoは なにいroの おはし でしたか。

   _____

4. おとうさんの purezentoは なんでしたか。

   _____

5. Kimuさんは、にほんが きraいですか。

   _____

❏ **5. Short dialogue**
While talking with Mr. Hino, Mr. Honda realizes that he forgot his girlfriend's birthday.

ほんださん:	Kyoうは、なんにちですか。
ひのさん:	ここのかです。
ほんださん:	えっ、なのか jaないですか。
ひのさん:	いいえ、あしたは、とおかです。
ほんださん:	どうしよう…。きのうは、かのjoの たんjoうびでした。
ひのさん:	ほんとうですか。

New words and expressions in the dialogue

Progressive	Kana	Kanji	English
どうしよう	どうしよう	どうしよう	What shall I do?
ほんとうですか。	ほんとうですか。	本当ですか。	Really?

❑ 6. Short dialogue activities
1. Practice reading the dialogue in pairs.
2. Talk about the dates for today, yesterday, and tomorrow.

❑ 7. More words you can write
You should practice writing these words a minimum of five times each. Not only will you be practicing the new hiragana, but you will also learning new words.

やね	roof	たんさん	carbonation
ゆうえんち	fun park	ようちえん	kindergarten
およめさん	bride	しわ	wrinkles
きんようび	Friday	しんかんせん	bullet train
いわ	rock	うわさ	a rumor
みずを のむ	to drink water		

8 │ Drill ドリル

If you're not sure what these sentences mean, we recommend that you review the lesson up to this point before continuing.

1. Kyoうは なんにち ですか。
2. あなたの たんjoうびは なんがつですか。
3. あしたは はつかですか。

8 | Sentence Building ぶんのつくり

In each lesson we build on a previous sentence. Watch it grow and transform each time new concepts are introduced.

> **あなたの おかあさんの たんjoうびは いつですか。**
> **When is your mother's birthday?**

Compare how the sentence has changed from the prior lessons:

Lesson 5:　　あなたの おかあさんは なにいroの くruまが すきですか。

　　　　　　What color car does your mother like?

Lesson 6:　　あなたの おかあさんは なにいroの くruまが ほしいですか。

　　　　　　What color car does your mother want?

Lesson 7:　　あなたの おかあさんの くruまは どこですか。

　　　　　　Where is your mother's car?

8 | Answer Key

❑ Word practice (answers)

1. わらう
2. だいこん
3. みずを のむ
4. わるい
5. わたし
6. ほんを かう
7. こんや
8. わすreru
9. えいがを みru
10. きんぞく
11. かんたん
12. すしを たべru

❑ Hiragana matching (answers)

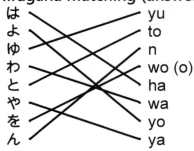

は   yu
よ   to
ゆ   n
わ   wo (o)
と   ha
や   wa
を   yo
ん   ya

❑ Reading comprehension (translation)

① My name is Kim.
② Yesterday was my birthday.
③ I am 27 years old.
④ My birthday is (on) Christmas.
⑤ My friend's present was (a set of) red chopsticks.
⑥ My father's present was a Japanese language book.
⑦ I really like Japan.

❑ 1. Questions (sample answers)

1. When is your father's birthday?　Juがつ にjuいちにちです。
2. What month and what day is Christmas?　Juにがつ にjuごにちです。
3. What month do you like?　ごがつが すきです。
4. What month and what day is today?　Kyoうは、さんがつ とおかです。
5. What month and what date was yesterday?　きのうは、さんがつ ここのかでした。
6. Is Children's Day is July 4th?　いいえ、ちがいます。
いいえ、ごがつ いつかです。

❑ 2. Dates (sample answers)

1. Mother's birthday　しちがつ みっか
2. Constitution Day　ごがつ みっか
3. March 15　さんがつ juごにち
4. Culture Day　juいちがつ みっか
5. Children's Day　ごがつ いつか
6. April 20　しがつ はつか

❑ 3. Japanese translation (answers)

Imai san:　When is your birthday?
Yamada san:　It is March 23rd. And yours?
Imai san:　My birthday is tomorrow.
Yamada san:　Congratulations! How old are you? (How old will you be?)
Imai san:　38 years old.

❑ 4. Reading comprehension questions (answers)

1. When was Kim's birthday?   きのうでした。/ 12 がつ 25 にちでした。
2. How old is Kim today?   にjuうななさいです。
3. What color chopsticks were her friend's present?   あかい おはしでした。
4. What was her dad's present?   にほんごの ほんでした。
5. Does Kim dislike Japan?   いいえ、にほんが だいすきです。

❑ 5. Short dialogue (translation)

Mr. Honda:	What day of the month is it today?
Mr. Hino:	It's the ninth.
Mr. Honda:	What? Isn't it the seventh?
Mr. Hino:	No, tomorrow is the tenth.
Mr. Honda:	What am I going to do? Yesterday was my girlfriend's birthday!
Mr. Hino:	Really!?

Vocabulary Groups

K   food and drink

Progressive	Kana	Kanji	English
たまご	たまご	卵	egg
ごはん	ごはん	ご飯	boiled rice
miruku	ミルク	ミルク	milk
みず	みず	水	water
ju–su	ジュース	ジュース	juice
くri	くり	栗	chestnut
pan	パン	パン	bread
ke–ki	ケーキ	ケーキ	cake
aisu kuri–mu	アイス・クリーム	アイス・クリーム	ice cream
にんじん	にんじん	人参	carrot
tomato	トマト	トマト	tomato
だいこん	だいこん	大根	radish
たまねぎ	たまねぎ	玉ねぎ	onion
こshoう	こしょう	こしょう	pepper
しお	しお	塩	salt
えび	えび	海老	shrimp
にく	にく	肉	meat
poteto	ポテト	ポテト	potato

たまご

アイス・クリーム

ケーキ

Lesson 9 Level ① — Days, Weeks, and Years
Next week, next month

9   About This Lesson このレッスンについて

Before The Lesson

1. Be able to write and read やゆよわをん.
2. Be able to say dates and months in Japanese and how to use でした.
3. Review vocabulary group K.

Lesson Goals

1. Learn the days of the week and years.

From The Teachers

1. The new words in this lesson are important in everyday conversations. Since some of the words are similar spend some extra time memorizing them.

9   New Words あたらしい ことば

Progressive	Kana	Kanji	English
なんようび	なんようび	何曜日	what day of the week?
なんねん	なんねん	何年	what year?
いま	いま	今	now
おととい	おととい	一昨日	day before yesterday
あさって	あさって	明後日	day after tomorrow
せんshuう	せんしゅう	先週	last week
こんshuう	こんしゅう	今週	this week
raいshuう	らいしゅう	来週	next week
せんげつ	せんげつ	先月	last month
こんげつ	こんげつ	今月	this month
raいげつ	らいげつ	来月	next month

kyoねん	きょねん	去年	last year
ことし	ことし	今年	this year
raいねん	らいねん	来年	next year
せいねんがっぴ	せいねんがっぴ	生年月日	date of birth
がんたん	がんたん	元旦	New Year's Day
pa–ti–	パーティー	パーティー	party

Days of the Week ようび

Monday	げつようび	月曜日
Tuesday	かようび	火曜日
Wednesday	すいようび	水曜日
Thursday	もくようび	木曜日
Friday	きんようび	金曜日
Saturday	どようび	土曜日
Sunday	にちようび	日曜日

9 New Phrases あたらしい かいわ

1. なんねん うまれですか。   In what year were you born?

2. _____ねん うまれ です。   I was born in the year _____.

9 Culture Clip: Japan's New Year

❏ **9-1. New Year's Day in Japan**

In Japan, the New Year is the most important holiday period. It's as important in Japan as Christmas is in the United States. From January 1st until one week after, Japan almost comes to a stop. Many stores and companies are closed while everyone celebrates the New Year.

9 Grammar ぶんぽう

❑ 9-2. Expressing the year

ねん literally means "year." To say a year, you simply say the number of the year and add ねん to it. In Japanese, years cannot be represented as they are in English. For example, you cannot express 1998 as "nineteen—ninety—eight." The full number must be stated.

Examples

the year 1980	せん kyuうhyaく はちjuうねん
the year 1801	せん はっpyaく いちねん
the year 2010	にせん juうねん
the year 2017	にせん juうななねん

❑ 9-3. Saying complete dates including the year

Complete dates in Japanese always start with the year, then are followed by month and day of the month. Just remember the order is always from the largest time span to the smallest.

> **YEAR + MONTH + DAY OF MONTH**

Examples

1. May 11, 2005
    にせんごねん ごがつ juういちにち

2. January 20, 2011
    にせんjuういちねん いちがつ はつか

3. April 5, 1999
    せんkyuうhyaく kyuうjuう kyuう ねん しがつ いつか

4. August 30, 2015
    にせんjuうごねん はちがつ さんjuうにち

❑ **9-4. Next Friday, last March, etc.**

When saying things like "Monday of last week" or "May of next year", you must link the words together with の. In the following examples, の means "of". Just as in saying complete dates, the order is always from the largest time span to the smallest.

> **Examples**
>
> 1. raいshuうの きんようび   Friday of next week
> 2. こんshuうの げつようび   Monday of this week
> 3. raいげつの juうごにち   the 15th of next month
> 4. せんげつの ついたち   the 1st of last month
>
> 5. ことしの さんがつ   March of this year
> 6. kyoねんの はちがつ   August of last year
>
> 7. せんkyuうhyaくごjuうねんの にがつ   February of 1950
> 8. にせんごhyaくねんの roくがつ   June of 2500

9   Q&A しつもんと こたえ English→Japanese

1. **What day is it?**   なんようび ですか。
   It's Monday.   げつようび です。
   It's Friday.   きんようび です。
   It's Wednesday.   すいようび です。

2. **What day is today?**   Kyoうは なんようび ですか。
   Today is Saturday.   Kyoうは どようび です。
   Today is Sunday.   Kyoうは にちようび です。
   I don't know.   わかriません。

3. **When is the party?**   Pa–ti–は いつですか。
   The party is the day after tomorrow.   Pa–ti–は あさって です。
   The party is today.   Pa–ti–は kyoう です。
   It's Friday of next week.   Raいshuうの きんようび です。
   It was yesterday.   きのう でした。

4. **When is Thanksgiving?**   かんshaさいは いつですか。
   It's on November 27th.   Juういちがつ にjuうななにち です。
   It was last week.   せんshuう でした。
   It was last month.   せんげつ でした。
   It's Thursday of next week.   raいshuうの もくようび です。

5. **What day was the Christmas of 1935?**
    せんkyuうhyaく さんjuうごねんの kurisumasuは なんようび でしたか。

    Maybe it was Thursday.   たぶん、もくようび でした。
    It was Wednesday.   すいようび でした。

---

9 ⬛ Reading Comprehension どっかい

Read the sentences below. Use the information to answer the reading comprehension questions later in this lesson.

① Kyoうは juうにがつ さんjuうにちです。

② あさっては がんたんです。

③ ことしの がんたんは もくようびです。

④ Kyoねんの がんたんは すいようびでした。

Hiragana らりるれろ

ら   New Hiragana あたらしい ひらがな

Make sure you learn the correct stroke order since correct stroke order will mean neater characters when writing fast.

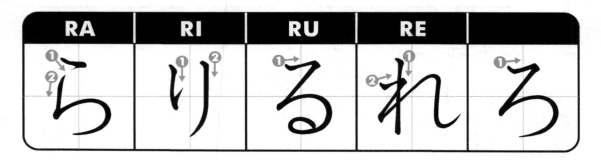

ら   Various Styles スタイル

Write each character as neatly as you can and compare it to the different versions.

らりるれろ　らりるれろ　らりるれろ　らりるれろ　らりるれろ

ら Writing Practice れんしゅう

To practice correct stroke order, first trace the light gray characters, then write each character six times for practice.

ra	ら	ら					
ri	り	り					
ru	る	る					
re	れ	れ					
ro	ろ	ろ					

ら Word Practice ことばの れんしゅう

Fill in the appropriate hiragana in the blanks for each word.

1. あた＿＿しい (new)
   ra

2. し＿＿ (to know)
   ru

3. ＿＿んあい (love; romance)
   re

4. ＿＿んご (apple)
   ri

5. みせ＿＿ (to show)
   ru

6. ＿＿んshuう (practice)
   re

7. べん＿＿ (convenient)
   ri

8. う＿＿おい (moisture)
   ru

9. かく＿＿んぼ　(hide and seek)
   re

10. どう＿＿　(road)
    ro

11. ＿＿うか　(hallway)
    ro

12. まわ＿＿みち　(detour)
    ri

ら　Everyday Hiragana Words にちじょうの ことば

ねる
to sleep; go to bed

いくら
salted salmon eggs

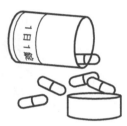

くすり
medicine

ろうそく
candle

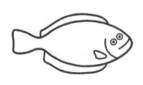

かれい
flounder

かみなり
thunder; lightning

ら　Words You Can Write かける ことば

Write the following words using the hiragana that you just learned. This is a great way to increase your Japanese vocabulary.

り か
(science)

よる
(night)

れい
(example)

まる
(circle)

こおり
(ice)

あひる
(duck)

かえる
(frog)

りんご
(apple)

べんり
(convenient)

ひだり
(left)

みずいろ
(light blue)

きいろ
(yellow)

ろうそく
(candle)

さる
(monkey)

ら **Hiragana Matching ひらがな マッチング**

Connect the dots between each hiragana and the correct ro–maji.

る ·　　　　· ru

し ·　　　　· shi

り ·　　　　· re

ろ ·　　　　· i

ぬ ·　　　　· ro

れ ·　　　　· ra

い ·　　　　· nu

ら ·　　　　· ri

9 Lesson Activities

❑ 1. Event dates

Write the corresponding events and dates in Japanese for the following pictures.

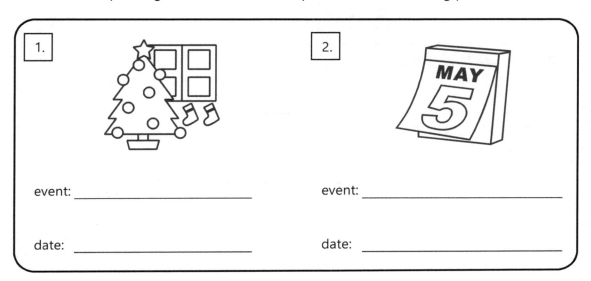

1.

event: _____

date: _____

2.

event: _____

date: _____

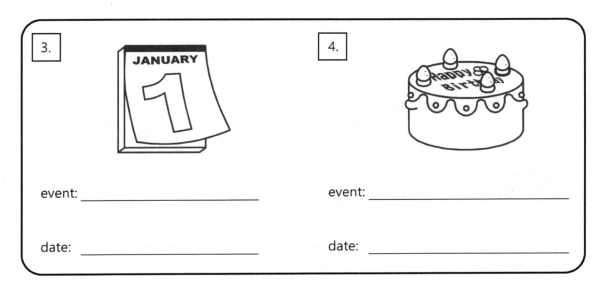

3.

event: _____

date: _____

4.

event: _____

date: _____

❑ 2. Questions

Answer the following questions as if they were being asked to you directly. Use the hiragana that you have learned when writing your answers.

1. あさっては なんようび ですか。

   _____

2. おとといは なんがつ なんにち でしたか。

   _____

3. たんjoうびは、なんがつ なんにち ですか。

   _____

4. Kyoねんは なんねん でしたか。

   _____

5. せんげつの ついたちは なんようび でしたか。

   _____

6. らいshuうの もくようびは なんにち ですか。

   _____

7. せんshuうの どようびは なんにち でしたか。

   _____

8. らいねんは、なんねんですか。

   _____

❏ 3. Japanese translation
Translate the reading comprehension in this lesson into English.

①	
②	
③	
④	

❏ 4. Short dialogue
Youko and Takahiro are talking about their birthdays.

ようこ:	こんshuうの きんようびは わたしの たんjoうびです。
たかひろ:	そうですか。たんjoうび おめでとう。
ようこ:	ありがとう。
たかひろ:	なんねんうまれですか。
ようこ:	せんkyuうhyaく ななjuう さんねんうまれです。
たかひろ:	わたしも です。わたしの たんjoうびは せん kyuうhyaく ななjuう さんねんの ろくがつ みっかです。
ようこ:	ほんとう？
たかひろ:	たんjoうびpa–ti–は、いつですか。
ようこ:	こんshuうの どようびです。

New words and expressions in the dialogue

Progressive	Kanji	English
ほんとう？	本当？	Is that true? Really?
わたしも	私も	Me too.

❏ **4. Short dialogue activities**
Practice reading the dialogue in pairs.
Talk about your birthday (including the year) with
your partner.

Use the following questions:
1. たんjoうびは いつですか／なんがつ なんにちですか。
2. なんねんうまれですか。

❏ **5. More words you can write**
You should practice writing these words a minimum of five times each. Not only will you be
practicing new hiragana, but you will also learn new words.

らんぼう	violence	こんらん	confusion
あらし	a storm	れんらく	contact
かみなり	thunder; lightning	どろぼう	a thief
どんぐり	acorn	ろうじん	old person
れいぞうこ	refrigerator	らくがき	graffiti
りゆう	a reason	ろうか	hallway
かいろ	heat pad	わすれもの	forgotten item
めじるし	landmark	めずらしい	rare (adj.)
くるま	car		

9 Drill ドリル

If you're not sure what these sentences mean, we recommend that you review the lesson up to
this point before continuing.

1. Kyoうは なんようび ですか。
2. きんようびは なんにちですか。
3. らいshuうの にちようびは わたしの ともだちの たんjoうび です。
4. Kyoねんの にがつは さむかったですか。

9 Sentence Building ぶんのつくり

In each lesson we will build on a previous sentence. The previous sentence was あなたの おかあさん のたんjoうびは いつですか.

> ### ことし、あなたの おかあさんの たんjoうびは なんようび でしたか。
> ### On what day of the week was your mother's birthday this year?

Compare how the sentence has changed from the prior lessons:

Lesson 6: あなたの おかあさんは なにいろの くるまが ほしいですか。

What color car does your mother want?

Lesson 7: あなたの おかあさんの くるまは どこですか。

Where is your mother's car?

Lesson 8: あなたの おかあさんの たんjoうびは いつですか。

When is your mother's birthday?

9 Answer Key

❏ Word practice (answers)

1. あたらしい
2. しる
3. れんあい
4. りんご
5. みせる
6. れんshuう
7. べんり
8. うるおい
9. かくれんぼ
10. どうろ
11. ろうか
12. まわりみち

❏ Hiragana matching (answers)

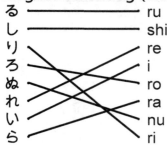

る —————— ru
し —————— shi
り   re
ろ   i
ぬ   ro
れ   ra
い   nu
ら   ri

❏ 1. Event dates (answers)

1. Kurisumasu — juうにがつ にjuうごにち
2. こどものひ — ごがつ いつか
3. がんたん — いちがつ ついたち
4. (わたしの) たんjoうび — ___がつ___にち

❏ 2. Questions (answers vary based on when answered)

1. What day of the week is the day after tomorrow? — ～ようびです。
2. What day was the date and month before yesterday? — ～がつ～にちでした。
3. What is the date and month of your birthday? — (answers vary)
4. What year was last year? — にせん～ねんでした。
5. What day of the week was the 1st of last month? — ～ようびでした。
6. What day is next Thrusday? — ～にちです。
7. What day was last Saturday? — ～にちでした。
8. What year is next year? — にせん～ねんです。

❏ 3. Japanese translation (answers)

① Today is December 30th.
② The day after tomorrow is New Year's Day.
③ This year's New Year's Day is Thursday.
④ Last year it was Wednesday.

❏ 4. Short dialogue translation (answers)

Yoko: This Friday is my birthday.
Takahiro: Really? Happy birthday!
Yoko: Thanks.
Takahiro: What year were you born?
Yoko: I was born in 1973.
Takahiro: Me, too! My birthday is June 3rd, 1973.
Yoko: Really?
Takahiro: When is your birthday party?
Yoko: It's this Saturday.

Vocabulary Groups

L nature

Progressive	Kanji	English
やま	山	mountain
あめ	雨	rain
たいよう	太陽	sun
つき	月	moon
ゆき	雪	snow
はる	春	spring
なつ	夏	summer
あき	秋	autumn; fall
ふゆ	冬	winter

Lesson
10
Level ①

Asking for Things

Give me something, please.

10 About This Lesson このレッスンについて

Before The Lesson

1. Be able to write and read らりるれろ.
2. Review vocabulary group L.

Lesson Goals

1. Learn how to ask for things using "please".
2. Learn how to specify one item over another using "this" and "that".

From The Teachers

1. Memorize the new phrases in this lesson. They will come in handy later.

10 New Phrases あたらしい かいわ

1. いらっshaいませ。   Welcome! (at a place of business)
2. Shoう shoう、おまちください。   Please wait a moment. (very polite)
3. Choっと、まってください。   Wait a minute. (informal)

4. なにが いいですか。   What would you like?
    This can also mean "what is good?" depending on the conversation.

5. _____ が いいです。   I would like a _____.
    This is a response to なにが いいですか。

6. ありがとう ございました。   Thank you very much. (past tense)
    This is used to say "thank you" for something that has already been done.

7. どうぞ。   Here you go. / Go ahead.

10 New Words あたらしい ことば

Progressive	Kana	Kanji	English
いくら	いくら	いくら	How much?
menyu–	メニュー	メニュー	menu
poteto	ポテト	ポテト	French fries
chi–zuba–ga–	チーズバーガー	チーズバーガー	cheeseburger
piza	ピザ	ピザ	pizza
supagetti	スパゲッティ	スパゲッティ	spaghetti
bi–fu	ビーフ	ビーフ	beef
sandoicchi	サンドイッチ	サンドイッチ	sandwich
sando	サンド	サンド	sandwich (short vers.)
deza–to	デザート	デザート	dessert
あっ！	あっ！	あっ！	Oh!
おつり	おつり	お釣	change
(お)のみもの	(お)のみもの	お飲み物	a drink
たべもの	たべもの	食べ物	food
おかし	おかし	お菓子	a snack
みそしる	みそしる	味噌汁	miso soup
おひや	おひや	お冷	cold drinking water

10 Grammar ぶんぽう

❑ 10-1. Please give me (standard)

ください is an equivalent of the English word "please." ください is always used in a sentence and cannot be used by itself. The direct object particle を marks the object being requested.

> **Give me [*something*], please.**
> **[*something*] を ください。**

Examples sentences
1. Give me some water, please.   みずを ください。
2. Please give me a pencil.   えんぴつを ください。
3. An apple, please.   りんごを ください。

❑ 10-2. Please give me (polite)

おねがいします basically means "please" or "I request of you." It's used the same way
ください is used, but is more polite. The object marker を marks the object being requested.

> **Would you please give me [something]?**
> **[something] を おねがいします。**

Example sentences

1. みずを おねがいします。   Would you please give me some water?
2. えんぴつを おねがいします。   Would you please give me a pencil?
3. りんごを おねがいします。   Would you please give me an apple?

Unlike ください, おねがいします can be used alone to just say "please" or "I request."

Example conversation

1. A: のみものが ほしい ですか。   Do you want a drink?
   B: おねがいします。   Please.
   A: はい、どうぞ。   Here you go.
   B: ありがとう ございます。   Thank you.

❑ 10-3. The difference between ください and おねがいします

ください and おねがいします are both polite. You can use ください without being considered rude
at all. In situations where you are requesting something from someone above you in status,
or in situations where you wish to be more polite, then おねがいします should be used.

❑ 10-4. The particle も

The particle も means "too" or "also". Like the other particles you have learned, it comes
after the word it is referring to. When it is applied to the topic of the sentence, it takes the
place of は or が completely.

Example Conversations

1. A: なにが すきですか。   What do you like?
   B: Bananaが すきです。りんごも すきです。   I like bananas. I like apples, <u>too</u>.

2. A: なにが いいですか。   What would you like?
   B: Robusuta–と おちゃを ください。   Give me a lobster and tea, please.
   A: わたしも おちゃを ください。   Give me tea <u>also</u>.

3. A: わたしは じてんshaが きらいです。   I dislike bicycles.
   B: わたし<u>も</u> きらいです。   I <u>also</u> dislike them.

4. A: わたしは 1998 ねん うまれです。   I was born in 1998.
   B: わたし<u>も</u> 1998 ねん うまれです。   I was <u>also</u> born in 1998.
       みかchaん<u>も</u> 1998 ねん うまれです。   Mika was <u>also</u> born in 1998.

❑ 10-5. A funny problem with particle choice

Even native Japanese speakers make the common mistake of telling a girl, "You are pretty today," by saying:

> **Kyoう<u>は</u> きれい です。**
> **You are pretty today.**

The trap is how the particle は puts emphasis on kyoう. You are saying, "As for today, you are pretty," and this implies all other days she is not pretty! Avoid this by changing は to も:

> **Kyoう<u>も</u> きれい です。**
> **You are pretty today <u>also</u>.**

This problem can happen anytime you give someone a compliment. So make sure to choose your particles wisely!

❑ 10-6. Sizes

Japanese sizes are *esu* (S), *emu* (M), and *eru* (L). As you can tell, the sizes words are borrowed from English. These sizes are common for clothing or food served in fast food restaurants. To say, "large cola," you must make *eru* into a の adjective by adding の. This is the pattern for all size words.

Examples

1. Esuの ko–raと emuの potetoを おねがいします。
   Please give me a small cola and medium fries.

2. Eruの pizaが ほしいです。
   I want a large pizza.

10 Mini Conversations ミニ かいわ Japanese→English

1. Conversation between a waitress and a customer

A: いらっshaいませ。

B: おはよう ございます。ここは なにが おいしいですか。

A: ここは chikin sandoが おいしいです。Supagetti–も おいしいです。

B: Jaあ、supagetti–を ください。

A: Welcome to the store.

B: Good morning. What tastes good here?

A: The chicken sandwich is delicious. The spaghetti is also delicious.

B: Well then, some spaghetti, please.

2. Conversation in a sandwich shop

A: すみません、chikin su–puは いくらですか。

B: さんbyaくえん です。

A: Jaあ、ko–raと chikin su–puを ください。

A: Excuse me, how much is chicken soup?

B: It's 300 yen.

A: Well then, give me a cola and chicken soup, please.

3. Conversation at a fast food restaurant counter

A: Chi–zuba–ga–をください。あっ、potetoも ください。

B: おのみものは？

A: Ko–hi–を ください。

B: はい、shoう shoう、おまちください。

A: A cheeseburger, please. Oh, and fries too, please.

B: Would you like a drink?

A: A coffee, please.

B: Please wait a few moments.

4. Conversation in a pizza restaurant

A: Pizaを おねがいします。Ko–raも おねがいします。

B: はい、わかりました。

A: Would you please give me some pizza? A cola also, please.

B: Okay.

10 | Mini Conversations ミニ かいわ English→Japanese

1. Conversation at a friend's house

A: Would you please give me some chopsticks?
B: What?
A: Chopsticks, please.

A: おはしを おねがいします。
B: なん ですか。
A: おはしを ください。

2. Conversation in a pizza restaurant

A: Excuse me. I want a pizza. How much are they?
B: Pizzas are 1200 yen.
A: They sure are cheap.

A: すみません。Pizaが ほしいです。いくら ですか。
B: Pizaは せんにhyaくえん です。
A: やすい ですね。

3. Conversation in a restaurant

A: Excuse me. What is good (delicious) today?
B: The beef soup is good today. But the chicken soup is also good.
A: Well then, give me the beef soup, please.

A: すみません。kyoうは なにが おいしいですか。
B: Kyoうは bi–fu su–puが おいしいです。でも、chikin su–puも おいしいです。
A: Jaあ, bi–fu su–puを ください。

4. Conversation in a restaurant

A: Some miso soup, please.
B: Ok, please wait a few minutes.
B: (5 minutes later) Here you go.
A: Some cold water also, please.

A: みそしるを おねがいします。
B: はい、shoう shoう、おまちください。
B: (5 minutes later) はい、どうぞ。
A: おひやも おねがいします。

10 | Reading Comprehension どっかい

Read the conversations below. If you don't understand them, review this lesson's grammar.

The following conversation takes place in a restaurant in Japan.
A customer enters a restaurant...
Waitress: いらっshaいませ！
Customer: menyu–を おねがいします。
5 minutes later...
Customer: すみません。
Waitress: はい。
Customer: supagetti を ください。
Waitress: おのみものは なにが いいですか。
Customer: みずを ください。
Waitress: はい、shoう shoう、おまちください。
10 minutes later...
Waitress: はい、どうぞ
Customer: ありがとう。おchaと ko–ra もください。
Waitress: はい、shoう shoう、おまちください。
40 minutes later...
Customer: いくら ですか
Waitress: にせん ごhyaく にjuう いちえんです。
Customer: はい。
Waitress: おつりは よんhyaく ななjuう kyuうえんです。 ありがとう ございました。

Compound Hiragana

The final hiragana are easy! There are only 33 official hiragana left to learn - but don't let that number scare you. They are all made up of the hiragana that you already know. Just by looking at them you should already have an idea of the sound that they represent.

> **Examples**
>
> き (ki)   +   や (ya)   =   きゃ (kya)
>
> し (shi)   +   ゆ (yu)   =   しゅ (shu)
>
> ち (chi)   +   よ (yo)   =   ちょ (cho)

きゃ Writing Points かくポイント

❑ **10-7. The correct way to write compound hiragana**

When writing compound hiragana, make sure that the second character is visibly smaller than the first character.

ro–maji	correct	incorrect
mya	みゃ	みや
ryo	りょ	りよ
chu	ちゅ	ちゆ
kya	きゃ	きや
pya	ぴゃ	ぴや

❑ 10-8. Compound Hiragana

The following are the compound hiragana. They are created using the hiragana you already know so you should have no problem learning these.

きゃ kya	きゅ kyu	きょ kyo		ひゃ hya	ひゅ hyu	ひょ hyo
ぎゃ gya	ぎゅ gyu	ぎょ gyo		びゃ bya	びゅ byu	びょ byo
しゃ sha	しゅ shu	しょ sho		ぴゃ pya	ぴゅ pyu	ぴょ pyo
じゃ ja	じゅ ju	じょ jo		みゃ mya	みゅ myu	みょ myo
ちゃ cha	ちゅ chu	ちょ cho		りゃ rya	りゅ ryu	りょ ryo
にゃ nya	にゅ nyu	にょ nyo				

きゃ | Writing Practice れんしゅう

To practice correct stroke order, first trace the light gray characters, then write each character six times for practice.

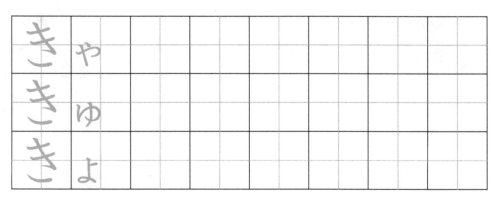

KYA

KYU

KYO

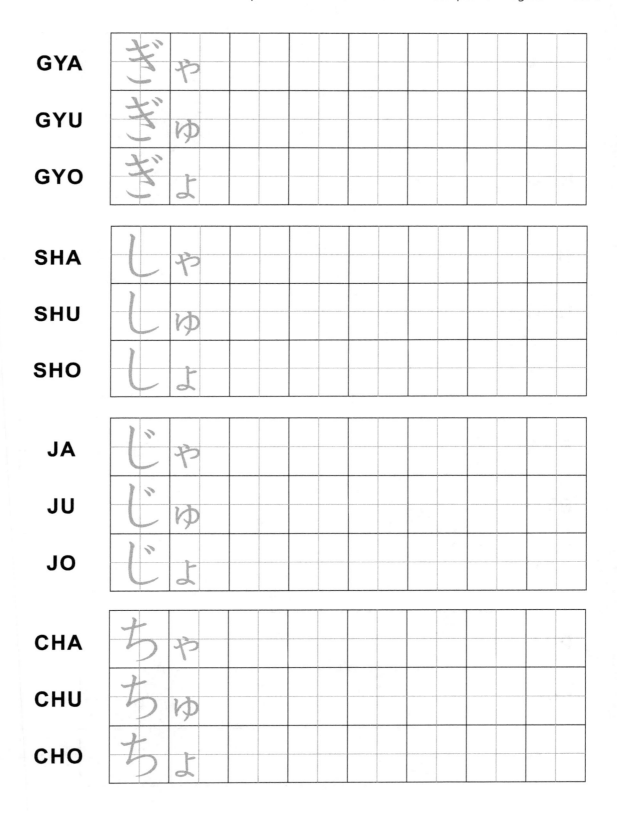

GYA ぎゃ

GYU ぎゅ

GYO ぎょ

SHA しゃ

SHU しゅ

SHO しょ

JA じゃ

JU じゅ

JO じょ

CHA ちゃ

CHU ちゅ

CHO ちょ

NYA	にゃ							
NYU	にゅ							
NYO	にょ							

HYA	ひゃ							
HYU	ひゅ							
HYO	ひょ							

BYA	びゃ							
BYU	びゅ							
BYO	びょ							

PYA	ぴゃ							
PYU	ぴゅ							
PYO	ぴょ							

MYA みゃ

MYU みゅ

MYO みょ

RYA りゃ

RYU りゅ

RYO りょ

きゃ Word Practice ことばの れんしゅう

Fill in the appropriate hiragana in the blanks for each word.

1. とう__く (arrival)
   　　cha

2. さん__く (three hundred)
   　　bya

3. と__かん (library)
   　sho

4. __う__う (cow's milk)
   gyu nyu

5. さん __く (mountain range)
   　　mya

6. __うばい (business; commerce)
   sho

7. __うたん (carpet)
   ju

8. でん__う (sales slip; voucher)
   　　pyo

9. __うだい (siblings)
   kyo

10. __う__う (dinosaur)
    kyo ryu

11. __うがく (study abroad)
    ryu

12. __ うどん (beef bowl)
    gyu

きゃ Words You Can Write かける ことば

Write the following words using the hiragana compounds that you've learned in this lesson. This is a great way to increase your Japanese vocabulary.

ちょう
(butterfly)

きゅう
(nine)
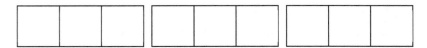

びょうき
(sick)
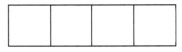

じゅう
(ten)

りゅう
(dragon)

ぎゃく
(reverse)

みょうじ
(last name)

しゅうり
(repair)

きょく
(a song)

きょうと
(Kyoto)

りょこう
(travel)

かいしゃ
(company)

でんしゃ
(train)

きんぎょ
(gold fish)

| | | | | | | | | |

ちゃわん
(bowl)

| | | | | | | | | |

きゃ   **Everyday Hiragana Words にちじょうの ことば**

ちきゅうぎ
globe

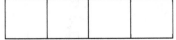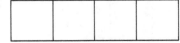

しゅう
state

おちゃ
tea

べんきょう
study

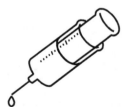

ちゅうしゃ
shot

しゅうり
repair

きゃ **Hiragana Matching ひらがな マッチング**

Connect the dots between each hiragana and the correct ro–maji.

ぎゃ ・   ・ nyu

みょ ・   ・ shu

しゅ ・   ・ rya

ぴょ ・   ・ ja

りゃ ・   ・ myo

ちょ ・   ・ pyo

じゃ ・   ・ cho

にゅ ・   ・ gya

10 Lesson Activities

❑ 1. Grammar drill 1

How would you order the following items at a restaurant? Use both ～をおねがいします and ～をください. Use と (and) if necessary.

1._____

2._____

3._____

4._____

❑ 2. Grammar drill 2

Answer the following questions in Japanese. Then add a second sentence using the particle も (also) or でも (but) as shown in the examples.

> **Ex. いぬが すきですか。**
> - はい、いぬが すきです。ねこも すきです。
> - いいえ、いぬが きらいです。ねこも きらいです。
> - いいえ、いぬが きらいです。でも、ねこは すきです。

1. あたらしいterebi が ほしいですか。

_____

2. はるが すきですか。

_____

3. Ko–raは、おいしいですか。

_____

4. あなたの くるまは、おおきいですか。

_____

❏ 3. Conversation creation
Using the hiragana you know, write a conversation from the concepts in this lesson.

❏ 4. Japanese translation
Translate the reading comprehension in this lesson into English.

A customer enters a restaurant...
Waitress: _____
Customer: _____
5 minutes later...
Customer: _____
Waitress: _____
Customer: _____
Waitress: _____
Customer: _____
Waitress: _____
10 minutes later...
Waitress: _____
Customer: _____
Waitress: _____

---

40 minutes later...

Customer: _____

Waitress: _____

Customer: _____

Waitress: _____

_____

❑ 5. Short dialogue

Sayuri and Chieko are at a Japanese restaurant ordering food and drinks.

Waitress:	いらっしゃいませ。Menyu– を どうぞ。
さゆり:	ここは てんぷらが おいしいです。
ちえこ:	そうですか。じゃあ、てんぷらが いいです。
さゆり:	わたしも てんぷらが すきです。でも、きょうは とんかつが いいです。
ちえこ:	じゃあ、てんぷらと とんかつを おねがいします。
Waitress:	かしこまりました。おのみものは なにが よろしいですか。
さゆり:	Aisu ti– を ください。
ちえこ:	わたしは おちゃを おねがいします。
Waitress:	かしこまりました。

New words and expressions in the dialogue

Progressive	Kanji	English
てんぷら	天ぷら	deep-fried vegetables or seafood
とんかつ	豚カツ	pork cutlet
なにが よろしいですか。*	何が よろしいですか。	What would you like?
かしこまりました。	かしこまりました。	Certainly; Very well.
aisu ti–	アイスティー	iced tea

* more polite version of なにが <u>いい</u>ですか？

❑ 6. Short dialogue activities
1. Practice reading the dialogue in pairs.
2. Imagine you are at a restaurant. Practice ordering food and a drink.

❑ 7. More words you can write
You should practice writing these words a minimum of five times each. Not only will you be practicing the new hiragana but you will also learn new words.

おきゃくさん	a customer or guest	しゅじゅつ	surgery
じょうだん	a joke	じゅうたん	carpet
かいじゅう	a monster	はっぴょう	an announcement

10 | Drill ドリル

If you're not sure what these sentences mean, we recommend that you review the lesson up to this point before continuing.

1. Supagetti–をください。
2. Menyu–を おねがいします。みずも おねがいします。
3. なにが いいですか。

10 | Sentence Building ぶんのつくり

In this lesson we are starting a new sentence to build on. Watch it grow and transform as new concepts are introduced.

> **Sandoを ください。**
> **A sandwich, please.**

10   Answer Key

❑ Word practice (answers)

1. とうちゃく
2. さんびゃく
3. としょかん
4. ぎゅうにゅう
5. さんみゃく
6. しょうばい
7. じゅうたん
8. でんぴょう
9. きょうだい
10. きょうりゅう
11. りゅうがく
12. ぎゅうどん

❑ Hiragana matching (answers)

ぎゃ — nyu
みょ — shu
しゅ — rya
ぴょ — ja
りゃ — myo
ちょ — pyo
じゃ — cho
にゅ — gya

❑ 1. Grammar drill 1 (answers)

1. Ke–ki を おねがいします／Ke–ki を ください。
2. Piza を おねがいします／Piza を ください。
3. Sandoicchi とju–su を おねがいします／ Sandoicchi とju–su を ください。
4. Hanba–ga– とPoteto を おねがいします／ Hanba–ga– とPoteto を ください。

❑ 2. Grammar drill 2 (sample answers)

1. はい、あたらしい terebiが ほしいです。あたらしい konpyu–ta–も ほしいです。
   いいえ、あたらしい terebiが ほしくないです。でも、あたらしい konpyu–ta–が ほしいです。

2. はい、はるが だいすきです。でも、なつは すきじゃないです。
   いいえ、はるが すきじゃないです。なつも すきじゃないです。

3. いいえ、ko–raは おいしくないです。ju–suも おいしくないです。
   はい、ko–raは おいしいです。おちゃも おいしいです。

4. いいえ、おおきくないです。でも、おかあさんの くるまは おおきいです。
   はい、おおきいです。おかあさんの くるまも おおきいです。

❑ 4. Japanese translation (answers)

Waitress: Welcome!
Customer: A menu please.

5 minutes later...
Customer: Excuse me.
Waitress: Yes.
Customer: Spaghetti, please.
Waitress: What would you like to drink?
Customer: Water, please.
Waitress: Okay, Please wait a few moments.

10 minutes later...

Waitress:	Here you go.
Customer:	Thank you. Please give me tea and a cola also.
Waitress:	Okay, Please wait a few moments.

40 minutes later...

Customer:	How much is it?
Waitress:	2,521 yen.
Customer:	Okay.
Waitress:	The change is 479 yen. Thank you very much.

❑ 5. Short dialogue translation (answers)

Waitress:	Welcome. Here is our menu.
Sayuri:	The tempura is tasty here.
Chieko:	Really? Well then, I would like tempura.
Sayuri:	I like tempura, too. But today I would like tonkatsu.
Chieko:	Ok then, tempura and tonkatsu please.
Waitress:	Certainly. What would you like for a drink?
Sayuri:	I would like an iced tea.
Chieko:	(Green) tea for me, please.
Waitress:	Certainly.

Vocabulary Groups

M direction words

Progressive	Kanji	English
みぎ	右	right
ひだり	左	left
うえ	上	up
した	下	down
きた	北	north
ひがし	東	east
みなみ	南	south
にし	西	west

N things around the house II

Progressive	Kanji	English
かさ	傘	umbrella
いえ	家	house
でんわ	電話	telephone
かぎ	鍵	key
いす	椅子	chair
ごみばこ	ごみ箱	trash can
toire	トイレ	toilet

ごみばこ

かぎ

いえ

Lesson 11
Level ①

Counting Objects
Various counting units

11 About This Lesson このレッスンについて

Before The Lesson

1. Be able to write and read compound ひらがな.
2. Understand Japanese basic counting and how to ask for things.
3. Review vocabulary groups M and N.

Lesson Goals

1. Learn how to count various objects depending on their characteristics.

From The Teachers

1. Pay special attention to the counters taught in this lesson. You will sound strange if you mix them up. Also, if you are not strong in the area of counting, now would be the time to review the Pre-Lesson on counting.

11 Explanation せつめい

Counting things in Japanese is not quite the same as in English. In Japanese, things are counted differently based on their shape or classification. Wow, that *is* strange! ...Or so many people say. If you think about it however, we have a similar system in English.

English also counts things differently based on what the item is. For example, "one *slice* of pizza," "two *head* of cattle," "a *school* of fish" or "a *flock* of birds" are all things we say in English without batting an eye. In this lesson we will introduce four of the most commonly used Japanese counting systems.

11 Counters カウンター

How Many?	General / Abstract Objects	Small / Round General Objects	Long / Cylindrical Objects	Thin and Flat Objects
	いくつ？	なんこ？	なんぼん？	なんまい？
1	ひとつ	いっこ	いっぽん	いちまい
2	ふたつ	にこ	にほん	にまい
3	みっつ	さんこ	さんぼん	さんまい
4	よっつ	よんこ	よんほん	よんまい
5	いつつ	ごこ	ごほん	ごまい
6	むっつ	ろっこ	ろっぽん	ろくまい
7	ななつ	ななこ	ななほん	ななまい
8	やっつ	はっこ	はっぽん／はちほん	はちまい
9	ここのつ	きゅうこ	きゅうほん	きゅうまい
10	とお	じっこ じゅっこ (spoken)	じっぽん じゅっぽん (spoken)	じゅうまい
11	じゅういっこ	じゅういっこ	じゅういっぽん	じゅういちまい
12	じゅうにこ	じゅうにこ	じゅうにほん	じゅうにまい
13	じゅうさんこ	じゅうさんこ	じゅうさんぼん	じゅうさんまい
14	じゅうよんこ	じゅうよんこ	じゅうよんほん	じゅうよんまい
15	じゅうごこ	じゅうごこ	じゅうごほん	じゅうごまい
16	じゅうろっこ	じゅうろっこ	じゅうろっぽん	じゅうろっまい
17	じゅうななこ	じゅうななこ	じゅうななほん	じゅうななまい
18	じゅうはっこ	じゅうはっこ	じゅうはっぽん	じゅうはっまい
19	じゅうきゅうこ	じゅうきゅうこ	じゅうきゅうほん	じゅうきゅうまい
20	にじっこ にじゅっこ (spoken)	にじっこ にじゅっこ (spoken)	にじっぽん にじゅっぽん (spoken)	にじゅうまい
100	ひゃっこ	ひゃっこ	ひゃっぽん	ひゃくまい
1000	せんこ	せんこ	せんぼん	せんまい

NOTE: As you can see, after ten items, each counter continues into infinity following the pattern of the first ten numbers and the basic rules of counting. After ten items, the いくつ counter follows the pattern of the なんこ counter.

General / Abstract Objects いくつ

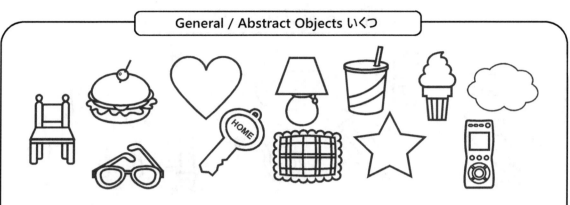

The いくつ counter is the most common and versatile counter. It can be used to count almost anything – physical objects as well as abstract objects, such as problems or ideas. It cannot be used to count people, animals, or animated living creatures, and is not normally used to count large objects such as airplanes. Many Japanese use this counter even though a more proper counter exists. Always try to use the correct counter to identify what you are counting, but when in doubt use this counter. This counter changes to the なんこ counter after 10.

Round / General Objects なんこ

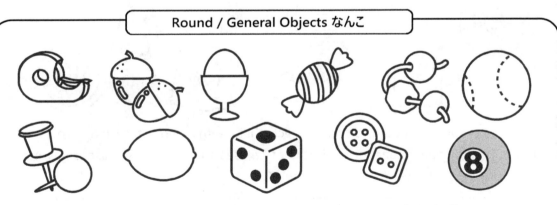

The なんこ counter is used when counting round objects such as fruit, balls, etc... The objects being counted do not have to be perfectly round. The なんこ counter can also be used as a general counter like いくつ. It cannot, however, be used to count abstract objects in the way that いくつ is used.

Long / Cylindrical Objects なんぼん

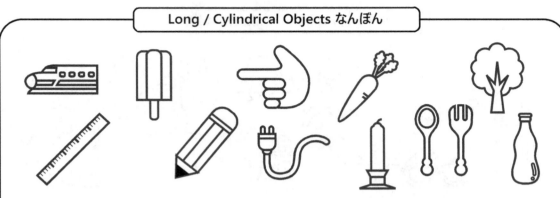

The なんぼん counter is used to count objects that are long and cylindrical in shape, such as bottles of cola, pens, legs and flowers (due to the stem). It is also used to count some items that might not seem to be long or cylindrical, such as video cassettes, teeth, and numbers of flights. Don't be surprised to hear this counter in a variety of situations.

Thin / Flat Objects なんまい

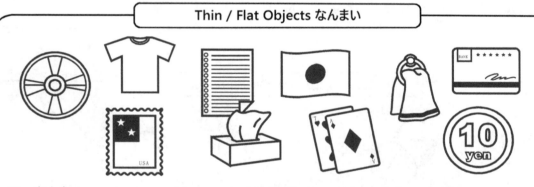

The なんまい counter is used to count objects that are thin and flat, such as paper, tickets, plates, and compact discs. It cannot be used to count books, magazines, etc. These use the published materials counter さつ.

11 New Words あたらしい ことば

Progressive	Kana	Kanji	English
いくつ	いくつ	いくつ	How many things?
なんこ	なんこ	何個	How many round objects?
なんぼん	なんぼん	何本	How many cylindrical objects?

なんまい	なんまい	何枚	How many thin and flat objects?
かみ	かみ	紙	paper
chiketto	チケット	チケット	tickets
はな	はな	花	flowers
はた	はた	旗	flag
ほし	ほし	星	star (in the sky)
karenda–	カレンダー	カレンダー	calendar

11 Grammar ぶんぽう

❑ 11-1. The counters and particles

In the previous lesson about ください and おねがいします, you learned that the object particle を follows the item being requested. However, this is only true for the object of a sentence and NOT the counter. No matter which counter is being used, particles are not necessary after the counters.

Examples

(general, abstract objects)
1. ひとつ、ください。   One, please.
2. まくらを みっつ、ください。   Three pillows, please.
3. いすを いつつ、ください。   Five chairs, please.

(round, general objects)
4. よんこ、ください。   Four, please.
5. りんごを にこ、ください。   Two apples, please.
6. Orenjiを じっこ、ください。   Ten oranges, please.

(long, cylindrical objects)
7. ろっぽん、ください。   Six, please.
8. えんぴつを いっぽん、ください。   One pencil, please.
9. Bananaを ななほん、ください。   Seven bananas, please.

(thin, flat objects)
10. よんまい、ください。   Four, please.
11. Pizaを にまい、ください。   Two slices of pizza, please.
12. かみを ごひゃくまい、ください。   Five hundred pieces of paper, please.

❏ 11-2. More

あと means "more," "else," "in addition" and sometimes "other." It is placed in front of numbered things in the following ways. It is okay to add は after あと.

Example Q&A

1. <u>あと</u> いくらですか。
   How much <u>more</u> is it?

   <u>あと</u> ごひゃくえんです。
   It's five hundred yen <u>more</u>.

2. <u>あとは</u> どこの resutoranが おいしいですか。
   What other restaurant is delicious?

   わたしの hoteruの resutoranが おいしいです。
   The restaurant in my hotel is delicious.

Example Conversations

1. Conversation between friends
   A: なにが すきですか。   What do you like?
   B: すしと pizaが すきです。   I like sushi and pizza.
   A: <u>あと</u>、なにが すきですか。   What <u>else</u> do you like?
   B: <u>あとは</u>、さしみが すきです。   <u>In addition</u>, I like sashimi.

2. Conversation between friends
   A: <u>あとは</u>、なにが いいですか。   What <u>else</u> would you like?
   B: みずと supu-nを ください。   Some water and a spoon, please.
   A: はい しょうしょう、おまちください。 Please wait a few moments.

---

11 Q&A しつもんと こたえ English→Japanese

1. **How many cups are there?**   Koppuは いくつ ですか。
   There are five cups.   Koppuは いつつ です。
   There is one.   ひとつ です。

2. **How many oranges are there?**   Orenjiは なんこ ／いくつ ですか。
   There are six oranges.   Orenjiは ろっこ / むっつ です。
   There are three.   みっつ です。/ さんこ です。

3. **How many pencils are there?**   えんぴつは なんぼん ですか。
    There are two pencils.   えんぴつは にほん です。
    There are 22 pencils.   えんぴつは にじゅうにほん です。
    There are ten.   じっぽん です。

4. **How many tickets are there?**   Chikettoは なんまい ですか。
    There are seven tickets.   Chikettoは ななまい です。
    There are 100 tickets.   Chikettoは ひゃくまい です。
    There are twelve.   じゅうにまいです。

5. **How many pink flowers are there?**   Pinkuの はなは なんぼん ですか。
    There is one pink flower.   Pinkuの はなは いっぽん です。
    There are three.   さんぼん です。

6. **How many purple stars are there?**   むらさきの ほしは いくつ ですか。
    There are 39 purple stars.   むらさきの ほしは さんじゅうきゅうこです。
    There are 70 purple stars.   むらさきの ほしは ななじっこです。

7. **What would you like?**   なにが いいですか。
    Three slices of pizza, please.   Pizaを さんまい、ください。
    Some water and a banana, please.   みずと bananaを いっぽん、ください。

11 Q&A しつもんと こたえ Japanese→English

1. **Karenda–は なんまい ですか。**   How many calendars are there?
    ななじゅういちまい です。   There are 71.
    ひゃく にじゅうごまい です。   There are 125.
    いちまん よんせんまい です。   There are 14,000.

2. **Ko–raは なんぼん ですか。**   How many colas are there?
    はっぽん です。   There are eight.
    よんほん です。   There are four.

3. **Ko–raは あと なんぼん ですか。**   How many more cans of cola?
    あと ろっぽん、ください。   Six more cans, please.
    あと いっぽん、ください。   One more can, please.

4. **あと いくつ ほしい ですか。**   How many more do you want?
    あと ふたつ、ほしい です。   I want two more.
    あと じゅうろっこ、ほしい です。   I want sixteen more.

5. Bananaは なんぼん ですか。　　　　　　How many bananas are there?
   じゅうごほん です。　　　　　　　　　There are 15.
   たぶん ろっぽん です。　　　　　　　　Maybe, there are six.

6. Pizaは なんまい、ほしい ですか。　　　How many pieces pizzas do you want?
   さんまい、ほしい です。　　　　　　　I want three.
   Pizaは ほしくない です。　　　　　　　I don't want any pizza.

---

11 Mini Conversations ミニ かいわ

1. Conversation at a ticket booth for a concert
   A: Four tickets, please.
   B: Okay.
   A: Oh! Two more tickets, please.
   B: Okay. Seven, right?
   A: No, that's wrong. Six tickets, please.

   A: Chikettoを よんまい、ください。
   B: はい。
   A: あっ、あと にまい、ください。
   B: はい。ななまい ですね。
   A: いいえ、ちがいます。Chikettoを ろくまい、ください。

2. Conversation at a drink stand at the beach
   A: Please give me some cola.
   B: How many?
   A: Two, please.

   A: Ko–raを ください。
   B: なんぼん ですか。
   A: にほん、ください。

Hiragana: Next Steps

Congratulations on learning hiragana!
Here are some tips to help you reinforce what you have learned:

Let's put hiragana in our daily lives!
Write words in hiragana on "post it" notes and then stick them on items around your house.
You can even write しお and こしょう on your salt and pepper shakers using a permanent marker.
This will enforce your skills even when you aren't thinking about it.

Read manga!
Some manga (Japanese comics) and children's books will have small hiragana next to any kanji
used in dialogue. When hiragana is used in this way it is called "furigana". Look for furigana
when purchasing manga to help you study. It's like Japanese on training wheels!

Keep on learning!
Your next step is to learn katakana! You have come this far, so keep up the momentum.
We are sure you will also enjoy learning katakana in "Japanese From Zero!" Book 2.

11 | Lesson Activities

❑ 1. Japanese questions

Answer the following questions as if they were being asked to you directly. Write all the answers in hiragana (except for the katakana words).

1. うまの あしは なんぼん ですか。

_____

2. Amerikaの はたの ほしは なんこ ですか。

_____

3. えんぴつが なんぼん ほしいですか。

_____

4. Pizaが なんまい ほしいですか。

_____

❑ 2. English questions

Translate then answer the following questions in Japanese. Write all your answers in hiragana.

1. How many white stars are there? ☆★★☆

_____

2. How many pencils are there? ✏✏✏✏✏✏✏

_____

3. How many fingers are there? (including thumbs!) ✋✋

_____

4. How many flags are there? 🚩🚩🚩🚩🚩🚩

_____

5. How many clocks are there? 🕐 🕐 🕐 🕐

_____

❏ 3. Grammar drill

How would you ask for the following items? Write the sentences with おねがいします and
ください. Make sure you use an appropriate counter and amount in each sentence.

Ke-ki を みっつ、ください。
Ke-ki を みっつ、おねがいします。

1. _____

   _____

2. _____

   _____

3. _____

   cheeseburgers _____

4. _____

   _____

5. _____

   _____

❏ **4. Short dialogue**

Jon and Masami are at a sushi bar.

Sushi chef:	いらっしゃい。
Jon:	すみません、いくらと はまちを ください。
Sushi chef:	はい！ そちらの おきゃくさんは？
まさみ:	わたしは おみそしるを ひとつと おちゃを おねがいします。きょうの おすすめは なんですか。
Sushi chef:	そうですね。きょうは あまえびが おいしいです。
まさみ:	じゃあ、それを ひとつ、ください。
Jon:	あと、えだまめも ください。
まさみ:	わたしも えだまめが ほしいです。 おさらを にまい、おねがいします。
Sushi chef:	はい、わかりました！

New words and expressions in the dialogue

Progressive	Kanji	English
いらっしゃい	いらっしゃい	welcome (rough form of いらっしゃいませ)
いくら	いくら	salmon eggs
はまち	ハマチ	yellow tail fish
おきゃくさん	お客さん	customer
おすすめ	お薦め	recommendation
あまえび	あまえび	sweet shrimp
えだまめ	枝豆	green soybeans
そちら	そちら	polite version of そっち (there)

❏ **5. Short dialogue activities**

1. Practice reading the dialogue in pairs.
2. Practice ordering things at a sushi bar.

11 Drill ドリル

If you're not sure what these sentences mean, we recommend that you review the lesson up to this point before continuing.

1. Ko–raを さんぼん、ください。
2. りんごを じっこ、おねがいします。
3. かみを ごまい、ください。
4. いくつ、ほしいですか。
5. あと ここのつ、ください。

11 Sentence Building ぶんのつくり

In each lesson we will build on a previous sentence. Watch it grow and transform each time new concepts are introduced.

> **Sandoを よっつ、ください。**
> **Four sandwiches, please.**

Compare how the sentence has changed from the prior lesson:

Lesson 10:   Sandoをください。

A sandwich, please.

11 Answer Key

❑ 1. Japanese questions (sample answers)
1. How many legs does a horse have?   よんほんです。
2. How many stars are there on the American flag?   ごじゅっこです。
3. How many pencils do you want?   ごほん、ほしいです。
4. How many pizzas do you want?   いちまい、ほしいです。

❑ 2. English questions (answers)
1. しろい ほしは いくつですか。   よっつです。／よんこです。
2. えんぴつは なんぼんですか。   はっぽんです。
3. ゆびは なんぼんですか。   じゅっぽんです。／じっぽんです。
4. はたは なんぼんですか。   ろっぽんです。

(flags on a pole use the なんぼん counter. If not on a pole, it would be the なんまい counter)

5. とけいは いくつですか。   よっつです。

❑ 3. Grammar drill (answers)
1. Chiketto を にまい、おねがいします／Chiketto を にまい、ください。
2. たまごを じゅうにこ、おねがいします／たまごを じゅうにこ、ください。
3. Chi–zuba–ga– を ふたつ、おねがいします／Chi–zuba–ga– を ふたつ、ください。
4. えんぴつを さんぼん、おねがいします／えんぴつを さんぼん、ください。
5. にんじんを よんほん、おねがいします／にんじんを よんほん、ください。

❑ 4. Short dialogue (translation)
Sushi Chef:	Welcome.
Jon:	Excuse me, please give me salmon roe (salmon eggs) and yellow tail.
Sushi Chef:	Okay! How about the customer there?
Masami:	I'll have one miso soup and green tea, please.
	What is today's recommendation?
Sushi Chef:	Let's see... The sweet shrimp is good today.
Masami:	Then give me one of those, please.
Jon:	Can I also have green soybeans, please?
Masami:	I want green soybeans, too. Give us two plates, please.
Sushi Chef:	Got it! (I have understood)

Vocabulary Groups

O at school

Progressive	Kanji	English
せんせい	先生	teacher
ほん	本	book
じしょ	辞書	dictionary
おてあらい	お手洗い	restroom
えんぴつ	鉛筆	pencil
おんがく	音楽	music

P at the office, etc.

Progressive	Kanji	English
けいたい (short for けいたいでんわ)	携帯(電話)	cellular phone
スマホ (short for スマートフォン)	スマホ	smart phone
おかね	お金	money
ko–hi–	コーヒー	coffee
たばこ	たばこ	cigarettes
めがね	めがね	glasses
pasokon	パソコン	PC (computer)
no–to pasokon	ノートパソコン	laptop computer
めいし	名刺	business card

Q insects

Progressive	Kanji	English
ごきぶり	ごきぶり	cockroach
あり	蟻	ant
はえ	蠅	house fly

おかね

コーヒー

パソコン

Lesson 12 Level ①

Japanese Verbs
Polite verb conjugation

Welcome to Japanese verbs. This is where Japanese becomes really fun! We will start out slowly with just four verbs and four forms. Learn them well and you should have no problem grasping the verb forms that follow.

12 About This Lesson このレッスンについて

Before The Lesson

1. Be able to write and read compound ひらがな.
2. Understand Japanese basic counting and how to ask for things.
3. Review vocabulary groups M and N.

Lesson Goals

1. Learn how to conjugate verbs into the polite forms.
2. Learn how to use the particle に.

From The Teachers

1. The dictionary form of a verb is the most important form. Put effort into memorizing them and all other verb forms that come up in other lessons.

12 New Words あたらしい ことば

Progressive	Kana	Kanji	English
なにご	なにご	何語	what language?
なにじん	なにじん	何人	what nationality?
rosanzerusu	ロサンゼルス	ロサンゼルス	Los Angeles
rasu begasu	ラスベガス	ラスベガス	Las Vegas
shikago	シカゴ	シカゴ	Chicago
kariforunia	カリフォルニア	カリフォルニア	California
kanada	カナダ	カナダ	Canada
かんこく	かんこく	韓国	Korea

ちゅうごく	ちゅうごく	中国	China
ぎんこう	ぎんこう	銀行	bank
ふく	ふく	服	clothing; clothes
~し	~し	~市	~ City
~しゅう	~しゅう	~州	~ State
~けん	~けん	~県	~ Prefecture
~ご	~ご	~語	~ language
~じん	~じん	~人	~ nationality

12 New Phrases あたらしい かいわ

1. おひさしぶりです。   It has been a long time.
2. なにごが はなせますか。   What languages can you speak?
3. _____が はなせます。   I can speak _____.

12 Grammar ぶんぽう

❑ 12-1. Polite versus informal speaking

In Japanese, it is common to use polite language with people you don't know, or who have higher social status than yourself. For example, when speaking to a stranger on the street or to your boss, you should use polite verb forms.

However, if you are talking to your family, friends, or people that are of lower or equal status than you, speaking informally will be more natural. Until your Japanese level becomes more advanced, we suggest that you stick to polite Japanese in order to form good speaking habits.

❑ 12-2. Conjugating verbs into the polite form

The "dictionary form" of a verb is the only version that is in the dictionary. It is the most basic form of the verb without any conjugation. From this form of the verb, you can conjugate the verbs into many other forms using simple patterns. Let's look at the four verbs we will learn in this lesson:

Dictionary Form	English Verb	Verb Type
いく	to go	regular
くる	to come	irregular
かえる	to return; go back; go home; come back; come home etc.	regular
わかる	to understand; know	regular

To conjugate the dictionary forms into other forms, the hiragana chart will be useful. This is a shortened chart – not all the hiragana are listed.

ら ra	ま ma	ば ba	な na	た ta	さ sa	が ga	か ka	あ a	**あ form**
り ri	み mi	び bi	に ni	ち chi	し shi	ぎ gi	き ki	い i	**い form**
る ru	む mu	ぶ bu	ぬ nu	つ tsu	す su	ぐ gu	く ku	う u	**う form**
れ re	め me	べ be	ね ne	て te	せ se	げ ge	け ke	え e	**え form**
ろ ro	も mo	ぼ bo	の no	と to	そ so	ご go	こ ko	お o	**お form**

The forms

Notice how the rows on the chart above have been labeled あ, い, う, え, お form. You may have noticed that every new verb in this lesson ends with a hiragana in the う form. This isn't just a coincidence - because *all verbs* in the Japanese language in the dictionary form end with うform hiragana.

For example, the verb いく (to go) ends in く. くる (to come) , わかる (to understand), and かえる (to return) all end in る. Both く and る are う form hiragana.

Verb types

Each verb in this lesson has been labeled as regular or irregular. The majority of Japanese verbs are regular verbs. We call them "regular" because there are so many of them and they all follow the exact same conjugation pattern.

Generally, irregular verbs do not follow any logical rule. The patterns of irregular verbs must be memorized. Luckily there are only a small amount of irregular verbs.

Making the conversion

To make the polite versions of regular verbs, the *final* hiragana of the dictionary form needs to be changed into the い form.

Step 1: Convert the last hiragana into the いform.

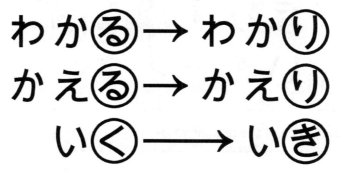

Look back at the hiragana chart at the beginning of this lesson. See the る? Move straight up the column to the り. The first step of conjugating regular verbs into their polite forms is to switch their final hiragana into the い form.

Remember that this pattern will NOT work for irregular verbs such as くる (to come), but only for regular verbs.

In "Japanese From Zero!" Book 2, you will learn how to use the hiragana chart to make more verb conjugations.

After changing the dictionary form into the い form, all you need to do is add one of the following endings to complete the verb:

Polite verb endings			
Present / Future Positive	Present / Future Negative	Past Positive	Past Negative
~ます will~, do~, am going to~	~ません won't~, don't~	~ました did~	~ません でした didn't~

Step 2: Add a stem.

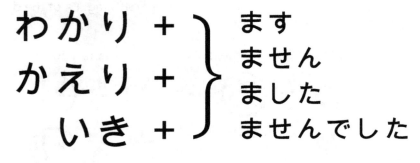

Now let's conjugate each of the regular verbs in this lesson.

わかり<u>ます</u>   do understand
わかり<u>ません</u>   do not understand; will not understand
わかり<u>ました</u>   understood; did understand
わかり<u>ませんでした</u>   didn't understand

いき<u>ます</u>   will go; do go
いき<u>ません</u>   won't go; don't go
いき<u>ました</u>   went
いき<u>ませんでした</u>   didn't go

かえり<u>ます</u>   will return; do return
かえり<u>ません</u>   will not return; do not return
かえり<u>ました</u>   returned
かえり<u>ませんでした</u>   didn't return

The only verb in this lesson that isn't regular is くる (come). Remember: irregular verbs don't follow the chart we showed you earlier - their patterns have to be memorized.

くる is conjugated as follows:

き<u>ます</u>	will come;, do come
き<u>ません</u>	won't come; don't come
き<u>ました</u>	came
き<u>ませんでした</u>	didn't come

❑ 12-3. Location particles に and へ

Now that we have verbs to get you moving, where are you going? That's what location particles are for.

に and へ (although written as へ, it's pronounced as え) are both location and destination particles. They are placed after locations. In English, に and へ can both mean "to."

There are differences where に and へ are used. に is used when going to an exact location, as in, "I am going to France" (Furansuに いきます). The particle へ is used when going in a general direction, as in "I am going to the south" (みなみへ いきます).

In modern Japan, most Japanese people freely mix に and へ without regard to grammatical rules. It would not be wrong to say Furansu へ いきます. The key point to remember is that locations require a location marker. In order to prevent confusion, from this point on we will use に as the standard location and destination marker.

に as a location marker

Examples

とうきょうに	<u>to</u> Tokyo
がっこうに	<u>to</u> school
ぎんこうに	<u>to</u> the bank
にほんに	<u>to</u> Japan

Now let's combine locations with the verbs.

Example Sentences

1. とうきょうに いきます。	I am going to Tokyo.
2. ぎんこうに いきました。	I went to the bank.
3. がっこうに いきませんでした。	I didn't go to school.
4. おおさかに いきません。	I am not going to Osaka.

❏ 12-4. Time particle に

に is also used to mark time. When used with time, it can mean "in", "on", or "at".

```
┌──────────── に as a time marker ────────────┐
│ Examples                                    │
│ いちがつに                    in January     │
│ かようびに                    on Tuesday     │
│ ろくじに                      at six o'clock  │
│                                             │
│ Example Sentences                           │
│ 1.  いちがつに いきます。       I am going in January.  │
│ 2.  かようびに いきました。     I went on Tuesday.      │
└─────────────────────────────────────────────┘
```

❏ 12-5. Time particle usage with きょう、せんしゅう、らいねん etc.

You don't need to add a time particle to words like きょう (today)、あした (tomorrow) etc. These words are not "specific times" like "Monday" or "January". Adding に would be as strange as saying "I'm going ON tomorrow" or "I didn't go ON yesterday".

The same rule applies to, "this week", "next month", "last year", etc. An easy way to remember this rule is: "If you don't use IN, ON, or AT in English, then don't use に."

```
┌─────────────────────────────────────────────┐
│ Example Sentences                           │
│ 1.  らいしゅう、いきます。      I am going next week.       │
│ 2.  きのう、いきました。        I went yesterday.           │
│ 3.  きょねん、いきませんでした。 I didn't go last year.      │
│ 4.  こんしゅう、いきません。     I am not going this week.   │
└─────────────────────────────────────────────┘
```

❏ 12-6. Sentence structure using verbs

Verbs always come last in Japanese sentences. And just like ですか is a question, you can add か after the verb to make a question.

```
┌─────────────────────────────────────────────┐
│ Example Q&A                                 │
│ 1. どこに いきますか。        Where are you going (to)?    │
│    にほんに いきます。         I am going to Japan.         │
│                                             │
│ 2. いえに かえりましたか。     Did you return home?        │
│    いいえ、ともだちの いえに いきました。  No, I went to a friend's house. │
│                                             │
│ 3. いつ きますか。           When are you coming?         │
│    さんがつに いきます。       I will go in March.          │
└─────────────────────────────────────────────┘
```

4. なんにちに いきますか。　　　　**What day of the month are you going?**
　 ふつかに いきます。　　　　　　　 I am going <u>on</u> the 2nd.

5. いつ にほんに いきますか。　　　 **When are you going to Japan?**
　 らいねんの いちがつに いきます。 I am going next January.

6. きのう、がっこうに いきましたか。 **Did you go to school yesterday?**
　 いいえ、いきませんでした。　　　 No, I didn't go.
　 でも、あした いきます。　　　　　 But I will go tomorrow.

❑ 12-7. Using the verb わかる

When using わかる (to understand) が marks the thing that you understand.

Example Sentences
1.　にほんごが わかります。　　　　 I understand Japanese.
2.　にほんごが わかりません。　　　 I don't understand Japanese.
3.　かれは えいごが わかりません。 He doesn't understand English.

❑ 12-8. Languages and nationalities

By adding ご (language) and じん (people) after a country, you can create languages and nationalities. For example, Spain in Japanese is "supein", so "Spanish language" is **supeinご**. Russia in Japanese is "roshia" so a Russian person is **roshiaじん**.

English	Country	People	Language
Japan	にほん	にほんじん	にほんご
Korea	かんこく	かんこくじん	かんこくご
China	ちゅうごく	ちゅうごくじん	ちゅうごくご
Spain	supein	supeinじん	supeinご

Note: Some countries don't follow the pattern.

English	Country	People	Language
America	amerika	amerikaじん	えいご
Phillipines	firipin	firipinじん	tagaraguご
Mexico	mekishiko	mekishikoじん	supeinご

Example Sentences
1.　Furansuごが わかりますか。　　　 Do you understand French?
2.　Jonさんは kanadaじん です。　　 Jon is Canadian.
3.　ようこさんは supeinごが はなせます。 Youko can speak Spanish.

12 | Q&A しつもんと こたえ English→Japanese

1. **When are you coming back?**
   I will return in May.
   I will return on the 22nd.
   I will return next week.

   いつ、かえりますか。
   5 がつに かえります。
   22 にちに かえります。
   らいしゅう、かえります。

2. **Are you going?**
   Yes, I'm going.
   No, I'm not going.

   いきますか。
   はい、いきます。
   いいえ、いきません。

3. **Where are you going?**
   I'm going to Miyazaki City.
   I'm going to a friend's house.
   I'm going to Hyogo Prefecture.

   どこに いきますか。
   みやざきしに いきます。
   ともだちの いえに いきます。
   ひょうごけんに いきます。

4. **Are you going to Tokyo?**
   Yes, I am going to Tokyo.
   No, I am not going to Tokyo.

   とうきょうに いきますか。
   はい、とうきょうに いきます。
   いいえ、とうきょうに いきません。

5. **Are you coming to the party?**
   Yes, I am going.
   No, I am not going.

   Pa–ti–に きますか。
   はい、いきます。
   いいえ、いきません。

6. **Did you go to Japan?**
   Yes, I went to Japan.
   No, I didn't go to Japan.

   にほんに いきましたか。
   はい、にほんに いきました。
   いいえ、にほんに いきませんでした。

7. **When are you coming back?**
   I will return tomorrow.
   I will return on Sunday.

   いつ、かえりますか。
   あした、かえります。
   にちようびに かえります。

8. **Will you come (over) tomorrow?**
   Yes, I will go.
   No, I won't go.
   No, I will go the day after tomorrow.

   あした、きますか。
   はい、いきます。
   いいえ、いきません。
   いいえ、あさって いきます。

9. **When did you return to Canada?**
   I didn't return.
   I came back on Wednesday.

   いつ kanadaに かえりましたか。
   かえりませんでした。
   すいようびに かえりました。

10. **What nationality are you?** なにじん ですか。
    I'm Mexican. Mekishikoじん です。
    I'm Korean. かんこくじん です。
    I'm Chinese. ちゅうごくじん です。
    I'm American. Amerikaじん です。

12 Q&A しつもんと こたえ Japanese→English

1. ふるたさんは ちゅうごくごが わかりますか？ **Does Mr. Furuta understand Chinese?**
   いいえ。でも、かんこくごが わかります。 No. But he understands Korean.

2. なにごが はなせますか。 **What languages do you speak?**
   Supeinごと えいごが はなせます。 I can speak Spanish and English.
   ちゅうごくごと かんこくごと にほんごが はなせます。 I can speak Chinese, Korean and Japanese.

12 Mini Conversations ミニ かいわ Japanese→English

1. **Conversation between friends**
   A: どこに いきますか。
   B: おじいさんの いえに いきます。
   A: おじいさんの いえは どこですか。
   B: Rasu begasuです。

   A: Where are you going?
   B: I am going to my grandfather's house.
   A: Where is your grandfather's house?
   B: Las Vegas.

2. **Conversation on the phone between friends**
   A: いつ、amerikaに かえりますか。
   B: すいようびに かえります。
   A: あなたの おかあさんも かえりますか。
   B: はい、おかあさんも かえります。

   A: When will you come back to America?
   B: I'll return on Wednesday.
   A: Will your mother also come back?
   B: Yes, my mother will also return.

3. Conversation between friends who haven't met in a while
A: おひさしぶりです。
B: いつ、かえりましたか。
A: おととい、かえりました。

A: It's been a long time.
B: When did you return?
A: I came back the day before yesterday.

4. Conversation between friends
A: だれが pa–ti–に きますか。
B: よしこさんと けいこさんが きます。
A: よしこさんと けいこさんは だれですか。
B: わたしの ともだちです。

A: Who is coming to the party?
B: Yoshiko and Keiko are coming.
A: Who are Yoshiko and Keiko?
B: They're my friends.

5. Conversation between two co-workers
A: いつ、amerikaに いきましたか。
B: Amerikaに いきませんでした。
A: じゃあ、どこに いきましたか。
B: かんこくに いきました。

A: When did you go to America?
B: I didn't go to America.
A: Well then, where did you go?
B: I went to Korea.

6. Conversation at work
A: なにごが はなせますか。
B: ちゅうごくごと えいごと にほんごが はなせます。
A: すごいですね。なにじんですか。
B: にほんじんです。

A: What languages can you speak?
B: I can speak Chinese, English, and Japanese.
A: That's amazing. What nationality are you?
B: I'm Japanese.

12 Reading Comprehension どっかい

Read the sentences below. Use the information to answer the reading comprehension questions later in this lesson.

① ここは amerikaの shikagoし です。

② まりさんは、じゅうがつ みっかに にほんに いきました。

③ きのう、shikagoしに かえりました。

④ まりさんと ともだちの よしこさんは あした、pa–ti–に いきます。

⑤ まりさんの ふくは しろです。

⑥ よしこさんのは orenji です。

⑦ あしたは harowi–n (Halloween) です。

⑧ まりさんは pa–ti–が だいすき です。

⑨ くがつに よしこさんの おとうさんの たんじょうび pa–ti–に いきました。

⑩ らいねんの しちがつ とおかに かんこくに いきます。

12 Lesson Activities

❑ 1. Grammar drill

Fill in the blanks with appropriate verb forms.

Dictionary Form	Polite Forms			
	Present / Future		Past	
	positive	negative	positive	negative
いく	いきます			
くる		きません		
かえる			かえりました	
わかる				わかりませんでした

❑ 2. Substitution drill

Replace the underlined word with the words provided.

> **Ex. あした <u>kanada</u>に いきます。**
>
> → Japan   あした にほんに いきます。

1. きょう <u>ぎんこうに</u> いきません。

    → school   _____

    → McDonald's   _____

    → friend's house _____

2. たなかさんは、<u>おととい</u> とうきょうに かえりました。

    → yesterday   _____

    → last Friday   _____

    → 5th of last month _____

3. やまもとさんは、<u>にほんに</u> かえりませんでした。

   → America   _____

   → Los Angeles   _____

   → Chicago   _____

4. やまださんは、<u>さんがつに</u> ここに きます。

   → 2nd of next month   _____

   → next Saturday   _____

   → May of next year _____

5. おかあさんの いえに <u>いきます</u>。

   → won't go   _____

   → went   _____

   → didn't go   _____

6. たむらさんの おとうさんは、<u>にほんごが</u> わかります。

   → English   _____

   → computer   _____

   → hiragana and katakana   _____

❏ 3. Reading comprehension questions

Answer the following questions about the reading comprehension in this lesson.

1. まりさんは きのう どこに かえりましたか。

   _____

2. まりさんの ともだちの なまえは なんですか。

   _____

3. きょうは なんがつ なんにち ですか。

   _____

4. まりさんは くがつに どこに いきましたか。

   _____

5. まりさんは らいねん どこに いきますか。

   _____

6. ここは どこですか。

   _____

7. まりさんは はちがつに どこに いきましたか。

   _____

❏ 4. Short dialogue

Mr. Tanaka sees Ms. Smith (Sumisu) on the street and they start a conversation.

Sumisuさん:	たなかさん、こんにちは。
たなかさん:	Sumisuさん、こんにちは。きょうは あついですね。
Sumisuさん:	はい、あついです。
たなかさん:	どこに いきますか。
Sumisuさん:	いまから ①がっこうに いきます。
たなかさん:	②なんの がっこう ですか。
Sumisuさん:	③にほんごがっこう です。
たなかさん:	そうですか。わたしは いまから ④しごとに いきます。

New words and expressions in the dialogue

Progressive	Kanji	English
いまから	今から	from now / from now on
なんの？	何の？	What? Which? What kind of?
きょうは あついですね。	今日は暑いですね。	Today sure is hot.

❏ 5. Short dialogue activities

Practice reading the above dialogue in pairs.
Substitute ①-④ with the following words and try
the conversation again.

A) ① Movies (えいが)
   ② What movie is it?
   ③ Any movie
   ④ I'm going to the bank

B) ① Party
  ② What (kind of) party is it?
  ③ school party
  ④ I'm going home

C) ① McDonald's
  ② Where is it?
  ③ It's over there
  ④ I'm going to school

❑ 6. Japanese translation
Translate the following conversation into Japanese.

1.	
Ryouhei:	I am going to China.
Nobuko:	I went last year. When are you going?
Ryouhei:	On the 20th of next month.
Nobuko:	When will you return?
Ryouhei:	Maybe on the 30th.
Nobuko:	That's nice.
Ryouhei:	
Nobuko:	
Ryouhei:	
Nobuko:	
Ryouhei:	
Nobuko:	

12 | Drill ドリル

If you're not sure what these sentences mean, we recommend that you review the lesson up to this point before continuing.

1. どこに いきますか。
2. いつ かえりますか。
3. きんようびに いきました。
4. にほんごが わかりますか。
5. なんがつに いきますか。

12 | Sentence Building ぶんのつくり

In this lesson we are starting a new sentence to build on. Watch it grow and transform as new concepts are introduced.

> あした、にほんに いきます。
> Tomorrow, I am going to Japan.

12 Answer Key

❑ Reading comprehension translation
① This is America's Chicago city.
② Mari went to Japan on October 3rd.
③ Yesterday she returned to Chicago.
④ Mari and her friend Yoshiko are going to a party tomorrow.
⑤ Mari's clothing (for the party) is white.
⑥ Yoshiko's are orange.
⑦ Tomorrow is Halloween.
⑧ Mari really likes parties.
⑨ In September, she went to Yoshiko's Father's birthday party.
⑩ Next year on July 10th, she is going to Korea.

❑ 1. Grammar drill (answers)

Dictionary Form	Polite Forms			
	Present/Future		Past	
	positive	negative	positive	negative
いく	いきます	いきません	いきました	いきませんでした
くる	きます	きません	きました	きませんでした
かえる	かえります	かえりません	かえりました	かえりませんでした
わかる	わかります	わかりません	わかりました	わかりませんでした

❑ 2. Substitution drill (answers)
1. きょう、ぎんこうに いきません。
   きょう、がっこうに いきません。
   きょう、makudonarudoに いきません。
   きょう、ともだちのいえに いきません。

2. たなかさんは、おととい とうきょうに かえりました。
   たなかさんは、きのう とうきょうに かえりました。
   たなかさんは、せんしゅうのきんようびに とうきょうに かえりました。
   たなかさんは、せんげつのいつかに とうきょうに かえりました。

3. やまもとさんは、にほんに かえりませんでした。
   やまもとさんは、amerikaに かえりませんでした。
   やまもとさんは、rosanzerusuに かえりませんでした。
   やまもとさんは、shikagoに かえりませんでした。

4. やまださんは、さんがつに ここに きます。
   やまださんは、らいげつのふつかに ここに きます。
   やまださんは、らいしゅうのどようびに ここに きます。
   やまださんは、らいねんのごがつに ここに きます。

5. おかあさんの いえに いきます。
   おかあさんの いえに いきません。
   おかあさんの いえに いきました。
   おかあさんの いえに いきませんでした。

6. たむらさんの おとうさんは、にほんごが わかります。
   たむらさんの おとうさんは、えいごが わかります。
   たむらさんの おとうさんは、konpyu–ta–が わかります。
   たむらさんの おとうさんは、ひらがなとかたかなが わかります。

❑ 3. Reading comprehension questions (answers)

1. Where did Mari return to yesterday?
   Shikagoに かえりました。

2. What is Mari's friend's name?
   よしこさん です。

3. What is the month and day of the month today?
   じゅうがつ さんじゅうにちです。
   (because tomorrow is Halloween in sentence 7)

4. Where did Mari go in September?
   よしこさんの おとうさんの たんじょうびpa–ti–に いきました。

5. Where is Mari going next year?
   かんこくに いきます。

6. Where is here?
   Shikagoしです。OR AmerikaのShikagoしです。

7. Where did Mari go in August?
   Did this one confuse you? It should have because we don't really know where Mari went in August. So the answer is: わかりません。

❑ 4. Short dialogue (translation)

Ms. Smith:	Good afternoon, Mr. Tanaka.
Mr. Tanaka:	Good afternoon, Ms. Smith. It sure is hot, isn't it?
Ms. Smith:	Yes, it's hot.
Mr. Tanaka:	Where are you going?
Ms. Smith:	I'm going to school (from) now.
Mr. Tanaka:	What school is it?
Ms. Smith:	It's Japanese language school.
Mr. Tanaka:	I see. I'm going to work now.

❑ 6. Japanese translation (answers)

Ryouhei:	ちゅうごくに いきます。
Nobuko:	わたしは きょねん、いきました。いつ いきますか。
Ryouhei:	らいげつの はつかです。
Nobuko:	いつ かえりますか。
Ryouhei:	たぶん、さんじゅうにちです／たぶん、さんじゅうにちに かえります。
Nobuko:	いいですね。

Lesson 13 — Level ① · Telling Time
Hours and minutes

13 About This Lesson このレッスンについて

Before The Lesson

1. Review all of the vocabulary groups.
2. Know how to conjugate verbs into the polite forms.

Lesson Goals

1. Learn how to tell time in Japanese.
2. Learn how to use から (from) and まで (until).

From The Teachers

1. から (from) and まで (until) are used for both time and location and are very handy particles. Make sure you take the time to learn how they are used.
2. Review everything you have learned in this book. It sets the stage for Level 2. Good Luck!

13 New Words あたらしい ことば

Progressive	Kana	Kanji	English
なんじ	なんじ	何時	what time?
はん	はん	半	half past (:30)
ごぜん	ごぜん	午前	AM (also means morning)
ごご	ごご	午後	PM (also means afternoon)
くうこう	くうこう	空港	airport
じゅぎょう	じゅぎょう	授業	class
arubaito	アルバイト	アルバイト	part-time job
やすみ	やすみ	休み	day off, break

13   Time じかん

o'clock - じ					
one o'clock	いちじ	一時	seven o'clock	しちじ	七時
two o'clock	にじ	二時	eight o'clock	はちじ	八時
three o'clock	さんじ	三時	nine o'clock	くじ	九時
four o'clock	よじ	四時	ten o'clock	じゅうじ	十時
five o'clock	ごじ	五時	eleven o'clock	じゅういちじ	十一時
six o'clock	ろくじ	六時	twelve o'clock	じゅうにじ	十二時

さんじ   しちじ   よじ   じゅういちじ   くじ

minutes - ふん, ぷん		
1 minute	いっぷん	一分
2 minutes	にふん	二分
3 minutes	さんぷん	三分
4 minutes	よんぷん	四分
5 minutes	ごふん	五分
6 minutes	ろっぷん	六分
7 minutes	ななふん	七分
8 minutes	はっぷん／はちふん	八分
9 minutes	きゅうふん	九分
10 minutes	じっぷん／じゅっぷん	十分
11 minutes	じゅういっぷん	十一分
12 minutes	じゅうにふん	十二分
13 minutes	じゅうさんぷん	十三分
14 minutes	じゅうよんぷん	十四分
15 minutes	じゅうごふん	十五分
16 minutes	じゅうろっぷん	十六分

17 minutes	じゅうななふん	十七分
18 minutes	じゅうはっぷん／じゅうはちふん	十八分
19 minutes	じゅうきゅうふん	十九分
20 minutes	にじっぷん／にじゅっぷん	二十分
25 minutes	にじゅうごふん	二十五分
30 minutes	さんじっぷん／さんじゅっぷん	三十分
35 minutes	さんじゅうごふん	三十五分
40 minutes	よんじっぷん／よんじゅっぷん	四十分
45 minutes	よんじゅうごふん	四十五分
50 minutes	ごじっぷん／ごじゅっぷん	五十分
55 minutes	ごじゅうごふん	五十五分
60 minutes	ろくじっぷん／ろくじゅっぷん	六十分

| しちじ よんぷん. | じゅうじ はっぷん | くじ じゅういっぷん | よじ よんじゅっぷん | しちじ にじゅうごふん |

13 Grammar ぶんぽう

☐ 13-1. AM and PM

ごぜん means both morning and AM ごご means both afternoon and PM. They are always placed in front of the time.

> **Examples**
> 1. <u>ごぜん</u> ごじ   5:00 AM
> 2. <u>ごぜん</u> じゅうにじ じゅっぷん   12:10 AM
> 3. <u>ごご</u> ろくじ   6:00 PM
> 4. <u>ごご</u> しちじ いっぷん   7:01 PM
> 5. <u>ごご</u> いちじ よんじゅうごふん   1:45 PM

❑ 13-2. Half past

はん means half past. It always comes after the hour.

Examples	
1. じゅうじ はん	10:30
2. さんじ はん	3:30
3. にじ はん	2:30

Example sentences	
1. にじはんに いきます。	I am going at 2:30.
2. しちじはんに かえります。	I will return at 7:30.
3. ともだちは じゅうじはんに きました。	My friend came at 10:30.

❑ 13-3. Using the particle から

から means "from" or "since," depending on the context. It comes after a time or location to say "from this time" or "from this location". It is used much like its English equivalent.

から with time

Examples	
1. なんじ から	from what time?
2. はちがつ から	from August
3. いつ から	from when?
4. さんじはん から	from 3:30
5. げつようびから	from Monday

から with location

Examples	
1. どこ から	from where?
2. あそこ から	from that place over there
3. にほん から	from Japan
4. しごと から	from work
5. ともだちのいえから	from a friend's house

Example Q&A

1. なんじ<u>から</u> いきますか。
   ごじ<u>から</u> いきます。

   <u>From</u> what time will you go?
   I will go <u>from</u> five o'clock.

2. しごとは なんじ<u>から</u> ですか。
   しちじはん<u>から</u> です。

   <u>From</u> what time is your work?
   It's <u>from</u> 7:30.

3. どこ<u>から</u> きましたか。
   あおもりけん<u>から</u> きました。
   みやざきし<u>から</u> きました。

   Where did you come <u>from</u>?
   I came <u>from</u> Aomori Prefecture.
   I came <u>from</u> Miyazaki City.

4. いつ にほん<u>から</u> かえりますか。
   あした かえります。

   When will you return <u>from</u> Japan?
   I will return tomorrow.

5. なつは きょう<u>から</u>ですか。

   いいえ、あさって<u>から</u>です。

   Is summer <u>from</u> today?
   (Does summer start today?)
   No, it is <u>from</u> the day after tomorrow.

❏ 13-4. Using the particle まで

まで means "until", "up until", or "as far as". It comes after a time or location to say "until this time" or "until this location". When まで is used with location, the location is the final destination. It can also mean "up until to" or just "to". Remember that まで and に are different. In most cases, に can be thought of as a single destination marker and まで can be thought of as a final destination marker.

まで with time	
Examples	
1. なんじ <u>まで</u>	<u>until</u> what time?
2. いつ <u>まで</u>	<u>until</u> when?
3. さんじ <u>まで</u>	<u>until</u> three o'clock
4. いちがつ <u>まで</u>	<u>until</u> January
5. きょう <u>まで</u>	<u>until</u> today

まで with location	
Examples	
1. とうきょう <u>まで</u>	<u>until</u> Tokyo
2. どこ <u>まで</u>	<u>until</u> where?
3. しごと <u>まで</u>	<u>until</u> work

Example Q&A

1. どこまで いきますか。
   ほっかいどうまで いきます。

   Up until where (how far) are you going?
   I am going to (as far as) Hokkaido.

2. しごとは なんじまで ですか。
   しちじはんまで です。

   Until what time is your work?
   It's until 7:30.

3. どこまで いきましたか。
   あおもりけんまで いきました。

   Up until where (how far) did you go?
   I went to (as far as) Aomori Prefecture.

4. がっこうは なんじまで ですか。
   さんじはんまで です。

   Until what time is school?
   It's until 3:30.

13 Mini Conversations ミニ かいわ Japanese→English

1. **Conversation between co-workers**
   A: しごとは なんじから なんじまで ですか。
   B: ごぜん はちじから ごご ごじまで です。
   A: いつ かえりますか。
   B: ごじはんに かえります。

   A: From what time until what time is your work?
   B: It's from 8 AM until 5 PM.
   A: When will you return home?
   B: I will return at 5:30.

2. **Conversation between friends**
   A: ふゆは いつから いつまで ですか。
   B: ふゆは じゅうがつから にがつまで です。
   A: ちがいます。
   B: ごめんなさい。ふゆは じゅうにがつから さんがつまで です。

   A: From when until when is winter?
   B: Winter is from October until February.
   A: That's wrong.
   B: Sorry. Winter is from December until March.

3. **Conversation between friends**
   A: Pa–ti–は なんじからなんじまで ですか。
   B: ごご ろくじから ごぜん いちじまで です。
   A: わかりました。ありがとう。

A: From what time until what time is the party?

B: It's from 6 PM until 1 AM.

A: Okay. Thanks.

4. Conversation between friends

A: きょう、どこから どこまで いきますか。

B: なごやしから ひめじしまで いきます。

A: でんしゃは なんじですか。

B: じゅういちじ よんじゅうさんぷん です。

A: From where to where are you going today?

B: I will go from Nagoya City to Himeji City.

A: What time is the train?

B: It's at 11:43.

5. Conversation between brothers

A: おかあさんは いつ きますか。

B: らいしゅうの どようびに きます。

A: なんじに?

B: ごぜん しちじに。

A: When will mother come?

B: She will come next Saturday.

A: At what time?

B: At 7 AM.

6. Conversation between friends

A: なんじの ひこうき ですか。

B: ひこうきは ごごはちじ じゅうななふん です。

A: くうこうに なんじに いきますか。

B: ろくじはんに いきます。

A: What time is your flight?   （ひこうき can mean "flight" and "plane."）

B: The plane (my flight) is 8:17 PM.

A: What time are you going to the airport?

B: I'm going at 6:30.

7. Conversation between neighbors

A: Kurisumasuのpa–ti–は いつですか。

B: らいしゅうの どようびの しちじからです。

A: なんじまでですか。

B: たぶん じゅうにじまで です。

A: When is the Christmas party?

B: It starts at seven o'clock next Saturday.

A: What time does it end?

B: Maybe until twelve o'clock.

13 Q&A しつもんと こたえ English→Japanese

1. **What time is it?**
   It is two o'clock.
   It is 6:12.

   なんじ ですか。
   にじ です。
   ろくじ じゅうにふん です。

2. **What time was it?**
   It was twelve o'clock.
   It was three o'clock.
   It was four o'clock.

   なんじ でしたか。
   じゅうにじ でした。
   さんじ でした。
   よじ でした。

3. **From what time is your work?**
   My work is from eight o'clock.
   My work is from seven o'clock.

   あなたの しごとは なんじから ですか。
   わたしの しごとは はちじから です。
   わたしの しごとは しちじから です。

4. **What time are you going?**
   I'm going at three o'clock.
   I'm not going.

   なんじに いきますか。
   さんじに いきます。
   いきません。

5. **What time will you go back?**
   I will go back at 6:30.
   I'm not going back.

   なんじに かえりますか。
   ろくじはんに かえります。
   かえりません。

6. **What time did you come here?**
   I came at 4:15.
   I came yesterday.

   ここに なんじに きましたか。
   よじ じゅうごふんに きました。
   きのう、きました。

7. **Until when is your break?**
   My break until August.
   It's until next week.

   やすみは いつまで ですか。
   やすみは はちがつまで です。
   らいしゅうまで です。

8. **Since when have you liked Japanese?**
   I have liked it since I was fifteen years old.
   I have liked it since last year.

   いつから にほんごが すき でしたか。
   じゅうごさいから すきでした。
   きょねんから すきでした。

13 Reading Comprehension どっかい

Read the sentences below. Use the information to answer the reading comprehension questions later in this lesson.

① ここは にほんごの がっこうです。

② ここに Samu (Sam) さんは ごぜん じゅうじに きました。

③ Jonさんは じゅうじ じゅうごふんに きました。

④ きょうの じゅぎょうは じゅうじはんから ごご いちじまで です。

⑤ Samuさんは にじに いえに かえります。

⑥ ごご よじに しごとに いきます。

⑦ Samuさんの しごとは よじはんから ごぜん いちじはんまで です。

⑧ Samuさんの しごとは hoteruの しごとです。

⑨ Jonさんは にじはんに supeinごの がっこうに いきます。

⑩ Supeinごの がっこうは さんじはんまで です。

⑪ いえに ろくじに かえります。

⑫ ごご はちじから arubaitoです。

⑬ しちじ ごじゅうごふんに いきます。

⑭ Arubaitoは じゅうにじまで です。

⑮ Jonさんの arubaito は makudonarudo です。

13 Lesson Activities

❑ 1. Drill
Write the time shown on each clock in Japanese.

1. _____   2. _____   3. _____

4. _____   5. _____   6. _____

7. _____   8. _____   9. _____

❑ 2. Question and answer
Answer the following questions as if they were being asked to you directly. Write all the answers in hiragana.

1. しごと／がっこうは なんじからですか。

_____

2. なんじに しごと／がっこうに いきますか。

_____

3. なんようびに しごと／がっこうに いきますか。

_____

4. なんじに いえに かえりますか。

_____

5. いま、なんじですか。

_____

6. にほんごの じゅぎょうは なんじから なんじまで ですか。

_____

7. あなたの にほんごのせんせいは だれですか。

_____

8. ふゆは なんがつから なんがつまで ですか。(December to February)

_____

9. なつは なんがつから なんがつまで ですか。(June to September)

_____

❑ 3. Reading comprehension questions

Answer the following questions about the reading comprehension in this lesson. Write all the answers in hiragana (except for the katakana words).

1. ここは どこですか。

_____

2. だれが にほんごの がっこうに じゅうじに きましたか。

_____

3. きょうの じゅぎょうは なんじから なんじまで ですか。

_____

4. Samuさんの しごとは なんじから なんじまでですか。

_____

5. Samuさんは いえに なんじに かえりましたか。

_____

6. Jonさんの arubaito は なんじから なんじまで ですか。

_____

7. Jonさんは なんじに にほんごのがっこうに きましたか。

_____

8. Jonさんは にじはんに どこに いきますか。

_____

❏ **4. Japanese translation**
Translate the following conversations into English.

1.

Aさん:	いつから しごとですか。
Bさん:	にがつ ようかから です。
Aさん:	しごとは なんじから なんじまで ですか。
Bさん:	ごぜん はちじから ごご よじまで です。

2.

Aさん:	いま なんじ ですか。
Bさん:	よじ にじゅっぷん です。
Aさん:	よじはんに いえに かえります。
Bさん:	いえは どこ ですか。
Aさん:	あそこ です。

3.

Aさん:	あしたから にほんに かえります。
Bさん:	いつまで ですか。
Aさん:	はちがつ じゅうごにちまで です。
Bさん:	そうですか。 いいですね。

❑ 5. English translation

Translate the following conversations into Japanese.

1.

Mr. A:	When did you come here?
Ms. B:	I came at nine.
Mr. A:	Where is your friend?
Ms. B:	My friend didn't come.
Mr. A:	Where is your friend now?
Ms. B:	He is at home now.

2.

Mrs. A:	What time is your airplane?
Mr. B:	It's 10:30 a.m.
Mrs. A:	What time are you going to the airport?
Mr. B:	I'll go at 9:00.
Mrs. A:	Got it.

3.

Mr. A:	From what time is your part time job?
Mr. B:	It's from 1:00 p.m.
Mr. A:	Do you like your part time job?
Mr. B:	No, I don't like it.

❑ 6. Particle drill
Fill in the blanks with appropriate particles.

1. わたし _____ しごと _____ はちじ _____ ごじ _____です。

2. せんげつ _____ じゅうごにち _____ もくようびでした。

3. なんじ _____ いえ _____ かえります _____？

4. やまださん _____ くるま _____ しろ _____ gure– です。

5. いぬ _____ すきです。でも、ねこ _____ きらいです。

6. あたらしい じてんしゃ _____ ほしいです。

7. どれ _____ たなかさん _____ ほん です_____？

8. かようび _____ とうきょう_____ いきます。

9. Hanba–ga– _____ poteto _____ おねがいします。

    Ko–ra _____ (also) おねがいします。

❑ 7. Short dialogue

Mr. Hashimoto is talking to Mr. Watanabe about his plans for the weekend.

わたなべさん:	はしもとさん、あしたも はちじから しごとですか。
はしもとさん:	いいえ、あしたは やすみです。
わたなべさん:	いいですね。あしたは どこに いきますか。
はしもとさん:	あしたは おおさかに いきます。
わたなべさん:	ひこうきですか。
はしもとさん:	はい。くじの ひこうきです。くうこうに はちじに いきます。
わたなべさん:	そうですか。いつ かえりますか。
はしもとさん:	らいしゅうの かようびに とうきょうに かえります。

❑ 8. Short dialogue activities

1. Practice reading the dialogue in pairs.
2. Talk about your weekend plans.
   - Use the new verbs: 〜に いきます／きます／かえります

13 │ Drill ドリル

If you're not sure what these sentences mean, we recommend that you review the lesson up to this point before continuing.

1. なんじに いきますか。
2. でんしゃは なんじですか。
3. がっこうは いちじから はちじまで です。
4. あなたの しごとは なんじから ですか。
5. ごぜん ろくじに くうこうに いきます。

13 │ Sentence Building ぶんのつくり

In each lesson we will build on a previous sentence. Watch it transform each time new concepts are introduced.

> **あした、ごご さんじに にほんに いきます。**
> **Tomorrow, I am going to Japan at 3 p.m.**

Compare how the sentence has changed from the prior lesson:

Lesson 12:　あした にほんに いきます。

Tomorrow, I am going to Japan.

13 Answer Key

❑ Reading comprehension (translation)
① This is a Japanese language school.
② Sam came here at 10:00AM
③ John came at 10:15.
④ Today's class is from 10:30 to 1:00PM.
⑤ Sam will return home at 2:00.
⑥ He will go to work at 4:00PM.
⑦ Sam's job is from 4:30 to 1:30AM.
⑧ Sam's job is a hotel job.
⑨ John will go to Spanish school at 2:30.
⑩ Spanish school is until 3:30.
⑪ He will return home at six.
⑫ He has a part time job from 8:00PM.
⑬ He goes at 7:55.
⑭ His part time job is until twelve.
⑮ John's part time job is McDonald's.

❑ 1. Grammar drill (answers)
1. ろくじ ごふん
2. くじ にじゅっぷん
3. さんじ よんじゅっぷん
4. はちじはん
5. じゅうじ よんじゅうごふん
6. じゅうにじ ごじゅうさんぷん
7. よじはん
8. にじ じゅうななふん
9. しちじ ななふん

❑ 2. Question and answer (answers may vary)
1. From what time does your work/school start?
2. What time do you go to work/school ?
3. What days of the week do you go to work/school?

4. What time do you go home?
5. What time is it now?

6. From what time to what time is your Japanese class?
7. Who is your Japanese teacher?
8. From what month to what month is winter?
9. From what month to what month is summer?

しごとは、くじからです。
はちじに がっこうに いきます。
げつようびから きんようびまで
がっこうに いきます。
ろくじに いえに かえります。
いま、よじはんです。

ごじから ろくじはんまでです。
やまだせんせいです。
じゅうにがつから にがつまでです。
ろくがつから くがつまでです。

❑ 3. Reading comprehension questions (answers)
1. Where is here?
にほんご(の)がっこうです。

2. Who came to school at ten o'clock?
Samuです。

3. From what time until what time is today's class?
じゅうじから ごごいちじまで です。

4. From what time until what time is Sam's work?
よじはんから ごぜんいちじまで です。

5. What time did Sam return home?
にじに かえりました。

6. From what time until what time is John's part time job?
ごごはちじから じゅうにじまでです。

7. What time did John come to Japanese school?
じゅうじ じゅうごふんに きました。

8. Where does John go at 2:30?
Supeinごの がっこうに いきます。

❏ 4. Japanese translation (answers)

1. A: From when do you work? / When does your work start?
   B: It starts from February 8th.
   A: From what time until what time is the job?
   B: It is from 8:00 A.M. to 4:00 P.M.

2. A: What time is it now?
   B: 4:20.
   A: I am going home at 4:30.
   B: Where is your house?
   A: It's over there.

3. A: I am returning to Japan from tomorrow. *(perfectly correct sentence in Japanese.)*
   B: Until when?
   A: Until August 15th.
   B: Is that so? That's nice.

❏ 5. English translation (answers)

1. A: いつ ここに きましたか。
   B: くじに きました。
   A: ともだちは どこですか。
   B: ともだちは きませんでした。
   A: いま、ともだちは どこですか。
   B: いま、うちです。

2. A: なんじの ひこうきですか。 / ひこうきは なんじですか。
   B: ごぜん じゅうじはんです。
   A: なんじに くうこうに いきますか。
   B: くじに いきます。
   A: わかりました。

3. A: Arubaitoは なんじから ですか。
   B: いちじから です。
   A: Arubaitoが すきですか。
   B: いいえ、すきじゃない です。

❏ 6. Particle drill (answers)

1. わたしの しごとは はちじから ごじまでです。
2. せんげつの じゅうごにちは もくようびでした。
3. なんじに いえに(へ) かえりますか。
4. やまださんの くるまは しろと gure-です。
5. いぬが すきです。でも、ねこは きらいです。
6. あたらしいじてんしゃが ほしいです。
7. どれが たなかさんの ほんですか。
8. かようびに とうきょうに(へ) いきます。
9. Hanba-ga-と potatoを おねがいします。Ko-raも おねがいします。

❑ **7. Short dialogue translation**

Mr. Watanabe:	Are you also working from 8:00 tomorrow, Mr. Hashimoto?
Mr. Hashimoto:	No, tomorrow I'm off.
Mr. Watanabe:	That's nice. Where are you going tomorrow?
Mr. Hashimoto:	I'm going to Osaka tomorrow.
Mr. Watanabe	(By) airplane?
Mr. Hashimoto:	Yes, (by) the nine o'clock plane. I'm going to the airport at eight.
Mr. Watanabe	Is that so? When are you coming back?
Mr. Hashimoto:	I'm coming back to Tokyo next Tuesday.

APPENDICES

Everyday Phrases

A Greetings あいさつ

1.	Good morning.	Ohayou gozaimasu. / Ohayou.
2.	Good afternoon.	Konnichiwa.
3.	Good evening.	Konbanwa.
4.	Good night.	Oyasuminasai. / Oyasumi.
5.	Goodbye.	Sayounara.
6.	Thank you.	Doumo arigatou. / Arigatou.
7.	Thank you very much.	Doumo arigatou gozaimasu.
8.	You are welcome.	Dou itashimashite.
9.	It's been a long time. / Long time no see.	Shibaraku deshita.
10.	It's been a long time. / Long time no see.	Ohisashiburi desu. (standard)
11.	It's been a long time. / Long time no see.	Gobusata shite orimasu. (formal)
12.	Happy Birthday.	Tanjoubi omedetou.
13.	Happy New Year.	Akemashite omedetou.
14.	Bye.	Bai bai.
15.	See you.	Jaa ne. / Jaa.
16.	See you again.	Jaa mata. / De wa mata.
17.	Farewell.	Sayounara.

B Self Introductions じこしょうかい

18.	Nice to meet you.	Hajimemashite.
19.	What is your name?	Onamae wa nan desu ka.
20.	I am Tanaka.	(polite and humble) Tanaka to moushimasu.
21.	I am Tanaka.	(simple but correct) Tanaka desu.
22.	Best regards.	Yoroshiku onegai shimasu.

There is not an exact translation, but this phrase is said when first meeting somebody, usually after stating your name. It is also used on many other occasions to mean, "I request of you," when one is requesting something of another.

23. Where did you come from?	Doko kara kimashita ka.
24. I came from ____.	_____ kara kimashita.
25. Where do you live?	Doko ni sundeimasu ka.
26. I live in ____.	_____ ni sundeimasu.
27. How old are you?	Nan-sai desu ka.
28. I am 25 years old.	Ni juu go sai desu.
29. How old do I look?	Nan-sai ni miemasu ka.
30. You look ____.	_____ ni miemasu.

C Communication コミュニケーション

31. I am studying Japanese.	Nihongo o benkyou shiteimasu.
32. Do you understand?	Wakarimasu ka.
33. Yes, I understand.	Hai, wakarimasu.
34. No, I don't understand.	iie, wakarimasen.
35. Can you speak Japanese?	Nihongo ga hanasemasu ka.
36. Can you speak English?	Eigo ga hanasemasu ka.
37. A little.	Sukoshi.
38. Not at all.	Zenzen.
39. Please say it once again.	Mou ichido itte kudasai.
40. Please speak more slowly.	Motto yukkuri itte kudasai.
41. Please speak more clearly. (this can be rude)	Motto hakkiri itte kudasai.
42. Wait a moment, please.	Chotto matte kudasai.
43. Go ahead. / Please.	Douzo.
44. Excuse me.	Sumimasen.
45. I am sorry. / Please forgive me.	Gomen nasai.
46. What is it in Japanese?	Nihongo de nan desu ka.
47. What is it in English?	Eigo de nan desu ka.

D Shopping ショッピング

48. How much is it?	Ikura desu ka.
49. It's 400 yen.	Yon hyaku en desu.
50. It's 22 dollars.	Ni juu ni doru desu.

51. It's _____ dollars.   _____ doru desu.
52. It's _____ yen.   _____ en desu.

53. It's expensive.   Takai desu.
54. It's cheap.   Yasui desu.

E   At a Restaurant / Eating レストランで

55. A menu, please.   Menyu– o kudasai.
56. Water, please.   Mizu o kudasai.
57. More, please.   Motto kudasai.
58. _____ please.   _____ o kudasai.
59. It's delicious.   Oishii desu.
60. It doesn't taste good.   Oishikunai desu.
61. I am hungry.   Onaka ga sukimashita.
62. I am thirsty.   Nodo ga kawakimashita.
63. I am full.   Onaka ga ippai desu.
64. I will receive.   Itadakimasu. (said just prior to eating)
65. It was a good meal.   Gochisou sama deshita.
    Said after a meal, normally when someone has cooked or paid for you.

F   Entering and Exiting はいるとき、でるとき

66. I'm going and I will come back.   Ittekimasu.
    Always said by person who will be returning.

67. Go and be careful.   Itterasshai.
    Always said to the person who will be back from the place they are leaving.

68. I'm home.   Tadaima.
69. Welcome home.   Okaerinasai.
70. Sorry to disturb you.   Ojama shimasu.
    Said upon entering someone's house.

71. Sorry to have disturbed you.   Ojama shimashita.
    Said upon leaving someone's house.

G   On the Phone でんわで

72. Hello.	Moshi moshi. (on the phone)
73. Is <u>Mr. Honda</u> there?	<u>Honda san</u> wa irasshaimasu ka.
74. Is _____ there?	_____ san wa irasshaimasu ka.

H   Commands / Requests

75. Please show me.	Misete kudasai.
76. Please guide me.	Annai shite kudasai.
77. Please eat it.	Tabete kudasai.
78. Please read it.	Yonde kudasai.
79. Please say it.	Itte kudasai.
80. Please write it.	Kaite kudasai.
81. Please look at it. / Please look.	Mite kudasai.
82. Please come.	Kite kudasai.
83. Please stop it.	Yamete kudasai.

Last Names

❑ **Common Japanese surnames and their meaning**

Some of these family names' meanings are easily understood, but others are mysteriously vague. You will notice that most of the names have meaning related to the natural world. The meanings of the names are determined by the kanji they are composed of.

Name	Hiragana	Kanji	Possible Meaning
Aoki	あおき	青木	blue (green) tree
Endou	えんどう	遠藤	far away wisteria
Fujita	ふじた	藤田	a field of wisteria
Hasegawa	はせがわ	長谷川	long valley river
Hashimoto	はしもと	橋本	main bridge
Hayashi	はやし	林	woods
Higashi	ひがし	東	east
Honda	ほんだ	本田	main rice paddy
Ikeda	いけだ	池田	pond rice paddy
Inoue	いのうえ	井上	above a well
Ishikawa	いしかわ	石川	stone river
Itou	いとう	伊藤	grand wisteria
Kawada	かわだ	川田	river rice paddy
Kawamoto	かわもと	川本	main river
Kimura	きむら	木村	tree village
Kobayashi	こばやし	小林	small woods
Matsumoto	まつもと	松本	main pine
Mikami	みかみ	三上	three above
Minami	みなみ	南	south
Mori	もり	森	forest
Nakajima	なかじま	中島	inner island
Nakamura	なかむら	中村	inner forest
Nakano	なかの	中野	inner field
Nishida	にしだ	西田	west rice paddy
Nishimura	にしむら	西村	west village
Ogawa	おがわ	小川	small river
Sasaki	ささき	佐々木	helping tree
Satou	さとう	佐藤	helping wisteria
Shimizu	しみず	清水	clear water
Suzuki	すずき	鈴木	bell tree
Takahashi	たかはし	高橋	tall bridge
Takenaka	たけなか	竹中	inside bamboo

Tamura	たむら	田村	rice paddy village
Tanaka	たなか	田中	inner rice paddy
Tashiro	たしろ	田代	substitute field
Uchida	うちだ	内田	inner field
Watanabe	わたなべ	渡辺	neighborhood crossing
Yamada	やまだ	山田	mountain rice paddy
Yamaguchi	やまぐち	山口	mountain exit
Yamamoto	やまもと	山本	main mountain
Yamashita	やました	山下	below mountian
Yamazaki	やまざき	山崎	mountain penisula
Yoshida	よしだ	吉田	good rice paddy

Girls' Given Names

❑ **Common Japanese given names for girls**

These are some common Japanese given names for girls. The meaning of each name depends on the kanji used. The possible kanji for each name is countless.

Name	Hiragana	Possible Kanji
Ai	あい	愛
Akemi	あけみ	明美
Akiko	あきこ	明子、秋子
Asami	あさみ	麻美
Asuka	あすか	飛鳥、明日香
Aya	あや	綾、彩、亜矢
Ayaka	あやか	綾香、亜矢香
Ayako	あやこ	綾子、亜矢子
Chikako	ちかこ	千賀子、千香子
Chiyoko	ちよこ	千代子、知世子
Erika	えりか	絵里か
Etsuko	えつこ	悦子、恵津子
Haruka	はるか	春香
Hideko	ひでこ	秀子、英子
Hiroko	ひろこ	弘子、広子
Hisako	ひさこ	久子、寿子、比沙子
Hitomi	ひとみ	瞳
Kaori	かおり	香、香里
Kazuko	かずこ	和子、員子
Keiko	けいこ	恵子、啓子
Kimiko	きみこ	君子、公子
Kiyoko	きよこ	清子、喜代子
Kumiko	くみこ	久美子、組子
Kyouko	きょうこ	京子、今日子
Maiko	まいこ	麻衣子、舞子
Manami	まなみ	真奈美、愛美
Marina	まりな	真里菜
Megumi	めぐみ	恵美
Michiko	みちこ	美智子、美知子
Mika	みか	美香
Miyoko	みよこ	美代子、三代子
Momoko	ももこ	桃子
Natsumi	なつみ	奈津美、夏美

Nobuko	のぶこ	信子、伸子
Nobuyo	のぶよ	信代
Nozomi	のぞみ	希
Reiko	れいこ	玲子、礼子
Rie	りえ	理恵、利恵
Rieko	りえこ	理恵子
Rina	りな	里奈
Risa	りさ	理沙
Sachiko	さちこ	幸子
Saori	さおり	沙織、佐緒里
Satoko	さとこ	聡子、智子
Satomi	さとみ	里美
Sayoko	さよこ	佐代子、沙代子
Sayuri	さゆり	小百合
Setsuko	せつこ	節子
Shizuka	しずか	静香
Shizuko	しずこ	静子
Tomoko	ともこ	智子、友子
Youko	ようこ	洋子、陽子
Yui	ゆい	唯、由比
Yuka	ゆか	由香、由佳
Yukari	ゆかり	由香里
Yuki	ゆき	由紀
Yumiko	ゆみこ	由美子
Yuuko	ゆうこ	裕子、優子

Boys' Given Names

❑ **Common Japanese given names for boys**

These are some common Japanese given names for boys. The meaning of each name depends on the kanji used. The possible kanji for each name is countless.

Name	Hiragana	Possible Kanji
Akira	あきら	明、
Daisuke	だいすけ	大輔、大介
Hidehiro	ひでひろ	英博、英裕
Hideki	ひでき	秀樹、英樹
Hideo	ひでお	秀雄
Hideto	ひでと	秀人、英人
Hideyuki	ひでゆき	秀行、英之
Isao	いさお	功、勲
Jouji	じょうじ	譲二、譲治
Ken	けん	健、賢
Kenichi	けんいち	健一、謙一
Kenji	けんじ	健二、憲次
Makoto	まこと	誠
Masaki	まさき	正樹、雅紀
Masaru	まさる	勝
Masato	まさと	正人
Minoru	みのる	実、稔
Mitsuo	みつお	光男、光夫
Noboru	のぼる	昇、登
Osamu	おさむ	修
Ryo	りょ	力、緑
Ryouta	りょうた	良太、亮太
Satoshi	さとし	聡、覚
Shingo	しんご	信吾
Shougo	しょうご	省吾
Tadashi	ただし	忠志、正
Tatsuya	たつや	達也、達矢
Tomohide	ともひで	智英、友秀
Tsubasa	つばさ	翼
Tsutomu	つとむ	勉、務
Yoshiharu	よしはる	義春
Yoshihiro	よしひろ	義弘

English Glossary

#

0 | *rei, maru, zero* | れい、まる、ゼロ
1 | *ichi* | いち
2 | *ni* | に
3 | *san* | さん
4 | *shi, yon* | し、よん
5 | *go* | ご
6 | *roku* | ろく
7 | *shichi, nana* | しち、なな
8 | *hachi* | はち
9 | *ku, kyuu* | く、きゅう
10 | *juu* | じゅう
1 minute | *ippun* | いっぷん
10 minutes | *juppun* | じゅっぷん
11 minutes | *juuippun* | じゅういっぷん
12 minutes | *juunifun* | じゅうにふん
13 minutes | *juusanpun* | じゅうさんぷん
14 minutes | *juuyonpun* | じゅうよんぷん
15 minutes | *juugofun* | じゅうごふん
16 minutes | *juuroppun* | じゅうろっぷん
17 minutes | *juunanafun* | じゅうななふん
18 minutes | *juuhachifun* | じゅうはちふん
18 minutes | *juuhachifun* | じゅうはちふん
19 minutes | *juukyuufun* | じゅうきゅうふん
2 minutes | *nifun* | にふん
20 minutes | *nijuppun* | にじゅっぷん
25 minutes | *nijuugofun* | にじゅうごふん
3 minutes | *sanpun* | さんぷん
30 minutes | *sanjuppun* | さんじゅっぷん
35 minutes | *sanjuugofun* | さんじゅうごふん
4 minutes | *yonpun* | よんぷん
40 minutes | *yonjuppun* | よんじゅっぷん
45 minutes | *yonjuugofun* | よんじゅうごふん
5 minutes | *gofun* | ごふん
50 minutes | *gojuppun* | ごじゅっぷん
55 minutes | *gojuugofun* | ごじゅうごふん
6 minutes | *roppun* | ろっぷん
60 minutes | *rokujuppun* | ろくじゅっぷん
7 minutes | *nanafun* | ななふん
8 minutes | *hachifun* | はちふん
8 minutes | *happun* | はっぷん
9 minutes | *kyuufun* | きゅうふん

A

a girl's first name | *satoko* | さとこ
a joke | *joudan* | じょうだん
acorn | *donguri* | どんぐり
actor | *haiyuu* | はいゆう
afternoon | *gogo* | ごご
airplane | *hikouki* | ひこうき
airport | *kuukou* | くうこう
AM | *gozen* | ごぜん
America | *amerika* | アメリカ
an announcement | *happyou* | はっぴょう
ant | *ari* | あり
apple | *ringo* | りんご
April | *shigatsu* | しがつ

B

August | *hachigatsu* | はちがつ

baby | *akachan* | あかちゃん
banana | *banana* | バナナ
bank | *ginkou* | ぎんこう
basketball | *basuketto booru* | バスケットボール
bath | *ofuro* | おふろ
bear | *kuma* | くま
bed | *beddo* | ベッド
beef | *bi–fu* | ビーフ
bell, chime | *kane* | かね
bicycle | *jitensha* | じてんしゃ
big | *ookii* | おおきい
bird | *tori* | とり
birthday | *tanjoubi* | たんじょうび
black (adj.) | *kuroi* | くろい
black (noun) | *kuro* | くろ
blanket | *moufu* | もうふ
blue (adj.) | *aoi* | あおい
blue (noun) | *ao* | あお
boiled rice | *gohan* | ごはん
book | *hon* | ほん
bowl | *ochawan, chawan* | おちゃわん, ちゃわん
Brad Pitt (actor) | *Braddo Pitto* | ブラッド・ピット
bread | *pan* | パン
brown (adj.) | *chairoi* | ちゃいろい
brown (noun) | *chairo* | ちゃいろ
bullet train | *shinkansen* | しんかんせん
bus | *basu* | バス
business card | *meishi* | めいし
but | *demo* | でも

C

cake | *keeki* | ケーキ
calendar | *karenda–* | カレンダー
California | *kariforunia* | カリフォルニア
camera | *kamera* | かめら
Canada | *kanada* | カナダ
car | *kuruma* | くるま
carbonation | *tansan* | たんさん
carpet | *juutan* | じゅうたん
carrot | *ninjin* | にんじん
cat | *neko* | ねこ
cellular phone | *keitaidenwa* | けいたいでんわ
chair | *isu* | いす
change | *otsuri* | おつり
cheeseburger | *chi–zuba–ga–* | チーズバーガー
chest | *mune* | むね
chestnut | *kuri* | くり
Chicago | *shikago* | シカゴ
chicken | *chikin* | チキン
Children's Day | *kodomonohi* | こどものひ
China | *chuugoku* | ちゅうごく
chopsticks | *ohashi, hashi* | おはし、はし
Christmas | *kurisumasu* | クリスマス

cigarettes | *tabako* | たばこ
city | *~shi* | ~し
class | *jugyou* | じゅぎょう
clear | *toumei* | とうめい
clock | *tokei* | とけい
clothing, clothes | *fuku* | ふく
cockroach | *gokiburi* | ごきぶり
coffee | *ko-hi-* | コーヒー
cola | *ko-ra* | コーラ
cold | *samui* | さむい
cold drinking water | *ohiya* | おひや
cold to the touch | *tsumetai* | つめたい
color | *iro* | いろ
computer | *konpyu-ta-* | コンピューター
confusion | *konran* | こんらん
Constitution Day | *kenpoukinenbi* | けんぽうきねんび
contact | *renraku* | れんらく
contents | *mokuji* | もくじ
cow | *ushi* | うし
crab | *kani* | かに
Culture Day | *bunkanohi* | ぶんかのひ
cup; glass | *koppu* | コップ
customer, guest | *okyakusan* | おきゃくさん

D

date of birth | *seinengappi* | せいねんがっぴ
day after tomorrow | *asatte* | あさって
day before yesterday | *ototoi* | おととい
day off, break | *yasumi* | やすみ
dear, longed for | *natsukashii* | なつかしい
December | *juunigatsu* | じゅうにがつ
dessert | *deza-to* | デザート
diagonal | *naname* | ななめ
diary | *nikki* | にっき
dictionary | *jisho* | じしょ
difficult | *muzukashii* | むずかしい
dinosaur | *kyouryuu* | きょうりゅう
dislike, hate | *kirai* | きらい
doesn't taste good | *oishikunai* | おいしくない
dog | *inu* | いぬ
dollars | *doru* | ドル
down | *shita* | した
drink, drinks | *onomimono* | おのみもの
drink, drinks | *nomimono* | のみもの
duck | *ahiru* | あひる

E

ear | *mimi* | みみ
east | *higashi* | ひがし
egg | *tamago* | たまご
eight o'clock | *hachiji* | はちじ
elephant | *zou* | ぞう
eleven o'clock | *juuichiji* | じゅういちじ
explosion | *bakuhatsu* | ばくはつ
eye | *me* | め

F

face | *kao* | かお
father | *otousan* | おとうさん
February | *nigatsu* | にがつ

finger | *yubi* | ゆび
fire truck | *shoubousha* | しょうぼうしゃ
fish | *sakana* | さかな
five o'clock | *goji* | ごじ
flag | *hata* | はた
flowers | *hana* | はな
food | *tabemono* | たべもの
foot; leg | *ashi* | あし
forgotten item | *wasuremono* | わすれもの
fork | *fo-ku* | フォーク
four o'clock | *yoji* | よじ
fox | *kitsune* | きつね
free time | *hima* | ひま
French fries | *poteto* | ポテト
Friday | *kinyoubi* | きんようび
friend | *tomodachi* | ともだち
frog | *kaeru* | かえる
from now / from now on | *imakara* | いまから
frost | *shimo* | しも
fruit | *furu-tsu* | フルーツ
fruit | *kudamono* | くだもの
fun park | *yuuenchi* | ゆうえんち
futon | *futon* | ふとん

G

gambling | *gyanburu* | ギャンブル
giraffe | *kirin* | きりん
glasses | *megane* | めがね
gold | *kiniro* | きんいろ
Golden Week | *goruden wi-ku* | ゴールデンウィーク
goldfish | *kingyo* | きんぎょ
golf | *gorufu* | ゴルフ
good afternoon | *konnichiwa* | こんにちは
good bye, farewell | *sayounara* | さようなら
good morning | *ohayou gozaimasu* | おはよう ございます
good night | *oyasuminasai* | おやすみなさい
graffiti | *rakugaki* | らくがき
grandfather | *ojiisan* | おじいさん
grandmother | *obaasan* | おばあさん
grapes | *budou* | ぶどう
grass | *shibafu* | しばふ
gray | *guree* | グレー
gray | *haiiro* | はいいろ
green | *midori* | みどり
green onion | *negi* | ねぎ
green tea | *ocha* | おちゃ
gun | *teppou* | てっぽう

H

half past (:30) | *han* | はん
halibut | *hirame* | ひらめ
hallway | *rouka* | ろうか
hand | *te* | て
Harrison Ford (actor) | *Harison Fo-do* | ハリソン・フォード
head | *atama* | あたま
heat pad | *kairo* | かいろ
hello (on the phone) | *moshimoshi* | もしもし
her, she, girlfriend | *kanojo* | かのじょ
here, this place | *koko* | ここ
high pressure | *kouatsu* | こうあつ
him, he, boyfriend | *kare* | かれ

hobby | *shumi* | しゅみ
homework | *shukudai* | しゅくだい
horse | *uma* | うま
hot | *atsui* | あつい
house | *ie* | いえ
house fly | *hae* | はえ
How are you? (Are you fine?) | *genki desu ka* | げんき です か
How many cylindrical objects? | *nanbon* | なんぼん
How many round objects? | *nanko* | なんこ
How many thin and flat objects? | *nanmai* | なんまい
How many things? | *ikutsu* | いくつ
How much? | *ikura* | いくら

I

I, me (male or female) | *watashi* | わたし
I, me (males only) | *boku* | ぼく
ice cream | *aisu kuri–mu* | アイス・クリーム
I'm fine | *genki desu* | げんき です
imitation | *mane* | まね
Independence Day | *dokuritsu kinenbi* | どくりつきねんび
inside | *naka* | なか
internet | *inta–netto* | インターネット

J

January | *ichigatsu* | いちがつ
Japan | *nihon* | にほん
Japanese language | *nihongo* | にほんご
Japanese teacher | *nihongo no sensei* | にほんごの せんせい
juice | *ju–su* | ジュース
July | *shichigatsu* | しちがつ
June | *rokugatsu* | ろくがつ

K

key | *kagi* | かぎ
kindergarten | *youchien* | ようちえん
Kobe (city) | *koube* | こうべ
Korea | *kankoku* | かんこく

L

landmark | *mejirushi* | めじるし
language | *~go* | ~ご
laptop computer | *no–to pasokon* | ノートパソコン
Las Vegas | *rasu begasu* | ラスベガス
last month | *sengetsu* | せんげつ
last week | *senshuu* | せんしゅう
last year | *kyonen* | きょねん
left | *hidari* | ひだり
lemon | *remon* | レモン
lettuce | *retasu* | レタス
light blue | *mizuiro* | みずいろ
like | *suki* | すき
lion | *raion* | ライオン
liquid, fluid | *ekitai* | えきたい
lizard | *tokage* | とかげ
lobster | *robusuta–* | ロブスター
Los Angeles | *rosanzerusu* | ロサンゼルス
low pressure | *teiatsu* | ていあつ

M

magazine | *zasshi* | ざっし
March | *sangatsu* | さんがつ
married couple | *fuufu* | ふうふ
May | *gogatsu* | ごがつ
maybe | *tabun* | たぶん
meat | *niku* | にく
menu | *menyu–* | メニュー
milk | *miruku* | ミルク
mirror | *kagami* | かがみ
miso soup | *misoshiru* | みそしる
Monday | *getsuyoubi* | げつようび
money | *okane* | おかね
monkey | *saru* | さる
monster | *kaijuu* | かいじゅう
moonlight | *gekkou* | げっこう
morning | *gozen* | ごぜん
mother | *okaasan* | おかあさん
mouse | *nezumi* | ねずみ
mouth | *kuchi* | くち
movie | *eiga* | えいが
Mr., Ms., Mrs., Miss | *~san (after name)* | さん
music | *ongaku* | おんがく

N

name | *namae* | なまえ
nationality | *~jin* | ~じん
new | *atarashii* | あたらしい
New Year's Day | *gantan* | がんたん
newspaper | *shinbun* | しんぶん
next month | *raigetsu* | らいげつ
next week | *raishuu* | らいしゅう
next year | *rainen* | らいねん
nice, good | *ii、yoi* | いい 、よい
nine o'clock | *kuji* | くじ
no | *iie* | いいえ
north | *kita* | きた
nose | *hana* | はな
November | *juuichigatsu* | じゅういちがつ
now | *ima* | いま

O

October | *juugatsu* | じゅうがつ
of course | *mochiron* | もちろん
Oh! | *a!!* | あっ
old | *furui* | ふるい
old person | *roujin* | ろうじん
one o'clock | *ichiji* | いちじ
onion | *tamanegi* | たまねぎ
orange (color) | *orenji* | オレンジ
orange (fruit) | *mikan / orenji* | みかん / オレンジ
outside | *soto* | そと
over there, that place over there | *asoko* | あそこ

P

panda | *panda* | パンダ
pants | *zubon* | ズボン
paper | *kami* | かみ
part-time job | *arubaito* | アルバイト
party | *pa–ti–* | パーティー

patrol car | *patoka–* | パトカー
PC (computer) | *pasokon* | パソコン
peach | *momo* | もも
pen | *pen* | ペン
pencil | *enpitsu* | えんぴつ
pepper | *koshou* | こしょう
pig | *buta* | ぶた
pigeon; dove | *hato* | はと
pillow | *makura* | まくら
pink | *pinku* | ピンク
pizza | *piza* | ピザ
plate | *(o) sara* | (お) さら
PM | *gogo* | ごご
potato | *poteto* | ポテト
prefecture | *~ken* | ~けん
present, gift | *purezento* | プレゼント
purple | *murasaki* | むらさき

R

rabbit | *usagi* | うさぎ
radish | *daikon* | だいこん
rare (adj.) | *mezurashii* | めずらしい
really dislike, really hate | *daikirai* | だいきらい
really like, like a lot | *daisuki* | だいすき
reason | *riyuu* | りゆう
red | *aka* | あか
red | *akai* | あかい
refrigerator | *reizouko* | れいぞうこ
region | *chiiki* | ちいき
restaurant | *resutoran* | レストラン
restroom | *otearai* | おてあらい
right | *migi* | みぎ
rise in price | *neage* | ねあげ
rock | *iwa* | いわ
roof | *yane* | やね
rumor | *uwasa* | うわさ

S

salt | *shio* | しお
sand box | *sunaba* | すなば
sandwich | *sandoicchi* | サンドイッチ
sandwich (short vers.) | *sando* | サンド
Saturday | *doyoubi* | どようび
school | *gakkou* | がっこう
screw | *neji* | ねじ
September | *kugatsu* | くがつ
seven o'clock | *shichiji* | しちじ
sheep | *hitsuji* | ひつじ
shiny | *pikapika* | ぴかぴか
ship; boat | *fune* | ふね
shoe | *kutsu* | くつ
shopping | *kaimono* | かいもの
shrimp | *ebi* | えび
sightseeing | *kankou* | かんこう
silver | *giniro* | ぎんいろ
six o'clock | *rokuji* | ろくじ
small | *chiisai* | ちいさい
snack, snacks | *okashi* | おかし
snake | *hebi* | へび
soap | *sekken* | せっけん
soccer | *sakka–* | サッカー

soldier | *heitai* | へいたい
south | *minami* | みなみ
spaghetti | *supagetti–* | スパゲッティー
spring | *haru* | はる
spoon | *supu–n* | スプーン
Sports Day | *taiikunohi* | たいいくのひ
squid | *ika* | いか
star (in the sky) | *hoshi* | ほし
state | *~shuu* | ~しゅう
storm | *arashi* | あらし
strawberry | *ichigo* | いちご
Sunday | *nichiyoubi* | にちようび
surgery | *shujutsu* | しゅじゅつ
sushi | *sushi* | すし

T

tastes good, delicious | *oishii* | おいしい
teacher | *sensei* | せんせい
telephone | *denwa* | でんわ
television | *terebi* | テレビ
ten o'clock | *juuji* | じゅうじ
thank you, thanks | *arigatou* | ありがとう
that one (out of 2) | *socchi* | そっち
that one (out of 3 or more) | *sore* | それ
that one over there (out of 2) | *acchi* | あっち
that one over there (out of 3 or more) | *are* | あれ
That's great. / That's awesome. | *sugoi desu ne* | すごい です ね
there, that place | *soko* | そこ
thief | *dorobou* | どろぼう
this month | *kongetsu* | こんげつ
this one (out of 2) | *kocchi* | こっち
this one (out of 3 or more) | *kore* | これ
this week | *konshuu* | こんしゅう
this year | *kotoshi* | ことし
three o'clock | *sanji* | さんじ
thunder; lightning | *kaminari* | かみなり
Thursday | *mokuyoubi* | もくようび
tickets | *chiketto* | チケット
to come | *kuru* | くる
to drink water | *mizuwo nomu* | みずを のむ
to go | *iku* | いく
to move an item | *hakobu* | はこぶ
to return | *kaeru* | かえる
to stand out | *medatsu* | めだつ
to understand, know | *wakaru* | わかる
to undress | *nugu* | ぬぐ
today | *kyou* | きょう
toilet | *toire* | トイレ
tomato | *tomato* | トマト
tomorrow | *ashita* | あした
tooth, teeth | *ha* | は
toothbrush | *haburashi* | ハブラシ
tortoise; turtle | *kame* | かめ
towel | *taoru* | タオル
train | *densha* | でんしゃ
trash can | *gomibako* | ごみばこ
travel | *ryokou* | りょこう
tricycle | *sanrinsha* | さんりんしゃ
Tuesday | *kayoubi* | かようび
tuna | *maguro* | まぐろ
twelve o'clock | *juuniji* | じゅうにじ

two o'clock | *niji* | にじ

U

umbrella | *kasa* | かさ
up | *ue* | うえ

V

vegetable | *yasai* | やさい
violence | *ranbou* | らんぼう

W

want | *hoshii* | ほしい
warm, luke warm | *nurui* | ぬるい
water | *mizu* | みず
watermelon | *suika* | すいか
Wednesday | *suiyoubi* | すいようび
Well, then~ | *ja, jaa* | じゃ、じゃあ
west | *nishi* | にし
what color? | *nani iro* | なにいろ
what day of the month? | *nannichi* | なんにち
what day of the week? | *nanyoubi* | なんようび
what language? | *nanigo* | なにご
what month? | *nangatsu* | なんがつ
what nationality? | *nanijin* | なにじん
what time? | *nanji* | なんじ
what year? | *nannen* | なんねん
what? | *nani* | なに
what?, which?, what kind of? | *nanno ?* | なんの？
when? | *itsu* | いつ
where?, what place? | *doko* | どこ
which one (three or more) | *dore* | どれ
which one (two items) | *docchi* | どっち
white (adj.) | *shiroi* | しろい
white (noun) | *shiro* | しろ
who? | *dare* | だれ
wife | *oyomesan* | およめさん
window | *mado* | まど
wisdom | *chie* | ちえ
work | *shigoto* | しごと
wrinkles | *shiwa* | しわ

Y

yellow (adj.) | *kiiroi* | きいろい
yellow (noun) | *kiiro* | きいろ
yen | *en* | えん
yes | *hai* | はい
yesterday | *kinou* | きのう
Yoshio - common boy's first name | *Yoshio* | よしお
you | *anata* | あなた

Ro–maji Glossary

A

a!! / Oh!あっ！
acchi / that one over there (out of 2)あっち
ahiru / duckあひる
aisu kuri–mu | ice creamアイス・クリーム
aka / redあか
akachan | babyあかちゃん
akai / redあかい
amerika | Americaアメリカ
anata / youあなた
ao / blue (noun)あお
aoi / blue (adj.)あおい
arashi / a stormあらし
are / that one over there (out of 3 or more)あれ
ari / antあり
arigatou | thank you, thanksありがとう
arubaito | part-time jobアルバイト
asatte / day after tomorrowあさって
ashi / foot; legあし
ashita / tomorrowあした
asoko / over there, that place over thereあそこ
atama / headあたま
atarashii | newあたらしい
atsui / hotあつい

B

bakuhatsu | explosionばくはつ
banana | bananaバナナ
basu / busバス
basuketto booru | basketballバスケットボール
beddo / bedベッド
bi–fu | beefビーフ
boku / I, me (males only)ぼく
Braddo Pitto | Brad Pitt (actor)ブラッド・ピット
budou | grapesぶどう
bunkanohi | Culture Dayぶんかのひ
buta / pigぶた

C

chairo / brown (noun)ちゃいろ
chairoi / brown (adj.)ちゃいろい
chawan / bowlちゃわん
chie / wisdomちえ
chiiki / regionちいき
chiisai / smallちいさい
chiketto | ticketsチケット
chikin / chickenチキン
chi–zuba–ga– | cheeseburgerチーズバーガー
chuugoku | Chinaちゅうごく

D

daikirai | really dislike, really hate | だいきらい
daikon | radish | だいこん

D (continued)

dare / who? | だれ
demo / but | でも
densha | train | でんしゃ
denwa | telephone | でんわ
deza–to | dessert | デザート
docchi / which one (two items) | どっち
doko / where?, what place? | どこ
dokuritsu kinenbi | Independence Day | どくりつきねんび
donguri | acorn | どんぐり
dore / which one (three or more) | どれ
dorobou | a thief | どろぼう
doru / dollars | ドル
doyoubi | Saturday | どようび

E

ebi / shrimp | えび
eiga / movie | えいが
ekitai / liquid, fluid | えきたい
en / yen | えん
enpitsu | pencil | えんぴつ

F

fo–ku / fork | フォーク
fuku / clothing, clothes | ふく
fune / ship; boat | ふね
furui / old | ふるい
furu–tsu | fruit | フルーツ
futon / futon | ふとん
fuufu / married couple | ふうふ

G

gakkou | school | がっこう
gantan | New Year's Day | がんたん
gekkou | moonlight | げっこう
genki desu | I'm fine | げんき です
genki desu ka | How are you? (Are you fine?) | げんき です か
getsuyoubi | Monday | げつようび
giniro / silver | ぎんいろ
ginkou | bank | ぎんこう
go / ~ language | ~ご
go / 5 | ご
gofun / 5 minutes | ごふん
gogatsu | May | ごがつ
gogo / PM (also means afternoon) | ごご
gohan / boiled rice | ごはん
goji / five o'clock | ごじ
gojuppun | 50 minutes | ごじゅっぷん
gojuugofun | 55 minutes | ごじゅうごふん
gokiburi | cockroach | ごきぶり
gomibako | trash can | ごみばこ

goruden wi–ku | Golden Week | ゴールデンウィーク
gorufu | golf | ゴルフ
gozen | AM (also means morning) | ごぜん
guree | gray | グレー
gyanburu | gambling | ギャンブル

H

ha | tooth, teeth | は
haburashi | toothbrush | ハブラシ
hachi | 8 | はち
hachifun | 8 minutes | はちふん
hachigatsu | August | はちがつ
hachiji | eight o'clock | はちじ
hae | house fly | はえ
hai | yes | はい
haiiro | gray | はいいろ
haiyuu | actor | はいゆう
hakobu | to move an item | はこぶ
han | half past (:30) | はん
hana | flowers | はな
hana | nose | はな
happun | 8 minutes | はっぷん
happyou | an announcement | はっぴょう
Harison Fo–do | Harrison Ford (actor) | ハリソン・フォード
haru | spring | はる
hashi | chopsticks | はし
hata | flag | はた
hato | pigeon; dove | はと
hebi | snake | へび
heitai | soldier | へいたい
hidari | left | ひだり
higashi | east | ひがし
hikouki | airplane | ひこうき
hima | free time | ひま
hirame | halibut | ひらめ
hitsuji | sheep | ひつじ
hon | book | ほん
hoshi | star (in the sky) | ほし
hoshii | want | ほしい

I

ichi | 1 | いち
ichigatsu | January | いちがつ
ichigo | strawberry | いちご
ichiji | one o'clock | いちじ
ie | house | いえ
ii、yoi | nice, good | いい 、よい
iie | no | いいえ
ika | squid | いか
iku | to go | いく
ikura | How much? | いくら
ikutsu | How many things? | いくつ
ima | now | いま
imakara | from now / from now on | いまから
inta–netto | internet | インターネット
inu | dog | いぬ
ippun | 1 minute | いっぷん
iro | color | いろ
isu | chair | いす
itsu | when? | いつ

iwa | rock | いわ

J

ja, jaa | well, then~ | じゃ、じゃあ
jin | ~ nationality | ~じん
jisho | dictionary | じしょ
jitensha | bicycle | じてんしゃ
joudan | a joke | じょうだん
jugyou | class | じゅぎょう
juppun | 10 minutes | じゅっぷん
ju–su | juice | ジュース
juu | 10 | じゅう
juugatsu | October | じゅうがつ
juugofun | 15 minutes | じゅうごふん
juuhachifun | 18 minutes | じゅうはちふん
juuhachifun | 18 minutes | じゅうはちふん
juuichigatsu | November | じゅういちがつ
juuichiji | eleven o'clock | じゅういちじ
juuippun | 11 minutes | じゅういっぷん
juuji | ten o'clock | じゅうじ
juukyuufun | 19 minutes | じゅうきゅうふん
juunanafun | 17 minutes | じゅうななふん
juunifun | 12 minutes | じゅうにふん
juunigatsu | December | じゅうにがつ
juuniji | twelve o'clock | じゅうにじ
juuroppun | 16 minutes | じゅうろっぷん
juusanpun | 13 minutes | じゅうさんぷん
juutan | carpet | じゅうたん
juuyonpun | 14 minutes | じゅうよんぷん

K

kaeru | frog | かえる
kaeru | to return | かえる
kagami | mirror | かがみ
kagi | key | かぎ
kaijuu | a monster | かいじゅう
kaimono | shopping | かいもの
kairo | heat pad | かいろ
kame | tortoise; turtle | かめ
kamera | camera | かめら
kami | paper | かみ
kaminari | thunder; lightning | かみなり
kanada | Canada | カナダ
kane | bell, chime | かね
kani | crab | かに
kankoku | Korea | かんこく
kankou | sightseeing | かんこう
kanojo | her, she, girlfriend | かのじょ
kao | face | かお
kare | him, he, boyfriend | かれ
karenda– | calendar | カレンダー
kariforunia | California | カリフォルニア
kasa | umbrella | かさ
kayoubi | Tuesday | かようび
keeki | cake | ケーキ
keitaidenwa | cellular phone | けいたいでんわ
ken | ~ Prefecture | ~けん
kenpoukinenbi | Constitution Day | けんぽうきねんび
kiiro | yellow (noun) | きいろ
kiiroi | yellow (adj.) | きいろい
kingyo | goldfish | きんぎょ

kiniro / gold | きんいろ
kinou / yesterday | きのう
kinyoubi | Friday | きんようび
kirai / dislike, hate | きらい
kirin / giraffe | きりん
kita / north | きた
kitsune | fox | きつね
kocchi / this one (out of 2) | こっち
kodomonohi | Children's Day | こどものひ
ko–hi– / coffee | コーヒー
koko / here, this place | ここ
kongetsu | this month | こんげつ
konnichiwa | good afternoon | こんにちは
konpyu–ta– | computer | コンピューター
konran | confusion | こんらん
konshuu | this week | こんしゅう
koppu | cup; glass | コップ
ko–ra | cola | コーラ
kore / this one (out of 3 or more) | これ
koshou | pepper | こしょう
kotoshi | this year | ことし
kouatsu | high pressure | こうあつ
koube | Kobe (city) | こうべ
ku / 9 | く
kuchi / mouth | くち
kudamono | fruit | くだもの
kugatsu | September | くがつ
kuji / nine o'clock | くじ
kuma / bear | くま
kuri / chestnut | くり
kurisumasu | Christmas | クリスマス
kuro / black (noun) | くろ
kuroi | black (adj.) | くろい
kuru | to come | くる
kuruma | car | くるま
kutsu | shoe | くつ
kuukou | airport | くうこう
kyonen | last year | きょねん
kyou / today | きょう
kyouryuu | dinosaur | きょうりゅう
kyuu / 9 | きゅう
kyuufun | 9 minutes | きゅうふん

M

mado / window | まど
maguro | tuna | まぐろ
makura | pillow | まくら
mane / imitation | まね
maru / circle, zero | まる
me / eye | め
medatsu | to stand out | めだつ
megane | glasses | めがね
meishi | business card | めいし
mejirushi | landmark | めじるし
menyu– | menu | メニュー
mezurashii | rare (adj.) | めずらしい
midori | green | みどり
migi | right | みぎ
mikan / orenji | orange (fruit) | みかん / オレンジ

mimi / ear | みみ
minami | south | みなみ
miruku | milk | ミルク
misoshiru | miso soup | みそしる
mizu / water | みず
mizuiro | light blue | みずいろ
mizuwo nomu | to drink water | みずを のむ
mochiron | of course | もちろん
mokuji | contents | もくじ
mokuyoubi | Thursday | もくようび
momo / peach | もも
moshimoshi | hello (on the phone) | もしもし
moufu | blanket | もうふ
mune / chest | むね
murasaki | purple | むらさき
muzukashii | difficult | むずかしい

N

naka / inside | なか
namae | name | なまえ
nana / 7 | なな
nanafun | 7 minutes | ななふん
naname | diagonal | ななめ
nanbon | How many cylindrical objects? | なんぼん
nangatsu | what month? | なんがつ
nani / what? | なに
nani iro | what color? | なにいろ
nanigo | what language? | なにご
nanijin | what nationality? | なにじん
nanji | what time? | なんじ
nanko | How many round objects? | なんこ
nanmai | How many thin and flat objects? | なんまい
nannen | what year? | なんねん
nannichi | what day of the month? | なんにち
nanno ? | what? which? what kind of? | なんの ?
nanyoubi | what day of the week? | なんようび
natsukashii | dear, longed for | なつかしい
neage / a rise in price | ねあげ
negi / green onion | ねぎ
neji / a screw | ねじ
neko / cat | ねこ
nezumi | mouse | ねずみ
ni / 2 | に
nichiyoubi | Sunday | にちようび
nifun | 2 minutes | にふん
nigatsu | February | にがつ
nihon / Japan | にほん
nihongo | Japanese language | にほんご
nihongo no sensei | Japanese teacher | にほんごの せんせい
niji / two o'clock | にじ
nijuppun | 20 minutes | にじゅっぷん
nijuugofun | 25 minutes | にじゅうごふん
nikki / diary | にっき
niku / meat | にく
ninjin / carrot | にんじん
nishi / west | にし
nomimono | a drink, drinks | のみもの
no–to pasokon | laptop computer | ノートパソコン

nugu / to undress | ぬぐ
nurui / warm, luke warm | ぬるい

O

obaasan | grandmother | おばあさん
ocha / green tea | おちゃ
ochawan | bowl | おちゃわん
ofuro | bath | おふろ
ohashi | chopsticks | おはし
ohayou gozaimasu | good morning | おはよう ございます
ohiya / cold drinking water | おひや
oishii / tastes good, delicious | おいしい
oishikunai / doesn't taste good | おいしくない
ojiisan / grandfather | おじいさん
okaasan | mother | おかあさん
okane / money | おかね
okashi / a snack | おかし
okyakusan | a customer or guest | おきゃくさん
ongaku | music | おんがく
onomimono | a drink | おのみもの
ookii | big | おおきい
orenji / orange (color) | オレンジ
osara / plate | おさら
otearai | restroom | おてあらい
ototoi / day before yesterday | おととい
otousan | father | おとうさん
otsuri / change | おつり
oyasuminasai | good night | おやすみなさい
oyomesan | wife | およめさん

P

pan / bread | パン
panda / panda | パンダ
pasokon | PC (computer) | パソコン
pa-ti- / party | パーティー
patoka- | patrol car | パトカー
pen / pen | ペン
pikapika | shiny | ぴかぴか
pinku / pink | ピンク
piza / pizza | ピザ
poteto / French fries | ポテト
poteto / potato | ポテト
purezento | present, gift | プレゼント

R

raigetsu | next month | らいげつ
rainen | next year | らいねん
raion / lion | ライオン
raishuu | next week | らいしゅう
rakugaki | graffiti | らくがき
ranbou | violence | らんぼう
rasu begasu | Las Vegas | ラスベガス
rei / zero, 0 | れい
reizouko | refrigerator | れいぞうこ
remon | lemon | レモン
renraku | contact | れんらく
resutoran | restaurant | レストラン
retasu / lettuce | レタス
ringo / apple | りんご

riyuu / a reason | りゆう
robusuta- | lobster | ロブスター
roku | 6 | ろく
rokugatsu | June | ろくがつ
rokuji | six o'clock | ろくじ
rokujuppun | 60 minutes | ろくじゅっぷん
roppun | 6 minutes | ろっぷん
rosanzerusu | Los Angeles | ロサンゼルス
roujin / old person | ろうじん
rouka / hallway | ろうか
ryokou | travel | りょこう

S

sakana | fish | さかな
sakka- | soccer | サッカー
samui / cold | さむい
san / 3 | さん
san (after name) | Mr., Ms., Mrs., Miss | さん
sando / sandwich (short vers.) | サンド
sandoicchi | sandwich | サンドイッチ
sangatsu | March | さんがつ
sanji / three o'clock | さんじ
sanjuppun | 30 minutes | さんじゅっぷん
sanjuugofun | 35 minutes | さんじゅうごふん
sanpun | 3 minutes | さんぷん
sanrinsha | tricycle | さんりんしゃ
sara / plate | さら
saru / monkey | さる
satoko / a girl's first name | さとこ
sayounara | good bye, farewell | さようなら
seinengappi | date of birth | せいねんがっぴ
sekken | soap | せっけん
sengetsu | last month | せんげつ
sensei / teacher | せんせい
senshuu | last week | せんしゅう
shi / ~ City | ~し
shi / 4 | し
shibafu | grass | しばふ
shichi | 7 | しち
shichigatsu | July | しちがつ
shichiji | seven o'clock | しちじ
shigatsu | April | しがつ
shigoto | work | しごと
shikago | Chicago | シカゴ
shimo / frost | しも
shinbun | newspaper | しんぶん
shinkansen | bullet train | しんかんせん
shio / salt | しお
shiro / white | しろ
shiroi / white | しろい
shita / down | した
shiwa / wrinkles | しわ
shoubousha | fire truck | しょうぼうしゃ
shujutsu | surgery | しゅじゅつ
shukudai | homework | しゅくだい
shumi / hobby | しゅみ
shuu / ~ State | ~しゅう
socchi | that one (out of 2) | そっち
soko | there, that place | そこ
sore / that one (out of 3 or more) | それ
soto / outside | そと

sugoi desu ne | That's great. / That's awesome. | すごい です ね
suika / watermelon | すいか
suiyoubi | Wednesday | すいようび
suki / like | すき
sunaba | sand box | すなば
supagetti– | spaghetti | スパゲッティー
supu–n | spoon | スプーン
sushi / sushi | すし

T
tabako | cigarettes | たばこ
tabemono | food | たべもの
tabun / maybe | たぶん
taiikunohi | Sports Day | たいいくのひ
tamago | egg | たまご
tamanegi | onion | たまねぎ
tanjoubi | birthday | たんじょうび
tansan / carbonation | たんさん
taoru / towel | タオル
te / hand | て
teiatsu / low pressure | ていあつ
teppou | gun | てっぽう
terebi / television | テレビ
toire / toilet | トイレ
tokage | lizard | とかげ
tokei / clock | とけい
tomato | tomato | トマト
tomodachi | friend | ともだち
tori / bird | とり
toumei | clear | とうめい
tsumetai | cold to the touch | つめたい

U
ue / up | うえ
uma / horse | うま
usagi / rabbit | うさぎ
ushi / cow | うし
uwasa / a rumor | うわさ
W
wakaru | to understand, know | わかる
wasuremono | forgotten item | わすれもの
watashi | I, me (male or female) | わたし

Y
yane / roof | やね
yasai / vegetable | やさい
yasumi | day off, break | やすみ
yoji / four o'clock | よじ
yon / 4 | よん
yonjuppun | 40 minutes | よんじゅっぷん
yonjuugofun | 45 minutes | よんじゅうごふん
yonpun | 4 minutes | よんぷん
Yoshio | a common boy's first name | よしお
youchien | kindergarten | ようちえん
yubi / finger | ゆび
yuuenchi | fun park | ゆうえんち

Z
zasshi / magazine | ざっし
zero / zero, 0 | ゼロ
zou / elephant | ぞう
zubon / pants | ズボン

Kana Glossary

あ

アイス・クリーム | ice cream | *aisu kuri–mu*
あお | blue (noun) | *ao*
あおい | blue (adj.) | *aoi*
あか | red | *aka*
あかい | red | *akai*
あかちゃん | baby | *akachan*
あさって | day after tomorrow | *asatte*
あし | foot; leg | *ashi*
あした | tomorrow | *ashita*
あそこ | over there, that place over there | *asoko*
あたま | head | *atama*
あたらしい | new | *atarashii*
あっ！ | Oh! | *a!!*
あつい | hot | *atsui*
あっち | that one over there (out of 2) | *acchi*
あなた | you | *anata*
あひる | duck | *ahiru*
アメリカ | America | *amerika*
あらし | a storm | *arashi*
あり | ant | *ari*
ありがとう | thank you, thanks | *arigatou*
アルバイト | part-time job | *arubaito*
あれ | that one over there (out of 3 or more) | *are*

い

いい 、よい | nice, good | *ii, yoi*
いいえ | no | *iie* *
いえ | house | *ie*
いか | squid | *ika*
いく | to go | *iku*
いくつ | How many things? | *ikutsu*
いくら | How much? | *ikura*
いす | chair | *isu*
いち | 1 | *ichi*
いちがつ | January | *ichigatsu*
いちご | strawberry | *ichigo*
いちじ | one o'clock | *ichiji*
いつ | when? | *itsu*
いっぷん | 1 minute | *ippun*
いぬ | dog | *inu*
いま | now | *ima*
いまから | from now / from now on | *imakara*
いろ | color | *iro*
いわ | rock | *iwa*
インターネット | internet | *inta–netto*

う

うえ | up | *ue*
うさぎ | rabbit | *usagi*
うし | cow | *ushi*
うま | horse | *uma*
うわさ | a rumor | *uwasa*

え

えいが | movie | *eiga*
えきたい | liquid, fluid | *ekitai*
えび | shrimp | *ebi*
えん | yen | *en*
えんぴつ | pencil | *enpitsu*

お

おいしい | tastes good, delicious | *oishii*
おいしくない | doesn't taste good | *oishikunai*
おおきい | big | *ookii*
おかあさん | mother | *okaasan*
おかし | a snack | *okashi*
おかね | money | *okane*
おきゃくさん | a customer or guest | *okyakusan*
おさら | plate | *osara*
おじいさん | grandfather | *ojiisan*
おちゃ | green tea | *ocha*
おちゃわん | bowl | *ochawan*
おつり | change | *otsuri*
おてあらい | restroom | *otearai*
おとうさん | father | *otousan*
おととい | day before yesterday | *ototoi*
おのみもの | a drink | *onomimono*
おばあさん | grandmother | *obaasan*
おはし | chopsticks | *ohashi*
おはよう ございます | good morning | *ohayou gozaimasu*
おひや | cold drinking water | *ohiya*
おふろ | bath | *ofuro*
おやすみなさい | good night | *oyasuminasai*
およめさん | wife | *oyomesan*
オレンジ | orange (color) | *orenji*
おんがく | music | *ongaku*

か

かいじゅう | a monster | *kaijuu*
かいもの | shopping | *kaimono*
かいろ | heat pad | *kairo*
かえる | frog | *kaeru*
かえる | to return | *kaeru*
かお | face | *kao*
かがみ | mirror | *kagami*
かぎ | key | *kagi*
かさ | umbrella | *kasa*
がっこう | school | *gakkou*
カナダ | Canada | *kanada*
かに | crab | *kani*
かね | bell, chime | *kane*
かのじょ | her, she, girlfriend | *kanojo*
かみ | paper | *kami*
かみなり | thunder; lightning | *kaminari*
かめ | tortoise; turtle | *kame*
かめら | camera | *kamera*
かようび | Tuesday | *kayoubi*
カリフォルニア | California | *kariforunia*
かれ | him, he, boyfriend | *kare*
カレンダー | calendar | *karenda–*

かんこう | sightseeing | *kankou*
かんこく | Korea | *kankoku*
がんたん | New Year's Day | *gantan*

き

きいろ | yellow (noun) | *kiiro*
きいろい | yellow (adj.) | *kiiroi*
きた | north | *kita*
きつね | fox | *kitsune*
きのう | yesterday | *kinou*
ギャンブル | gambling | *gyanburu*
きゅう | 9 | *kyuu*
きゅうふん | 9 minutes | *kyuufun*
きょう | today | *kyou*
きょうりゅう | dinosaur | *kyouryuu*
きょねん | last year | *kyonen*
きらい | dislike, hate | *kirai*
きりん | giraffe | *kirin*
きんいろ | gold | *kiniro*
ぎんいろ | silver | *giniro*
きんぎょ | goldfish | *kingyo*
ぎんこう | bank | *ginkou*
きんようび | Friday | *kinyoubi*

く

く | 9 | *ku*
くうこう | airport | *kuukou*
くがつ | September | *kugatsu*
くじ | nine o'clock | *kuji*
くだもの | fruit | *kudamono*
くち | mouth | *kuchi*
くつ | shoe | *kutsu*
くま | bear | *kuma*
くり | chestnut | *kuri*
クリスマス | Christmas | *kurisumasu*
くる | to come | *kuru*
くるま | car | *kuruma*
グレー | gray | *guree*
くろ | black (noun) | *kuro*
くろい | black (adj.) | *kuroi*

け

けいたいでんわ | cellular phone | *keitaidenwa*
ケーキ | cake | *keeki*
げっこう | moonlight | *gekkou*
げつようび | Monday | *getsuyoubi*
けん | ~ Prefecture | *~ken*
げんき です | I'm fine | *genki desu*
げんき です か | How are you? (Are you fine?) | *genki desu ka*
けんぽうきねんび | Constitution Day | *kenpoukinenbi*

こ

ご | ~ language | *~go*
ご | 5 | *go*
こうあつ | high pressure | *kouatsu*
こうべ | Kobe (city) | *koube*
コーヒー | coffee | *ko–hi–*
コーラ | cola | *ko–ra*
ゴールデンウィーク | Golden Week | *goruden wi–ku*

ごがつ | May | *gogatsu*
ごきぶり | cockroach | *gokiburi*
ここ | here, this place | *koko*
ごご | PM (also means afternoon) | *gogo*
ごじ | five o'clock | *goji*
ごじゅうごふん | 55 minutes | *gojuugofun*
ごじゅっぷん | 50 minutes | *gojuppun*
こしょう | pepper | *koshou*
ごぜん | AM (also means morning) | *gozen*
こっち | this one (out of 2) | *kocchi*
コップ | cup; glass | *koppu*
ことし | this year | *kotoshi*
こどものひ | Children's Day | *kodomonohi*
ごはん | boiled rice | *gohan*
ごふん | 5 minutes | *gofun*
ごみばこ | trash can | *gomibako*
ゴルフ | golf | *gorufu*
これ | this one (out of 3 or more) | *kore*
こんげつ | this month | *kongetsu*
こんしゅう | this week | *konshuu*
こんにちは | good afternoon | *konnichiwa*
コンピューター | computer | *konpyu–ta–*
こんらん | confusion | *konran*

さ

さかな | fish | *sakana*
サッカー | soccer | *sakka–*
ざっし | magazine | *zasshi*
さとこ | a girl's first name | *satoko*
さむい | cold | *samui*
さようなら | good bye, farewell | *sayounara*
さら | plate | *sara*
さる | monkey | *saru*
さん | 3 | *san*
さん | Mr., Ms., Mrs., Miss | *san (after name)*
さんがつ | March | *sangatsu*
さんじ | three o'clock | *sanji*
さんじゅうごふん | 35 minutes | *sanjuugofun*
さんじゅっぷん | 30 minutes | *sanjuppun*
サンド | sandwich (short vers.) | *sando*
サンドイッチ | sandwich | *sandoicchi*
さんぷん | 3 minutes | *sanpun*
さんりんしゃ | tricycle | *sanrinsha*

し

し | ~ City | *~shi*
し | 4 | *shi*
しお | salt | *shio*
シカゴ | Chicago | *shikago*
しがつ | April | *shigatsu*
しごと | work | *shigoto*
じしょ | dictionary | *jisho*
した | down | *shita*
しち | 7 | *shichi*
しちがつ | July | *shichigatsu*
しちじ | seven o'clock | *shichiji*
じてんしゃ | bicycle | *jitensha*
しばふ | grass | *shibafu*
しも | frost | *shimo*
じゃ、じゃあ | well, then~ | *ja, jaa*
しゅう | ~ State | *~shuu*

じゅう | 10 | *juu*
じゅういちがつ | November | *juuichigatsu*
じゅういちじ | eleven o'clock | *juuichiji*
じゅういっぷん | 11 minutes | *juuippun*
じゅうがつ | October | *juugatsu*
じゅうきゅうふん | 19 minutes | *juukyuufun*
じゅうごふん | 15 minutes | *juugofun*
じゅうさんぷん | 13 minutes | *juusanpun*
じゅうじ | ten o'clock | *juuji*
ジュース | juice | *ju–su*
じゅうたん | carpet | *juutan*
じゅうななふん | 17 minutes | *juunanafun*
じゅうにがつ | December | *juunigatsu*
じゅうにじ | twelve o'clock | *juuniji*
じゅうにふん | 12 minutes | *juunifun*
じゅうはちふん | 18 minutes | *juuhachifun*
じゅうはちふん | 18 minutes | *juuhachifun*
じゅうよんぷん | 14 minutes | *juuyonpun*
じゅうろっぷん | 16 minutes | *juuroppun*
じゅぎょう | class | *jugyou*
しゅくだい | homework | *shukudai*
しゅじゅつ | surgery | *shujutsu*
じゅっぷん | 10 minutes | *juppun*
しゅみ | hobby | *shumi*
じょうだん | a joke | *joudan*
しょうぼうしゃ | fire truck | *shoubousha*
しろ | white | *shiro*
しろい | white | *shiroi*
しわ | wrinkles | *shiwa*
じん | ~ nationality | *~jin*
しんかんせん | bullet train | *shinkansen*
しんぶん | newspaper | *shinbun*

す

すいか | watermelon | *suika*
すいようび | Wednesday | *suiyoubi*
すき | like | *suki*
すごい です ね | That's great. / That's awesome. | *sugoi desu ne*
すし | sushi | *sushi*
すなば | sand box | *sunaba*
スパゲッティー | spaghetti | *supagetti–*
スプーン | spoon | *supu–n*
ズボン | pants | *zubon*

せ

せいねんがっぴ | date of birth | *seinengappi*
せっけん | soap | *sekken*
ゼロ | zero, 0 | *zero*
せんげつ | last month | *sengetsu*
せんしゅう | last week | *senshuu*
せんせい | teacher | *sensei*

そ

ぞう | elephant | *zou*
そこ | there, that place | *soko*
そっち | that one (out of 2) | *socchi*
そと | outside | *soto*
それ | that one (out of 3 or more) | *sore*

た

たいいくのひ | Sports Day | *taiikunohi*
だいきらい | really dislike, really hate | *daikirai*
だいこん | radish | *daikon*
だいすき | really like, like a lot | *daisuki*
タオル | towel | *taoru*
たばこ | cigarettes | *tabako*
たぶん | maybe | *tabun*
たべもの | food | *tabemono*
たまご | egg | *tamago*
たまねぎ | onion | *tamanegi*
だれ | who? | *dare*
たんさん | carbonation | *tansan*
たんじょうび | birthday | *tanjoubi*

ち

ちいき | region | *chiiki*
ちいさい | small | *chiisai*
チーズバーガー | cheeseburger | *chi–zuba–ga–*
ちえ | wisdom | *chie*
チキン | chicken | *chikin*
チケット | tickets | *chiketto*
ちゃいろ | brown (noun) | *chairo*
ちゃいろい | brown (adj.) | *chairoi*
ちゃわん | bowl | *chawan*
ちゅうごく | China | *chuugoku*

つ

つめたい | cold to the touch | *tsumetai*

て

て | hand | *te*
ていあつ | low pressure | *teiatsu*
デザート | dessert | *deza–to*
てっぽう | gun | *teppou*
でも | but | *demo*
テレビ | television | *terebi*
でんしゃ | train | *densha*
でんわ | telephone | *denwa*

と

トイレ | toilet | *toire*
とうめい | clear | *toumei*
とかげ | lizard | *tokage*
どくりつきねんび | Independence Day | *dokuritsu kinenbi*
とけい | clock | *tokei*
どこ | where?, what place? | *doko*
どっち | which one (two items) | *docchi*
トマト | tomato | *tomato*
ともだち | friend | *tomodachi*
どようび | Saturday | *doyoubi*
とり | bird | *tori*
ドル | dollars | *doru*
どれ | which one (three or more) | *dore*
どろぼう | a thief | *dorobou*
どんぐり | acorn | *donguri*

な

なか | inside | *naka*

なつかしい | dear, longed for | *natsukashii*
なな | 7 | *nana*
ななふん | 7 minutes | *nanafun*
ななめ | diagonal | *naname*
なに | what? | *nani*
なにいろ | what color? | *nani iro*
なにご | what language? | *nanigo*
なにじん | what nationality? | *nanijin*
なまえ | name | *namae*
なんがつ | what month? | *nangatsu*
なんこ | How many round objects? | *nanko*
なんじ | what time? | *nanji*
なんにち | what day of the month? | *nannichi*
なんねん | what year? | *nannen*
なんの？ | what? which? what kind of? | *nanno ?*
なんぼん | How many cylindrical objects? | *nanbon*
なんまい | How many thin and flat objects? | *nanmai*
なんようび | what day of the week? | *nanyoubi*

に

に | 2 | *ni*
にがつ | February | *nigatsu*
にく | meat | *niku*
にし | west | *nishi*
にじ | two o'clock | *niji*
にじゅうごふん | 25 minutes | *nijuugofun*
にじゅっぷん | 20 minutes | *nijuppun*
にちようび | Sunday | *nichiyoubi*
にっき | diary | *nikki*
にふん | 2 minutes | *nifun*
にほん | Japan | *nihon*
にほんご | Japanese language | *nihongo*
にほんごの せんせい | Japanese teacher | *nihongo no sensei*
にんじん | carrot | *ninjin*

ぬ

ぬぐ | to undress | *nugu*
ぬるい | warm, luke warm | *nurui*

ね

ねあげ | a rise in price | *neage*
ねぎ | green onion | *negi*
ねこ | cat | *neko*
ねじ | a screw | *neji*
ねずみ | mouse | *nezumi*

の

ノートパソコン | laptop computer | *no–to pasokon*
のみもの | a drink, drinks | *nomimono*

は

は | tooth, teeth | *ha*
パーティー | party | *pa–ti–*
はい | yes | *hai*
はいいろ | gray | *haiiro*
はいゆう | actor | *haiyuu*
はえ | house fly | *hae*
ばくはつ | explosion | *bakuhatsu*

はこぶ | to move an item | *hakobu*
はし | chopsticks | *hashi*
バス | bus | *basu*
バスケットボール | basketball | *basuketto booru*
パソコン | PC (computer) | *pasokon*
はた | flag | *hata*
はち | 8 | *hachi*
はちがつ | August | *hachigatsu*
はちじ | eight o'clock | *hachiji*
はちふん | 8 minutes | *hachifun*
はっぴょう | an announcement | *happyou*
はっぷん | 8 minutes | *happun*
はと | pigeon; dove | *hato*
パトカー | patrol car | *patoka–*
はな | flowers | *hana*
はな | nose | *hana*
バナナ | banana | *banana*
ハブラシ | toothbrush | *haburashi*
ハリソン・フォード | Harrison Ford (actor) | *Harison Fo–do*
はる | spring | *haru*
はん | half past (:30) | *han*
パン | bread | *pan*
パンダ | panda | *panda*

ひ

ビーフ | beef | *bi–fu*
ひがし | east | *higashi*
ぴかぴか | shiny | *pikapika*
ひこうき | airplane | *hikouki*
ピザ | pizza | *piza*
ひだり | left | *hidari*
ひつじ | sheep | *hitsuji*
ひま | free time | *hima*
ひらめ | halibut | *hirame*
ピンク | pink | *pinku*

ふ

ふうふ | married couple | *fuufu*
フォーク | fork | *fo–ku*
ふく | clothing, clothes | *fuku*
ぶた | pig | *buta*
ぶどう | grapes | *budou*
ふとん | futon | *futon*
ふね | ship; boat | *fune*
ブラッド・ピット | Brad Pitt (actor) | *Braddo Pitto*
ふるい | old | *furui*
フルーツ | fruit | *furu–tsu*
プレゼント | present, gift | *purezento*
ぶんかのひ | Culture Day | *bunkanohi*

へ

へいたい | soldier | *heitai*
ベッド | bed | *beddo*
へび | snake | *hebi*
ペン | pen | *pen*

ほ

ぼく | I, me (males only) | *boku*
ほし | star (in the sky) | *hoshi*
ほしい | want | *hoshii*

ポテト | French fries | *poteto*
ポテト | potato | *poteto*
ほん | book | *hon*

ま

まくら | pillow | *makura*
まぐろ | tuna | *maguro*
まど | window | *mado*
まね | imitation | *mane*
まる | circle, zero | *maru*

み

みかん / オレンジ | orange (fruit) | *mikan / orenji*
みぎ | right | *migi*
みず | water | *mizu*
みずいろ | light blue | *mizuiro*
みずを のむ | to drink water | *mizuwo nomu*
みそしる | miso soup | *misoshiru*
みどり | green | *midori*
みなみ | south | *minami*
みみ | ear | *mimi*
ミルク | milk | *miruku*

む

むずかしい | difficult | *muzukashii*
むね | chest | *mune*
むらさき | purple | *murasaki*

め

め | eye | *me*
めいし | business card | *meishi*
めがね | glasses | *megane*
めじるし | landmark | *mejirushi*
めずらしい | rare (adj.) | *mezurashii*
めだつ | to stand out | *medatsu*
メニュー | menu | *menyu–*

も

もうふ | blanket | *moufu*
もくじ | contents | *mokuji*
もくようび | Thursday | *mokuyoubi*
もしもし | hello (on the phone) | *moshimoshi*
もちろん | of course | *mochiron*
もも | peach | *momo*

や

やさい | vegetable | *yasai*
やすみ | day off, break | *yasumi*
やね | roof | *yane*

ゆ

ゆうえんち | fun park | *yuuenchi*
ゆび | finger | *yubi*

よ

ようちえん | kindergarten | *youchien*
よじ | four o'clock | *yoji*

よしお | a common boy's first name | *Yoshio*
よん | 4 | *yon*
よんじゅうごふん | 45 minutes | *yonjuugofun*
よんじゅっぷん | 40 minutes | *yonjuppun*
よんぷん | 4 minutes | *yonpun*

ら

ライオン | lion | *raion*
らいげつ | next month | *raigetsu*
らいしゅう | next week | *raishuu*
らいねん | next year | *rainen*
らくがき | graffiti | *rakugaki*
ラスベガス | Las Vegas | *rasu begasu*
らんぼう | violence | *ranbou*

り

りゆう | a reason | *riyuu*
りょこう | travel | *ryokou*
りんご | apple | *ringo*

れ

れい | zero, 0 | *rei*
れいぞうこ | refrigerator | *reizouko*
レストラン | restaurant | *resutoran*
レタス | lettuce | *retasu*
レモン | lemon | *remon*
れんらく | contact | *renraku*

ろ

ろうか | hallway | *rouka*
ろうじん | old person | *roujin*
ろく | 6 | *roku*
ろくがつ | June | *rokugatsu*
ろくじ | six o'clock | *rokuji*
ろくじゅっぷん | 60 minutes | *rokujuppun*
ロサンゼルス | Los Angeles | *rosanzerusu*
ろっぷん | 6 minutes | *roppun*
ロブスター | lobster | *robusuta–*

わ

わかる | to understand, know | *wakaru*
わすれもの | forgotten item | *wasuremono*
わたし | I, me (male or female) | *watashi*

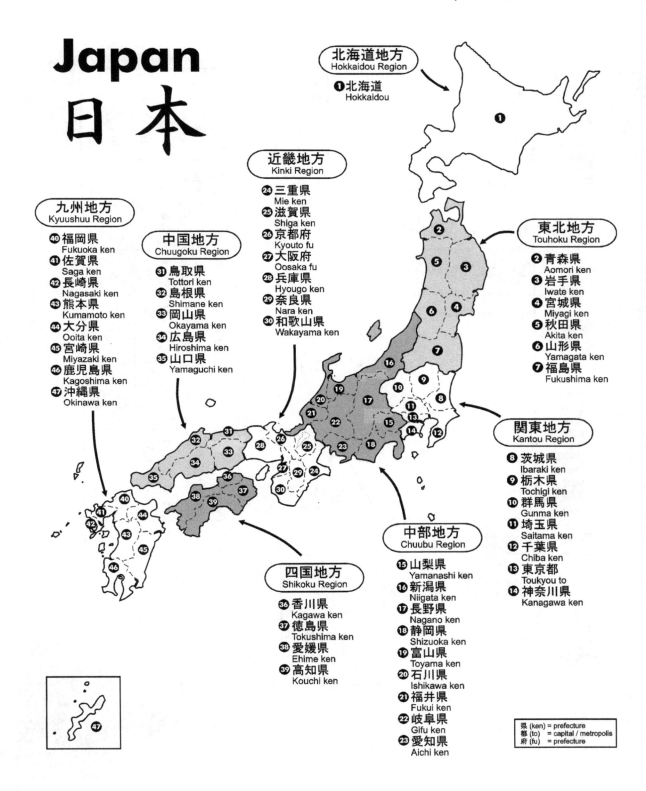

Japan
日本

北海道地方
Hokkaidou Region
❶北海道
Hokkaidou

近畿地方
Kinki Region
㉔三重県
Mie ken
㉕滋賀県
Shiga ken
㉖京都府
Kyouto fu
㉗大阪府
Oosaka fu
㉘兵庫県
Hyougo ken
㉙奈良県
Nara ken
㉚和歌山県
Wakayama ken

東北地方
Touhoku Region
❷青森県
Aomori ken
❸岩手県
Iwate ken
❹宮城県
Miyagi ken
❺秋田県
Akita ken
❻山形県
Yamagata ken
❼福島県
Fukushima ken

九州地方
Kyuushuu Region
㊵福岡県
Fukuoka ken
㊶佐賀県
Saga ken
㊷長崎県
Nagasaki ken
㊸熊本県
Kumamoto ken
㊹大分県
Ooita ken
㊺宮崎県
Miyazaki ken
㊻鹿児島県
Kagoshima ken
㊼沖縄県
Okinawa ken

中国地方
Chuugoku Region
㉛鳥取県
Tottori ken
㉜島根県
Shimane ken
㉝岡山県
Okayama ken
㉞広島県
Hiroshima ken
㉟山口県
Yamaguchi ken

関東地方
Kantou Region
❽茨城県
Ibaraki ken
❾栃木県
Tochigi ken
❿群馬県
Gunma ken
⓫埼玉県
Saitama ken
⓬千葉県
Chiba ken
⓭東京都
Toukyou to
⓮神奈川県
Kanagawa ken

中部地方
Chuubu Region
⓯山梨県
Yamanashi ken
⓰新潟県
Niigata ken
⓱長野県
Nagano ken
⓲静岡県
Shizuoka ken
⓳富山県
Toyama ken
⓴石川県
Ishikawa ken
㉑福井県
Fukui ken
㉒岐阜県
Gifu ken
㉓愛知県
Aichi ken

四国地方
Shikoku Region
㊱香川県
Kagawa ken
㊲徳島県
Tokushima ken
㊳愛媛県
Ehime ken
㊴高知県
Kouchi ken

県 (ken) = prefecture
都 (to) = capital / metropolis
府 (fu) = prefecture

Hiragana Chart

YesJapan Learn Japanese Today!

あ a	か ka	が ga	さ sa	ざ za	た ta	だ da	な na	は ha	ば ba	ぱ pa
い i	き ki	ぎ gi	し shi	じ ji	ち chi	ぢ ji	に ni	ひ hi	び bi	ぴ pi
う u	く ku	ぐ gu	す su	ず zu	つ tsu	づ zu	ぬ nu	ふ fu	ぶ bu	ぷ pu
え e	け ke	げ ge	せ se	ぜ ze	て te	で de	ね ne	へ he	べ be	ぺ pe
お o	こ ko	ご go	そ so	ぞ zo	と to	ど do	の no	ほ ho	ぼ bo	ぽ po

ま ma	や ya	ら ra	わ wa
み mi		り ri	
む mu	ゆ yu	る ru	を wo
め me		れ re	
も mo	よ yo	ろ ro	ん n

きゃ kya	きゅ kyu	きょ kyo
ぎゃ gya	ぎゅ gyu	ぎょ gyo
しゃ sha	しゅ shu	しょ sho
じゃ ja	じゅ ju	じょ jo
ちゃ cha	ちゅ chu	ちょ cho
にゃ nya	にゅ nyu	にょ nyo
ひゃ hya	ひゅ hyu	ひょ hyo
びゃ bya	びゅ byu	びょ byo
ぴゃ pya	ぴゅ pyu	ぴょ pyo
みゃ mya	みゅ myu	みょ myo
りゃ rya	りゅ ryu	りょ ryo

YesJapan.com

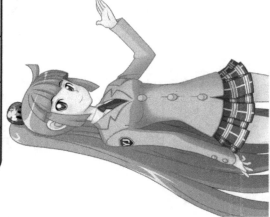